Reading and Writing Instruction *for*
PreK THROUGH FIRST-GRADE
Classrooms *in a* PLC at Work®

Erica Martin
Lisa May

EDITED BY
Mark Onuscheck
Jeanne Spiller

Solution Tree | Press

a division of
Solution Tree

555 North Morton Street
Bloomington, IN 47404
800.733.6786 (toll free) / 812.336.7700
FAX: 812.336.7790

email: info@SolutionTree.com
SolutionTree.com

Visit **go.SolutionTree.com/literacy** to download the free reproducibles in this book.

Printed in the United States of America

Library of Congress Cataloging-in-Publication Data

Names: Martin, Erica, author. | May, Lisa (Teacher), author.
Title: Reading and writing instruction for PreK through first-grade
    classrooms in a PLC at work / Erica Martin and Lisa May ; edited by Mark
    Onuscheck, Jeanne Spiller.
Description: Bloomington, IN : Solution Tree Press, 2020. | Series: Every
    teacher is a literacy teacher | Includes bibliographical references and
    index.
Identifiers: LCCN 2019057759 (print) | LCCN 2019057760 (ebook) | ISBN
    9781947604919 (paperback) | ISBN 9781947604926 (ebook)
Subjects: LCSH: Language arts (Early childhood) | Language arts
    (Elementary) | Professional learning communities--United States.
Classification: LCC LB1139.5.L35 M38 2020 (print) | LCC LB1139.5.L35
    (ebook) | DDC 372.6--dc23
LC record available at https://lccn.loc.gov/2019057759
LC ebook record available at https://lccn.loc.gov/2019057760

Solution Tree
Jeffrey C. Jones, CEO
Edmund M. Ackerman, President

Solution Tree Press
President and Publisher: Douglas M. Rife
Associate Publisher: Sarah Payne-Mills
Art Director: Rian Anderson
Managing Production Editor: Kendra Slayton
Senior Production Editor: Tonya Maddox Cupp
Content Development Specialist: Amy Rubenstein
Copy Editor: Mark Hain
Proofreader: Sarah Ludwig
Text and Cover Designer: Abigail Bowen
Editorial Assistants: Sarah Ludwig and Elijah Oates

ACKNOWLEDGMENTS

I consider myself extremely fortunate to work alongside the extraordinary teachers and administrators in Kildeer Countryside School District 96. Their hard work, dedication, and commitment to helping all students achieve at high levels inspires me each and every day. To my coauthor and editors, thank you for such a rewarding experience. I have learned so much from all of you and look forward to our continued friendship and collaboration. To my editor and friend, Jeanne: your leadership throughout this journey has been invaluable. I appreciate your unwavering encouragement, guidance, and support. Finally, thank you to my husband, Jeremy, and my children, Hannah and Ben, for their never-ending love and patience. You mean the world to me.

—Erica

This invaluable, rewarding, and challenging experience would not have been possible without the collaboration of my amazing book team and teammates in District 96. I've learned so much through this process. Thank you for your guidance and support. To Brené Brown, who came into my life precisely at the right time; because of her, I aspire to dare greatly. Thank you to my friend, Jeanne, for bringing her into my life and encouraging me to remove my armor and live boldly. To the swimming pool in my backyard . . . you've supported me in ways you will never know. Finally, to my husband, Johnny May, who teaches me every day about serving others. He is my constant cheerleader and biggest support along with my amazing kids, Brittany and TJ, who inspire me to be better every day. Everything I do, I do it for you!

—Lisa

Solution Tree Press would like to thank the following reviewers:

Mary Kelly
Principal
NB Galloway Elementary School
Channahon, Illinois

Elizabeth Love
Assistant Principal
Morrison Elementary and
Trusty Elementary
Fort Smith, Arkansas

Visit **go.SolutionTree.com/literacy** to download the free reproducibles in this book.

TABLE OF CONTENTS

Reproducible pages are in italics.

CHAPTER 4

Develop Collective Understanding of Mastery Expectations   93

CHAPTER 5

Respond to Data to Ensure All Students Learn: Response to Intervention   121

CHAPTER 6

Design Lessons Using the Gradual Release of Responsibility Instructional Framework   147

CHAPTER 7

Plan High-Quality Literacy Instruction   163

CHAPTER 8

Select Appropriate Instructional Strategies   217

ABOUT THE SERIES EDITORS

Mark Onuscheck is director of curriculum, instruction, and assessment at Adlai E. Stevenson High School in Lincolnshire, Illinois. He is a former English teacher and director of communication arts. As director of curriculum, instruction, and assessment, Mark works with academic divisions around professional learning, articulation, curricular and instructional revision, evaluation, assessment, social-emotional learning, technologies, and Common Core State Standards implementation. He is also an adjunct professor at DePaul University.

Mark was awarded the Quality Matters Star Rating for his work in online teaching. He helps to build curriculum and instructional practices for TimeLine Theatre's arts integration program for Chicago Public Schools. Additionally, he is a National Endowment for the Humanities grant recipient and a member of the Association for Supervision and Curriculum Development, the National Council of Teachers of English, and Learning Forward.

Mark earned a bachelor's degree in English and classical studies from Allegheny College and a master's degree in teaching English from the University of Pittsburgh.

Jeanne Spiller is assistant superintendent for teaching and learning for Kildeer Countryside Community Consolidated School District 96 in Buffalo Grove, Illinois. School District 96 is recognized on AllThingsPLC (www.AllThingsPLC.info) as one of only a small number of school districts where all schools in the district earn the distinction of a model professional learning community (PLC). Jeanne's work focuses on standards-aligned instruction and assessment practices. She supports schools and districts across the United States in gaining clarity about and implementing the four critical questions of professional learning communities. She is passionate about collaborating with schools to develop systems for teaching and learning that keep the focus on student results, and helping teachers determine how to approach instruction so that all students learn at high levels.

Jeanne received a Those Who Excel award from the Illinois State Board of Education in 2014 for significant contributions in administration to the state's public and nonpublic elementary schools. She is a graduate of the 2008 Learning Forward Academy, where she learned how to plan and implement professional learning that improves educator practice and increases student achievement. She has served as a classroom teacher, team leader, middle school administrator, and director of professional learning.

Jeanne earned a master's degree in educational teaching and leadership from Saint Xavier University, a master's degree in educational administration from Loyola University Chicago, and an educational administrative superintendent endorsement from Northern Illinois University.

To learn more about Jeanne's work, follow @jeeneemarie on Twitter.

To book Mark Onuscheck or Jeanne Spiller for professional development, contact pd@SolutionTree.com.

ABOUT THE AUTHORS

 **Erica Martin** is a literacy specialist at Kildeer Countryside School District 96, located in the northwest suburbs of Chicago. With over twenty years of experience as a literacy coach, reading interventionist, and English teacher, Erica has consulted with districts throughout the United States in literacy curriculum design, response to intervention, and data analysis. During Erica's service to Kildeer Countryside School District 96, the district has been recognized as a model PLC. She has also received a Those Who Excel award from the Illinois State Board of Education for excellence in literacy coaching.

Erica holds master's degrees in curriculum and instruction and literacy education, along with a reading specialist certification, from Northern Illinois University.

 **Lisa May** is a proud member of Kildeer Countryside School District 96, a model PLC school district. With over twenty years of education experience, she has classroom experience ranging from kindergarten through fourth grade. Lisa has also served as a reading specialist and interventionist. She was honored in 2014 with a Those Who Excel award in Illinois for excellence in elementary school literacy coaching.

Lisa earned a master's degree in curriculum and instruction from Concordia University Chicago and a master's degree as a reading specialist from Olivet Nazarene University.

To book Erica Martin or Lisa May for professional development, contact pd@ SolutionTree.com.

Every Teacher
Is a Literacy
Teacher

*Eventually we will send our students out into the wild, where newspapers of
record, college courses, bosses and colleagues, and increasingly health care providers,
bankers, and others will not provide them with accessible texts.*

—EILEEN MURPHY BUCKLEY

Every student must learn the fundamental skills necessary to navigate the wild
world of complex text. Literacy skills are so fundamental to learning that their
importance cannot be overstated. In fact, multiple studies show that avid readers demonstrate both superior literacy development and wide-ranging knowledge
across subjects (Allington, 2012; Hiebert & Reutzel, 2014; Sullivan & Brown,
2013). Our goal as educators must be to equip students with those necessary skills
so they can take control of their destinies, fulfill their potential, and thrive. We
contend that this mission begins with a highly intentional focus on the expectations outlined in the learning standards that guide teaching and learning in your
state, school, or district.

This book assists schools—more specifically, professional learning community–
based schools with collaborative teams—in designing standards-aligned instruction, assessment, and intervention that support all students' literacy development.

Chapter Organization and Four
Critical Questions

The content of this book is framed through the lens of Professional Learning
Communities (PLCs) at Work®, with each of the first five chapters focused on how

collaborative teams may begin to answer one or more of the four critical questions of PLCs (DuFour, DuFour, Eaker, Many, & Mattos, 2016, p. 59).

▶ **"What is it we want our students to know and be able to do?"** Chapter 1 addresses this question and introduces the pre-unit protocol (PREP), a tool designed to provide clarity about student learning expectations prior to beginning a unit of instruction.

▶ **"How will we know if each student has learned it?"** This question is addressed in chapters 2, 3, and 4. Chapter 2 reviews the various assessment types and questions best suited to literacy standards, provides an example of each type of assessment in a unit, and examines the unique nature of literacy assessment. Chapter 3 details a process for developing an instructional learning progression for each standard. This learning progression helps teams develop learning target–aligned assessments and high-quality instruction. Chapter 4 explores student proficiency, various rubric types and their development, student checklists, and collaborative scoring.

▶ **"How will we respond when some students do not learn it?"** Collaborative teams follow a data-inquiry process and, based on that information, take specific steps when students do not learn the intended outcomes, employing scaffolding or response to intervention (RTI). Chapter 5 discusses these topics.

▶ **"How will we extend the learning for students who have demonstrated proficiency?"** Extension opportunities are important when students have already learned what we want them to learn. RTI, explained in chapter 5, addresses extension as well as intervention. These topics are addressed in several sections of the book as well when referencing how teachers might respond to data.

In chapters 6, 7, 8, and 9, we focus on instructional processes. Topics include the gradual release of responsibility from teacher to student, planning high-quality instruction within the literacy block, selecting appropriate instructional strategies to facilitate high-quality literacy instruction, and the consideration of diversity and equity in literacy instruction.

The appendices offer various tools, including a blank reproducible version of the PREP template and other tools (appendix A), a guide for creating essential understandings and guiding questions (appendix B), and a list of figures and tables from the book (appendix C). Many of the examples in the appendices and included in other sections of the book are examples of how this work is implemented in Kildeer Countryside School District 96 in Buffalo Grove, Illinois. As practitioners in the district, we have used these tools and protocols in our work, allowing us the ability to offer a high level of insight and guidance in their use.

About This Series

This book is part of the *Every Teacher Is a Literacy Teacher* series that addresses literacy from prekindergarten through grade 12. The elementary segment of this series includes separate titles focused on instruction in grades preK–1, grades 2–3, and grades 4–5. The content and examples included in each title in the series address the discrete demands of each grade level. The secondary school segment focuses on how subject-area teachers approach literacy in various innovative ways, and the role every teacher must play in supporting literacy development in all subject areas throughout grades 6–12.

Each title in the elementary series includes full chapters on the steps collaborative teams must take prior to engaging in high-quality instruction. This is to ensure that readers are equipped with clarity about standards, assessment, learning progressions, mastery expectations, intervention, gradual release of responsibility, instructional time, instructional strategies, diversity, and equity. Specific collaborative team exercises are included in each chapter, making it simple for teams to engage in the work described in that chapter. Visit **go.SolutionTree.com/literacy** for a free reproducible version of all exercises.

The various secondary school books in this series each feature classroom literacy strategies for a subject area in grades 6–12, such as science or English language arts. The expert educators writing these secondary-level books approach literacy in varying and innovative ways and examine the role every teacher must play in supporting students' literacy development in all subject areas throughout their grades 6–12 schooling.

Woven throughout the books is the idea that collaboration is crucial to the success of any school dedicated to building effective teams in a PLC at Work culture (DuFour et al., 2016). When experts collaborate, innovative ideas emerge that support student learning and generate positive results. Across the world, schools are making a commitment to this core principle as teacher teams tackle longstanding concerns in education by making stronger curricular and instructional choices together. Such work is driven by teacher teams getting better and better at using assessment practices that support all students. Furthermore, schools that invest in a

PLC culture work in ways that are more unified and cohesive, prioritizing concerns and working together to innovate positive changes and continuous improvement. In this book, we are excited to share ways a PLC can radiate change when thoughtful educators dedicate themselves to support all students' literacy.

The Need for High-Quality Instruction in PreK Through First Grade

High-quality literacy instruction in the preK through first-grade years has a long-lasting and powerful impact on students' future academic achievement and success (Connor, Alberto, Compton, & O'Connor, 2014). Teachers at this level play a pivotal role in helping their students *learn to read* so that by fourth grade they *can read to learn* (Annie E. Casey Foundation, 2010). Unfortunately, many students struggle to make this critical transition. In fact, it is estimated that 66 percent of all U.S. fourth graders read so poorly that they failed to demonstrate even "partial mastery of prerequisite knowledge and skills" necessary to read and understand grade-level text (Lee, Grigg, & Donahue, 2007, p. 6).

As we know, students enter preK with varying levels of linguistic and cognitive abilities. Some students will learn to read easily regardless of the method of instruction, while others will require intensive intervention to master such a complex process. Sadly, students from economically disadvantaged families often come to our classrooms with the least exposure to early reading experiences. This, in turn, creates gaps in reading readiness and language development, leaving our neediest learners behind from the get-go.

With reading proficiency by third grade a key predictor of later academic success, we must change the trajectory of our struggling young readers so they do not fall behind forever (Annie E. Casey Foundation, 2010). Fortunately, research shows us that providing students with high-quality literacy instruction and intervention—teaching for students who have yet to master standards—during preK, kindergarten, and first grade can close the achievement gap, preventing reading problems early on before they become more difficult to remediate as students progress through the primary grades (Connor et al., 2014). To provide every student the opportunity for success, teachers must be prepared to implement varied, research-based teaching methods that will develop students' competence in language and literacy and foster their motivation to read and write for enjoyment, information, and communication. Literacy instruction in preK, kindergarten, and first grade is critical not only for ensuring students' future success throughout their academic years and beyond but also for cultivating a love of literacy for a lifetime of reading, writing, and communicating.

What High-Quality Instruction Looks Like in PreK Through First Grade

High-quality literacy instruction is imperative for all learners. Building the foundational skills necessary to read and write, including letter (name and sound) knowledge, phonological awareness, and an understanding of speech-sound relationships, is particularly important at preK through first grade. These skills are essential for students to learn how to become readers and writers. The National Early Literacy Panel (2008) finds that letter name and sound knowledge is the single best predictor of reading success in the primary grades. *Phonological awareness* refers to hearing and manipulating sound properties of words such as beginning sounds, syllables, and rhyming sounds. This is an important facet of the primary instructional program. *Phonemic awareness* specifically refers to the ability to hear and manipulate individual or single *phonemes*, the individual sounds (such as the three phonemes in *cat*: /c/ /a/ /t/), in spoken words and syllables.

Phonemic awareness and phonics are often confused as synonymous concepts. Phonemic awareness tasks, however, are most always oral, sounds in spoken words, while phonics involves the relationship between sounds and written symbols. Therefore, phonics instruction focuses on teaching sound-spelling relationships and is associated with print. The *alphabetic principle* is the understanding that specific letters or combinations of letters represent specific sounds in words; for example, understanding that the /s/ sound in speech is represented by the letter *s* in writing. This alphabetic principle relates to the comprehension of letter-sound correspondences, and understanding it is a major achievement that allows students to learn to decode and spell printed words using phonics. The alphabetic principle is also critical for students to enhance their thinking and reasoning abilities (Ehri & Roberts, 2006). Developing oral language comprehension and engaging students in meaningful conversation is crucial to literacy instruction, as they give meaning to what students are learning. *Oracy*—the ability to communicate through spoken language—is embedded within these foundational skills through letter (name and sound) knowledge, phonological awareness, and speech-sound relationships.

When students become skilled readers, they demonstrate a deep knowledge of these concepts as well as an understanding of messages communicated in texts. Research reveals that for students in these early grades to be successful readers, they must have a toolbox filled with these important foundational skills (Foorman et al., 2016). Classrooms filled with print, such as storybook reading, writing, and language and literacy play through dramatic play, allow students to experience the joy and power associated with reading and writing while also mastering basic literacy concepts that research shows are strong predictors of achievement (Roskos & Christie, 2011).

While the skills of reading and making meaning are certainly essential, a balanced approach to literacy is not complete without writing instruction. As any elementary teacher can tell you, students in preK through first grade have vivid imaginations and rather entertaining stories to tell. Through teacher modeling and mentor texts, students learn how to craft descriptive sentences and provide sensory details in a way that brings their stories to life. And believe it or not, these learners have some strong opinions, too! What makes someone brave? Should we have recess every day? They are eager to share their opinions, and as we guide them through the writing process, these little authors begin to understand the power of language and written expression.

Finally, it is important to keep attention span in mind. Research shows that normal attention span is three to five minutes per each year of a student's age; therefore, students in preK, kindergarten, and first grade cannot attend to any one task for more than twenty minutes at a time (Harstad, n.d.). Teachers must plan accordingly when creating learning experiences for these very young learners.

The Value of Professional Learning Communities in PreK Through First-Grade Literacy

Effective teachers produce greater achievement in student reading regardless of the curriculum materials, the reading programs, or their instructional routines (Allington, 2002; Blevins, 2017; Darling-Hammond, 1999; Pressley, Allington, Wharton-McDonald, Block, & Morrow, 2001). Simply put, good teachers can make a difference. The information provided by this book can help.

Take a moment to think about the typical preK, kindergarten, and first-grade classrooms. There may be a wide range of readers, from students who grew up in houses with no books and no library visits to those who read beyond grade level. In addition, our students come to us from a tremendously diverse array of backgrounds and cultures, with many speaking different languages and several just learning to speak English. We face the challenge of broadening our repertoire to build on the strengths and address the needs of a diversity of readers.

The reality is, however, that no individual teacher has all the skills, knowledge, and time necessary to accomplish this endeavor—at least not alone. If schools are committed to making meaningful changes in classroom practices that truly make a difference for all learners, then they are employing the collective efforts of a PLC at Work. When we integrate high-quality literacy instruction in a PLC, magic happens.

Throughout this book, we emphasize the importance of working together as a team of educators. Although collaborative team structures are highly variable depending on the needs and nature of the school community, all PLCs are focused on three big ideas: (1) a focus on learning, (2) a collaborative culture, and (3) a results orientation (DuFour et al., 2016). These ideas represent the core purpose of a PLC, and they are achieved by answering the four critical questions discussed earlier. Teachers in a PLC are organized into collaborative teams that work interdependently to achieve common goals for which members are mutually accountable (DuFour et al., 2016). You might have curriculum teams, grade-level teams, vertical teams spanning multiple grade levels, or even *singletons* (teams of one). Members clarify essential learning for all students, agree on unit pacing, and develop and administer common assessments to monitor learning and determine next steps in instruction. Teachers in a PLC also collaborate around sound instructional practices, sharing strategies that worked well, and, as a team, develop new differentiated lessons. Further, they openly discuss and analyze student data to make informed instructional decisions that forward students' learning. Through these collective efforts, teachers help establish a guaranteed and viable curriculum that ensures all students have an equal opportunity to learn by giving them access to the same content, knowledge, and skills regardless of their teacher (Marzano, 2003).

Put plainly, teachers within a PLC work *together* to ensure that every student, in every classroom, receives what he or she needs to master essential skills and pave the way for a promising future. To achieve this goal, it is important to collaborate with other professionals who can help support and guide you through the work of the PLC process. This book provides resources and tools to help teams operate effectively and maximize their collective strengths in the service of students.

While the size and scope of work in a PLC can differ greatly from one PLC to the next, the initial focus of teams is often a specific, discrete task that later evolves into more layered tasks and discussion topics. By simple definition, a *team* is a group of professionals working interdependently to achieve a common goal. PLC at Work architect Richard DuFour (2004) notes successful teams do the following.

- Have common time for collaboration on a regular basis

- Foster buy-in toward a discrete and overarching common goal

- Build a sense of community

- Engage in long-term work that continues from year to year

- Grow—but do not completely change—membership each year

With collaboration as one of the key concepts of a PLC, no doubt a collective effort is essential. But what happens when you are the sole content teacher at your grade level—a singleton (for example, the one kindergarten teacher in an elementary school or the only first grade teacher who teaches reading)? In these situations, it is important to collaborate with other professionals who can support and guide you (and for whom you can do the same) through the work of the PLC process. In many cases, a teacher from the preceding or following grade level can become a great working partner as he or she has a wealth of knowledge about the skills students have acquired or will need to acquire for the next school year. Grade-level partners who teach other content areas can also be helpful as you work collaboratively to provide a guaranteed and viable curriculum for every student in every classroom across the school. Finally, take advantage of an online, interconnected world to reach out to grade-level teachers in other PLC districts. Use technology to collaborate as you do the work of ensuring a consistent and viable, literacy-focused curriculum.

According to researcher and author Robert J. Marzano (2003), creating a guaranteed and viable curriculum is the "school-level factor with the most impact on student achievement" (p. 15). But for literacy instruction, this can be particularly challenging. Unlike other disciplines such as mathematics with less ambiguous standards, literacy consists of standards that can often be interpreted in many ways. For example, consider kindergarten reading literature standard 2 (RL.K.2) of the Common Core State Standards (CCSS): "With prompting and support, retell familiar stories, including key details" (National Governors Association Center for Best Practices [NGA] & Council of Chief State School Officers [CCSSO], 2010).

When the kindergarten teachers in District 96, where we work, began unwrapping this standard, they soon realized that each teacher understood the intended meaning of the words and phrases in the standard differently. For example, what does "with prompting and support" actually mean in practice? How much support should each teacher give a student and what should that support be like? Also, what exactly is a "key detail" and how is it different from a main idea? What does it mean to "retell" as opposed to simply give an account of a text? With all this ambiguity, the team risked having different interpretations and essentially different mastery expectations from one teacher to the next. If teachers do not unwrap and analyze these perplexing literacy standards collectively and come to consensus on what they mean, it is difficult to provide students with access to the same content, knowledge, and skills. Simply put, lack of clarity interferes with students' access to a guaranteed and viable curriculum. To develop a shared understanding of the words and phrases embedded in standards, members of our kindergarten team dedicate time to discussing interpretations, sharing ideas, and providing evidence of effective practices. Only when the team feels confident that they have reached a consensus do they move forward in their unit design.

The complex and important endeavor of teaching young people literacy becomes more manageable and tangible as we engage in the process as educators together, and the place to begin is getting clear as a team on what we want our students to know and be able to do. This is why, in chapter 1, we provide teachers with tools that will help them arrive at a collective understanding around the literacy standards and the specific learning outcomes necessary for proficiency. We'll provide a template to help your team examine and unwrap the standards and share strategies for focusing conversations as you dig into the often complicated and ambiguous wording of your literacy standards.

CHAPTER 1

Establish Clarity About Student Learning Expectations

The first critical question that drives PLC work—"What is it we want our students to know and be able to do?"—aligns to the need for a guaranteed and viable curriculum (DuFour et al., 2016, p. 59; Marzano, 2003). This pivotal question with regard to teaching literacy means, for example, that before introducing a complex text, launching into a writing activity, or conducting an assessment, teacher teams in a PLC must interpret English language arts (ELA) standards in the same way and use them to guide a robust, rigorous instruction and assessment plan. If teachers do not collaborate to analyze literacy standards and reach consensus on what they each mean, they will not afford students access to the same content, knowledge, and skills.

The answer to this first critical question requires carefully considering the following components, which work together to guide any effective instruction and assessment plan. In this text, we apply them to support students' literacy advancement.

▶ Standards

▶ Knowledge

▶ Skills

▶ Depth of knowledge (DOK; Webb, 1997, 1999)

▶ Learning targets

Teacher teams collaborate to become crystal clear about the specific knowledge and skills that all students must know and be able to do by the end of a particular unit. Defining consistent learning outcomes is vital in the preK through first-grade years since teachers will undoubtedly encounter a wide range of learners with a variety of literacy experiences. Often, learning opportunities differ significantly depending on family income and education, ethnicity, and language background (National Association for the Education of Young Children [NAEYC], 2009b). For instance, while some students come to us already knowing how to read and write, others might not have attended preK or even live in a state with kindergarten requirements.

To promote every child's early literacy development, the NAEYC (2009b) suggests implementing teaching practices "appropriate to children's age and developmental status, attuned to them as unique individuals, and responsive to the social and cultural contexts in which they live" (p. 1). This requires teachers "both meeting children where they are—which means that teachers must get to know them well—and enabling them to reach goals that are both challenging and achievable" (NAEYC, 2009b, p. 1).

Collectively, teams follow the PREP steps to focus on the most important standards in a unit, particularly those tied to literacy, and unwrap them so the team has a collective sense of the critical knowledge and skills that make up a standard. Without this deep and collective understanding, teachers will struggle to determine appropriate literacy goals to meet the array of learners in their classrooms. This chapter presents information and tools for teams to use as they follow the PREP protocol. Teams that want to extend the process can build essential understandings and guiding questions, guidance for which is in appendix B (page 269).

While *essential understandings* crystallize and articulate conceptual thinking for teachers to guide curriculum design more deeply, *guiding questions* set the purpose for students' learning. Teams often create essential understandings together to do two things: (1) synthesize the components gleaned from the PREP and (2) gain a deeper understanding of students' overall learning. Teams can then use these essential understandings to design student-friendly guiding questions that frame instruction and guide assessment throughout the unit. In addition, guiding questions encourage students to engage in the work ahead and make them aware of the connection between what they are doing and the learning outcomes.

Here, you will follow the example of a unit on friendship and acceptance in a kindergarten classroom at the beginning of the school year. In this fiction unit, teachers address early reading, writing, and foundational skills as these areas of literacy are intrinsically interconnected. When choosing a unit for prekindergarten, kindergarten, or first-grade students, teams will need to reflect on several factors impacting young learners. For example, in kindergarten, students often feel excited, anxious, or even a bit nervous for their first days of school. They might be entering a classroom setting for the very first time with limited experience engaging with peers, navigating a social landscape, or even approaching a potential new friend. To help students feel welcomed and at ease in classrooms, teachers might decide to start the year with a unit on friendship and acceptance. Using a variety of texts focused on the theme of friendship and acceptance, students learn to identify, discuss, and write about the literary elements of plot, character, setting, and key details while, at the same time, developing social skills and building tolerance toward others. The unit culminates with students drawing on specific textual evidence to craft a response to a text-dependent question.

PREP Steps

The six PREP steps are as follows. The rest of this chapter guides you through each of the steps to ensure you and your team will be able to use this process to create rich and rigorous curricula that are also guaranteed and viable.

1. Enter unit standards into the template.

2. Indicate priority standards.

3. Unwrap unit priority standards.

4. Identify knowledge items.

5. Determine skills.

6. Assign levels of rigor (DOK) for learning targets.

Content-area standards like the CCSS can be complex and often lead to various interpretations. Therefore, this process is vital as it safeguards student learning by establishing distinct expectations for learners across all classrooms. Participating in this process also sets the groundwork for subsequent collaborative efforts: building common assessments, critiquing the efficacy of existing units, and designing new lessons. However, the initial step involves establishing a collective clarity around targeted literacy standards in particular.

Figure 1.1 (pages 14–16) features a sample PREP template, completed by a collaborative team, with a breakdown of the knowledge and skills aimed for by the end of the three-week instructional period. (See pages 258–260 or visit **go.SolutionTree .com/literacy** for a free reproducible version of the "PREP Template.")

Unit of Instruction: Friendship and acceptance   **Duration:** Three weeks   **Grade:** K

Unit Standards (priority standards are in bold and italic typeface)

Strand: Reading for Literature

RL.K.1: With prompting and support, ask and answer questions about key details in a text.

RL.K.2: With prompting and support, retell familiar stories, including key details.

RL.K.3: With prompting and support, identify characters, settings, and major events in a story.

RL.K.4: Ask and answer questions about unknown words in a text.

RL.K.5: Recognize common types of texts (for example, storybooks, poems).

RL.K.7: With prompting and support, describe the relationship between illustrations and the story in which they appear.

RL.K.9: With prompting and support, compare and contrast the adventures and experiences of characters in familiar stories.

RL.K.10: Actively engage in group reading activities with purpose and understanding.

Strand: Reading for Foundational Skills

RF.K.1: Demonstrate understanding of the organization and basic features of print.

RF.K.1a: Follow words from left to right, top to bottom, and page by page.

RF.K.1b: Recognize that spoken words are represented in written language by specific sequences of letters.

RF.K.1c: Understand that words are separated by spaces in print.

RF.K.1d: Recognize and name all upper- and lowercase letters of the alphabet.

RF.K.3: Know and apply grade-level phonics and word analysis skills in decoding words.

RF.K.3a: Demonstrate basic knowledge of one-to-one letter-sound correspondences by producing the primary sound or many of the most frequent sounds for each consonant.

RF.K.3b: Associate the long and short sounds with common spellings (graphemes) for the five major vowels.

RF.K.3c: Read common high-frequency words by sight (for example, *the*, *of*, *to*, *you*, *she*, *my*, *is*, *are*, *do*, *does*).

RF.K.3d: Distinguish between similarly spelled words by identifying the sounds of the letters that differ.

Strand: Writing

W.K.3: Use a combination of drawing, dictating, and writing to narrate a single event or several loosely linked events, tell about the events in the order in which they occurred, and provide a reaction to what happened.

Strand: Language

L.K.1: Demonstrate command of the conventions of standard English grammar and usage when writing or speaking.

L.K.1b: Use frequently occurring nouns and verbs.

L.K.2: Demonstrate command of the conventions of standard English capitalization, punctuation, and spelling when writing.

L.K.2a: Capitalize the first word in a sentence and the pronoun *I*.

Unwrapped Unit Priority Standards (Words that appear in capital letters in this template are key verbs in the teaching unit; underlined words are key nouns and noun phrases.)	Knowledge Items	Skills (Learning Targets and DOK Level)
RL.K.1 With prompting and support, ASK and ANSWER questions about key details in a text.	• Readers understand the difference between a question and statement. • Questions can ask *who, what, when, where, why,* and *how.* • Readers ask questions of the author to help understand a text more deeply. • Readers use background knowledge and clues from the text to help understand a text more deeply. • Readers show understanding of key details by explaining their thinking.	• Ask questions to clarify understanding of a text. (DOK 2) • Answer questions about a character, setting, or event in a story, drawing on key details in the text. (DOK 2)
RL.K.3 With prompting and support, IDENTIFY characters, settings, and major events in a story.	• The elements of literature are *characters, setting,* and *events.* • Characters have traits, such as *brave, helpful,* or *selfish.* • Authors reveal character traits through their appearances, thoughts, and actions. • Setting can include both *when* (time) and *where* (place). • Events follow a sequence. • Temporal words (*first, next, last,* and so on) are important.	• Identify a character's traits using details from the story as support by focusing on what the character looks like, thinks or feels, and does. (DOK 1) • Explain where and when a story takes place. (DOK 1) • Describe how a setting changes throughout a story. (DOK 2) • Identify the main events in a story. (DOK 1)
RF.K.1d RECOGNIZE and NAME all upper- and lowercase letters of the alphabet.	• Words are made up of letters. • Each letter has a name. • Letters can be uppercase or lowercase.	• Recognize uppercase letters. (DOK 1) • Recognize lowercase letters. (DOK 1)
RF.K.3a DEMONSTRATE basic knowledge of one-to-one letter-sound correspondences by PRODUCING the primary sound or many of the most frequent sounds for each consonant.	• Each letter makes a sound or sounds. • Blending letter sounds helps decode words.	• Produce the primary sounds for each consonant. (DOK 1) • Blend individual letter sounds together to decode words. (DOK 1)

Figure 1.1: PREP template—Kindergarten example.

continued ➝

Unwrapped Unit Priority Standards	Knowledge Items	Skills (Learning Targets and DOK Level)
W.K.3 Use a combination of drawing, dictating and writing to NARRATE a single event or several loosely linked events, TELL about the events in the order in which they occurred, and PROVIDE a reaction to what happened.	• Stories include characters (who), settings (where), and events (what). • Stories can be told with pictures and words. • Story events happen in time order. • Characters have feelings about events. • Characters can take action as a result of another action. • Characters often say something as a result of an action.	• Draw pictures of characters and settings. (DOK 1) • Draw pictures of characters doing something. (DOK 1) • Tell, aloud, about the events in the story using the pictures. (DOK 1) • Write words that relate to the picture. (DOK 2)

Source for standards: NGA & CCSSO, 2010.

Although this example lists kindergarten literacy standards, teacher teams will complete the information based on their grade-level standards and collaborative team agreements. Also, this unit includes CCSS under the categories of literature, writing, and foundational skills, but teams can complete the process using whatever standards they are obligated to implement. This same process applies for teams in subject areas other than ELA as they address literacy standards. After all, students acquire content through complex text across all disciplines and should write to demonstrate comprehension. For example, those who teach science or social studies can identify one or more of these four literacy-focused strands, or domains—(1) reading, (2) writing, (3) speaking and listening, and (4) language—as crucial aspects of learning about habitats, weather, exploration, or why a community needs rules.

As you make your way through the rest of this and subsequent chapters, we encourage you and your teams to revisit this PREP template, as the new information you encounter will shed light on concepts embedded in the template and provide more direction on its practical application.

Taking a deep dive into a unit through the PREP affords grade-level teams the opportunity to fully define the nuances of those standards that are most essential to a student's academic success. The PREP also helps teams establish a clear and consistent vision for student learning throughout the unit. One benefit of using this tool is the way it facilitates teams chunking curriculum content. In *The New Art and Science of Teaching*, Robert J. Marzano (2017) emphasizes that teachers need to chunk content when teaching new information. Breaking hefty content into digestible pieces helps students learn since they "can hold only small amounts of information in their working memories" (Marzano, 2017, p. 30). Aside from the effectiveness of this approach for all learners, preK through first-grade students especially need each facet of a new literacy skill broken down. These young learners are notorious for their limited attention spans. Inside a typical classroom brimming with classmates and play centers, students will no doubt encounter plenty of distractions. Since they can only remember the content they can attend to, delivering instruction in small chunks is critical in enhancing young learners' literacy development.

Enter Unit Standards Into the Template

At the start of the PREP, an essential part of your team's discussions centers around the targeted standards for your unit of study. A myriad of concepts and skills reside in a single standard, and a unit typically addresses multiple standards. When considering a unit of instruction that consists of multiple standards across several strands (or *domains*) of literacy instruction the skill demands are multiplied.

A *unit* is a subdivision of instruction in a subject matter and might be interdisciplinary; it entails a series of standards-based interconnected lessons that together share a common focus. For example, language arts teachers might conduct a narrative unit in which students encounter various works of fiction and then craft their own stories. In social studies, a representative topic for a unit might focus on important historical figures or take a more thematic approach such as community workers or conflict and cooperation. In an interdisciplinary unit, students might study weather patterns, conduct research and write an information report, and design various graphs to track different weather conditions. Unit lengths vary from a mini-unit of two weeks to a comprehensive unit of perhaps eight weeks. Although teachers conduct various formative assessments all throughout a unit, a unit culminates in a summative assessment that measures the students' comprehensive understanding of all standards in the unit. See the discussion about assessments in chapter 2 (page 39) for more on this topic.

The exact compilation of standards that comprises a unit of literacy instruction will depend on three things.

1. Unit of study

2. Teaching resources

3. Curriculum pacing

If your district has purchased a packaged reading or writing program from a publisher, the learning standards may already be organized by unit or module. If your district has a content-specific curriculum map that outlines the learning standards for a unit or cycle of instruction, the standards would be transferred from the district outline.

In either case, entering every standard that will be addressed into the PREP template is an important first step in clarifying what students need to know and do to be proficient by the end of a unit. Teams may feel compelled to prioritize the standards, choosing only those that are absolutely essential. Step 2 of the PREP covers this process. For now, however, teams enter *every* standard pertaining to a specific unit.

Be cautious to not skip any remaining steps when you are transferring standards from a district or school list or purchased program. You might think the curriculum is spelled out, but teams of teachers must examine each learning standard and come to a collective agreement on its precise meaning and implications for instruction. While educators teach using various resources, such as published reading and writing programs, district curriculum materials, or teacher-generated units, the explicit and implicit skills embedded in the learning standards are what drive a well-designed and robust instructional plan and accompanying assessment.

Looking at the example in figure 1.1 (pages 14–16), you'll notice that some standards are written as general learning goals from which granular-level standards are established. Take, for example, RF.K.1: "Demonstrate understanding of the organization and basic features of print" (NGA & CCSSO, 2010). While this is the general learning goal for this foundational skills standard, the team has specifically broken down four detailed substandards (RF.K.1a, RF.K.1b, RF.K.1c, and RF.K.1d) students must master to be proficient in the foundational skills standard, or general learning goal. Foundational skills provide the building blocks necessary for becoming a competent and proficient reader. In preK through first grade, foundational skills instruction typically focuses on print concepts, phonological awareness, phonics and word recognition, and fluency.

Entering both the overall learning standards and substandards gives teams access to all components of student learning and helps provide additional specificity on student expectations.

EXERCISE

Enter Unit Standards Into the PREP Template

To prepare for the six-step PREP, write the entire set of standards for a targeted unit your team is planning to teach. As teams read about each step throughout this chapter, they may stop to participate in exercises and return to the PREP template to record more information. Alternatively, teams can read the entire chapter and work on all exercises in a fluid fashion.

Use the following questions to guide this exercise.

★ What unit will our team work on together to practice the PREP process? When will we teach this unit?

★ How can we work as a collaborative team to identify standards for this first step in the PREP process?

★ What plan can we put in place to address logistical decisions such as, When and where will we meet? Who will facilitate the meeting? Who will access the template and perhaps convert it to a Google Doc to share with others? Who will enter the information onto the template?

★ If I am in a situation where I do not have a collaborative team in my building or district (I am a singleton teacher), who can I reach out to from another school or district?

Indicate Priority Standards

So much to teach and not enough time. This seems to be a universal concern for teachers across grade levels. With dozens of standards, a multitude of essential skills, a sea of rich texts, and an array of lessons, one question lingers on the minds of educators everywhere: How do I fit it all in?

The next PREP step helps with this feeling of being overwhelmed. After entering all the unit standards into the PREP template, the next step is to *prioritize* the standards. Your collaborative team will decide what is most essential for students to learn; the corresponding standards, or *priority standards*, will become the emphasis for that unit of study. (Note that some educators call priority standards either *power* or *essential standards*, which are all interchangeable terms.)

Because there is simply not enough time in the school year to adequately and deeply teach all the standards listed in a district curriculum guide or provided for in a published literacy series, teams must determine which of the standards are priorities. If your team has already prioritized standards, you would simply identify the priority standards by bolding and italicizing them in the PREP template. The standards represent essential learning outcomes to be taught by all teachers in a unit. If your team has not yet established priority standards, follow along through the rest of step 2 to identify the standards that will become the basis for instruction, assessment, and intervention. Keep in mind that any one unit typically has no more than five priority standards.

Priority standards are, according to education consultant and former classroom teacher Larry Ainsworth (2013):

> a carefully selected *subset* of the total list of the grade-specific and course-specific standards within each content area that students must know and be able to do by the end of each school year in order to be prepared for the standards in the next grade level or course. (p. xv)

The list of prioritized standards becomes the focus of instruction and assessment as well as intervention when students do not learn them.

Standards not deemed a priority are not forgotten or neglected. Instead, they take on more of a supporting role (Ainsworth, 2013). Simply put, determining priority standards helps teams separate the "need to know" from the "nice to know" learning (DuFour et al., 2016):

> The process of prioritizing the standards has significant benefits. It creates greater clarity about what teachers will teach, which in turn, promotes more efficient planning and sharing of resources. Perhaps the greatest benefit of prioritizing the standards is that it encourages teachers to embrace more in-depth instruction by reducing the pressure to simply cover the material. (p. 117)

In essence, when we cram too many standards into a unit of instruction, we are forced to sprint through curriculum, "sacrificing deep, rich teaching, . . . chipping away at our students' motivation" (Gallagher, 2009, p. 10). Focusing on priority standards gives teachers permission to slow down the pace and engage students deeply in the standards that are most essential to their learning.

If teams have not prioritized standards, they can determine which merit priority designation using the following four-step process (Bailey, Jakicic, & Spiller, 2014; Reeves, 2002).

1. Teams review the task and criteria for determining priority standards.

2. Individuals review standards and critique them against criteria.

3. Individuals share impressions with the team.

4. Teams review other sources of information for vertical alignment and accountability to external assessments.

Teams Review the Task and Criteria for Determining Priority Standards

Before teams begin to prioritize, they get an overview of the standards' expectations, reading these criteria and gaining clarity about what each means (Ainsworth, 2013; Reeves, 2002). It is important to note, though, that each standard does not necessarily need to meet all of the following criteria to be deemed a priority.

▸ **Does the standard have *endurance*?** Are the skills and knowledge embedded in the standard critical for students to remember beyond the course or unit in which it is taught? For example, the ability to coherently summarize complex text is a skill that extends beyond a particular unit of instruction. Summarization is therefore an enduring skill worth teaching.

▸ **Does this standard have *leverage*?** Are the skills and knowledge applicable across several disciplines? For example, summarizing complex text might be taught in language arts when students experience a literary work, but it is equally valuable when reading content in social studies and science.

▸ **Is the standard needed for student *readiness*?** Does the standard include prerequisite skills and knowledge necessary for the next grade? For example, when students learn the structure and elements of an opinion paper, it equips them with needed skills and knowledge to tackle the more rigorous work of argumentation writing.

▸ **Is the standard needed for *high-stakes exams*?** Will students need to know and apply the standard's skills and knowledge on external exams? For example, in district, state or provincial, college, or vocational exams, students might need to respond to questions or to writing prompts geared to the standard. Teachers should take this into consideration when discussing which standards are necessary for student preparedness.

Through thoughtful conversations around the endurance, leverage, and readiness of each reading standard, the kindergarten team that completed the PREP template in figure 1.1 (pages 14–16) decided that targets RL.K.1 ("With prompting and support, ask and answer questions about key details in a text") and RL.K.3 ("With prompting and support, identify characters, settings, and major events in a story") carried significant weight in terms of their current impact on student achievement and lifelong learning (NGA & CCSSO, 2010). For example, during their discussions, team members recognized how these two prioritized reading standards focus on strengthening students' basic reading comprehension and ability to respond to a text, which leads the way to a deeper analysis of texts down the road. Because of the foundation they establish for students' comprehension of and response to fiction, these two standards were decided to meet the criteria for endurance, leverage, and readiness. Likewise, teachers agreed that often the questions on high-stakes exams demand mastery of these standards.

Take standard RL.K.1, for instance: "With prompting and support, ask and answer questions about key details in a text" (NGA & CCSSO, 2010). This standard has *endurance* in that students are expected to ask and answer questions related to key ideas in a text throughout most of their educational careers (and beyond). In fact, in examining the progression of the CCSS, students are expected to discuss the key ideas of literary texts at every successive grade level through high school. Similarly, this standard is necessary for student *readiness* as the skills embedded in it prepare students for the next level of learning. In looking ahead to the third-grade standard RL.3.1, students are eventually expected to "ask and answer questions to demonstrate understanding of a text, referring explicitly to the text as the basis for the answers" (NGA & CCSSO, 2010). Certainly, students will likely struggle with the more complex skill of using evidence to support their understanding of a text without first mastering the skills of asking and answering questions related to the key ideas in a text. To be ready to learn the concepts that will be addressed in the grades ahead of them, students must first be proficient in this priority kindergarten standard.

Finally, the team of kindergarten teachers talked about this standard's *leverage*, which sparked compelling questions and considerations. What value does this standard bring to other disciplines? Is it a universal skill that has the leverage to impact a student's overall academic success? While teachers likely noted that other content disciplines, such as science and social studies, typically require reading skills needed to comprehend informational texts, they all agreed that learning how to ask and answer questions about a text is a lifelong skill that cannot be ignored. And it is, after all, the primary way we engage in the reading and discussion of a text. Therefore, RL.K.1 became a priority standard for this unit of instruction.

As the team progressed through the prioritization process, an insightful dialogue emerged over the reading foundational skills standards of RF.K.1 and RF.K.3, which the CCSS further breaks down into four substandards each. Rather than prioritizing the entire standard, this kindergarten team chose to prioritize the following substandards—RF.K.1d: "Recognize and name all upper- and lowercase letters of the alphabet" and RF.K.3a: "Demonstrate basic knowledge of one-to-one letter-sound correspondences by producing the primary sound or many of the most frequent sounds for each consonant" (NGA & CCSSO, 2010).

These substandards meet the criteria of endurance, readiness, and leverage because recognizing letters and their corresponding sounds is a necessary first step in learning to read and write. Also, from an instructional standpoint, these foundational skill substandards are logically integrated during instruction. Rather than focusing a lesson solely on letter recognition, instructors can maximize student learning by teaching letter names and sounds, along with their written formation, together in an efficient and brain-friendly manner.

It is also important to note that supporting standards can and often do become priority standards later in the year. Teams should reassess priority standards at the end of each unit based on student data and results. For instance, if students struggled to master a particular standard, perhaps the standard is better suited for a unit later in the school year. To help fill in any gaps in students' learning, teams might also prioritize a different standard for a unit. For example, at the end of a fiction unit requiring first-grade students to comprehend grade-level texts, the teacher team might discover that their students need more practice decoding before they can master the more complex standard of reading with accuracy and fluency.

Standards the team does not identify as priority for a unit move to a supporting role that connects to or enhances the priority standards, and they "are taught within the context of the Priority Standards, but do not receive the same degree of instruction and assessment emphasis as do the Priority Standards" (Ainsworth, 2013, p. xv). While teachers may not place an emphasis on a particular standard during initial units of study, it may become a primary focus for instruction and assessment during subsequent units. For example, although reading standard RL.K.2 ("With prompting and support, retell familiar stories, including key details") is pivotal in helping kindergarteners develop the skills necessary to eventually determine the central idea of a text and explain how it is conveyed through key details, the kindergarten team decided not to prioritize it for this unit of study taught at the beginning of the school year (NGA & CCSSO, 2010). Since many kindergartners enter school with little experience with or exposure to text, the team chose first to focus instruction, intervention, and assessment on helping students engage, react, and respond to text before they tackled the more complicated skill of sequencing the key details of the plot in correct order. Later in the year when students are ready for the rigor of standard RL.K.2, the team can choose to make it a priority standard.

After determining priority standards for the target unit, the team now unwraps these standards to examine the specific knowledge and skills embedded in each one. This will help teams develop assessments and design instruction. In the next section, we explain what unwrapping entails and provide examples related to the kindergarten fiction unit on friendship and acceptance.

Once team members are clear on the task and criteria, they are ready to proceed.

Individuals Review Standards and Critique Them Against Criteria

Individuals on the team review each standard and determine to what degree each meets the criteria. Each team member applies professional knowledge and judgment to annotate the standards she or he believes meets one or more of the criteria. For example, electronically or by hand, teachers enter E for endurance, L for leverage, R for readiness, and H for high-stakes exams next to each standard. For those that do not meet any of these criteria, no mark is needed.

This silent exercise enables think time to foster individual accountability. Special educators should be full participants in this process if they teach the content and should approach this process with typical grade-level expectations in mind. While special educators will naturally consider their students' current gaps, they should not determine priority based on individual students. Base priority on high expectations for all grade-level students. You can set a time limit for this initial activity. Five minutes per standard will allow enough time for discussion.

Individuals Share Impressions With the Team

For the team to arrive at an initial list of priority standards, each teacher shares his or her choices using a round-robin structure. One person begins by identifying a standard he or she chooses as a priority, using the criteria—endurance, leverage, readiness, and high-stakes exams—as justification and explanation. Be wary of support that includes individual bias or personal feelings about continuing a long-standing trend. Team members should select only those standards that meet the criteria. If teammates have difficulty agreeing, or if the discussion gets too emotional, go back to step one to review the criteria for endurance, leverage, and readiness (Bailey et al., 2014). By referring to the specific guidelines detailed in the criteria, teammates can interject and disagree with each other in a more diplomatic way.

As team members share, naturally a discussion will ensue. Encourage that discussion, since it will likely uncover misconceptions about standards as well as provide clarity about them. For this step to be productive, teams can abide by the following.

- Assign a scribe to record the standards that are deemed priority and those that are supporting.
- Determine in advance how the team will handle a lack of consensus.
- Ask each team member to share his or her annotated standards until everyone is satisfied with an initial list of priority standards.

Teams Review Other Sources of Information for Vertical Alignment and Accountability to External Assessments

To make final decisions, team members consider how the standards align vertically and the expectations for external accountability assessments. For vertical alignment, teams review previous and subsequent grade-level, subject-area, and course standards. For instance, in reviewing first-grade reading standards for literature, a kindergarten team realizes that in addition to teaching students to identify characters, settings, and major events in a story, they should also instruct students on how to use key details to help identify those story elements, as this skill is necessary for students to master the next level of learning, in which they must describe the story elements with text evidence.

It is prudent for teams to share their initial set of priority standards in person or electronically with other grade-level teams and collect feedback to ensure proper alignment. If the entire school or district participates in this process, all teams or representatives from each grade-level team can work on vertical progression.

Teams will also want to pay attention to the amount of emphasis the state accountability assessment places on particular standards. States typically release test blueprints or other documents that identify the percentage of test items aligned to particular standards. Other district documents or assessment data can also be considered.

EXERCISE

Indicate (or Determine) Priority Standards

Review the standards you put in the PREP template. If your team has already prioritized standards, distinguish these priority standards from supporting ones by bolding, underlining, or color-coding them. If you haven't yet prioritized, do so following the steps given in this section and then mark them in the template.

Use the following questions to guide this exercise.

★ Which standards are most essential to a student's academic and lifelong success?

★ Which of our standards meet the criteria for endurance, leverage, and readiness?

★ Are there supporting standards that will become priority standards in a unit later in the school year?

Unwrap Unit Priority Standards

A common misconception among many teacher teams is that listing unit standards sufficiently represents the basis for all instructional decisions moving forward. One might think, "I've got a list of standards right here, so I'm ready to teach." However, this is not the case. To fully understand each priority standard and guarantee a consistent curriculum across all grade-level classrooms, teams must examine each content-area standard and arrive at a collective agreement about its precise meaning and implications for instruction, assessment, and intervention.

Kindergarten and first-grade standards might seem straightforward, but they are often open to interpretations. For example, carefully examine the RL.K.2 CCSS kindergarten reading standard: "With prompting and support, retell familiar stories, including key details" (NGA & CCSSO, 2010). As mentioned in the introduction (page 1), the phrase *with prompting and support*, which appears in many kindergarten standards, is highly subjective. To some teachers, prompting and support might mean providing students with sentence stems, such as *the first event in the story was* _____. To other teachers, it might mean prompting students with a series of questions, such as, "What happens first? What happens next? How did the story end?" In addition, teachers might have different opinions of the term *key details*. How many key details must students mention during a retell? Do students need to retell all the key details? What if they can retell most or just a few of them?

Discussions regarding the particular details of a standard come alive during the unwrapping process, helping teachers realize when they have conflicting interpretations that might lead to very different learning experiences for students from one classroom to the next. By working through their differences, teachers achieve greater clarity on what they will be teaching.

It is the explicit and implicit skills and knowledge embedded in standards from which they will design a robust instructional plan. According to authors Kim Bailey and Chris Jakicic (2017):

The goal of the unwrapping process is twofold: first, to build shared or collective understanding of what the standard asks students to know and do; and second, to identify the smaller increments of learning, or learning targets, that will create a step-by-step path leading to that standard. (p. 21)

As teams unwrap standards, they pay particular attention to the nouns and verbs that define and describe the desired learning outcomes. You can see how this is done by noting the words in all capital letters or underlined in figure 1.1 (pages 14–16).

To give credence to unwrapping and provide teachers an authentic reason for participating in this critical step, they might talk about how they teach to a standard and what evidence of learning they have asked students to produce. For example, consider priority standard RL.K.3: "With prompting and support, identify characters, settings, and major events in a story" (NGA & CCSSO, 2010). One team member might ask students to generate a list of the different characters, settings, or events from the story. Another teacher on the same team asks students to draw a picture of a character during a major event in the story and label the key details from the text depicted in the scene. These examples are illustrative in a continuum of various interpretations—one more rudimentary in its design and expectation, the other requiring a more in-depth application of the standard.

To unwrap, teams can annotate a standard using a protocol like the one in figure 1.2.

Since there are several layers to each standard, teachers on a grade-level team can interpret the words differently. When teams participate in the unwrapping process, close examination and analysis of every verb, noun, and conjunction leads to a richer understanding of the complexity.

- With prompting and support, ASK and ANSWER questions about key details in a text. (RL.K.1)

Source for standard: NGA & CCSSO, 2010.

Figure 1.2: Using annotation to unwrap priority standards.

Find and Capitalize, Boldface, or Circle Verbs

While unwrapping this standard, the teachers recognized that there are two verbs embedded in this one learning standard: (1) *ask* and (2) *answer*. To assess student proficiency, the team felt it would not be enough simply to require students to *ask* questions about key details in a text; to meet the *entirety* of the standard, students would need to *answer* questions about key details in a text as well. This requires a more complex and sophisticated extension of knowledge and understanding. To be able to ask questions is one essential skill, but to answer those questions by drawing on key details in a text is an entirely different expectation.

Underline Nouns or Noun Phrases That Represent the Instructed Content and Concepts

Underlining the nouns and phrases in a standard allows teachers to pinpoint the knowledge items and conditions necessary for mastery. In the same standard, teachers underlined the noun *questions* and prepositional phrases *with prompting and support* and *about key details in a text*. Although the prepositional phrases can be lengthy, they identify the context in which students will demonstrate their learning. In this example, the team decided students need to understand the key details of a text in order to ask and answer related questions, and if students require, teachers can provide prompting and support. This is an important implication because teams will need to set clear expectations regarding what prompting and support might consist of during instruction and assessment. See chapter 3 (page 61) for further examination.

Unwrapping standards provokes an intentional conversation about the specific skills and concepts necessary for instruction and assessment. Prior to participating in the collaborative unwrapping process, a teacher might, for example and at first glance, perceive a standard to require students to provide only simple questions and answers about the text. However, close examination and analysis of every noun and verb leads to a deeper understanding of the complexity and entirety of the reading standard.

Educators Heather Friziellie, Julie A. Schmidt, and Jeanne Spiller (2016) write:

> Unpacking standards enables every teacher who teaches the standard to develop a deep and consistent understanding of the standard and its component expectations. The outcome is that students will receive instruction that is truly aligned to the expected rigor and complexity of the standard. (p. 46)

Once they have annotated standards in the PREP template, teachers keep them readily available to use as they identify knowledge items in the following step.

EXERCISE

Unwrapping Unit Priority Standards

Collaborative teams work on unwrapping their standards to gain clarity about learning goals. To do so, refer to the targeted priority standards on the PREP template and mark them according to the steps articulated in this process step.

Use the following questions to guide this exercise.

★ What verbs and nouns do we notice in our priority standards?

★ What smaller, incremental learning goals, or learning targets, exist in each overarching standard?

★ Are there important conjunctions (like *and* or *or*) to decipher when unwrapping a standard?

Identify Knowledge Items

After (or even while) teams unwrap and annotate standards, together they answer the question, What do we want students to know? This includes the factual information that forms the foundation for addressing standards and understanding deeper concepts. *Knowledge* comprises facts, dates, people, places, examples, and vocabulary terms, although not all standards or units necessarily include all these items. *Knowledge items* delineate what we want students to know, so they are written using nouns and noun phrases.

When compiling knowledge items, teams must consider the explicitly *and* implicitly stated information that students will need to know in order to address a particular standard. To illustrate, refer back to the kindergarten reading standard RL.K.1: "With prompting and support, ask and answer questions about key details in a text" (NGA & CCSSO, 2010). When discussing this standard, teams ask themselves, "What will students need to know in order to successfully master the entirety of this standard?" While they will certainly list the explicitly stated nouns including *questions* and *key details*, they will also add inferential knowledge items.

It's important to note that not all knowledge items are explicitly stated within the standard; often teachers must "read between the lines" to determine any implied knowledge needed for mastery (Bailey et al., 2014, p. 64). As illustrated in figure 1.3, the kindergarten team determined that mastering the priority standard requires students to know that *questions can ask* who, what, when, where, why, *and* how, although this item is not explicitly mentioned in the standard.

Unit Priority Standard	Knowledge
RL.K.1 With prompting and support, ask and answer questions about key details in a text.	• Readers understand the difference between a question and statement. • Questions can ask *who, what, when, where, why,* and *how.* • Readers ask questions of the author to help understand a text more deeply. • Readers use background knowledge and clues from the text to help understand a text more deeply. • Readers show understanding of key details by explaining their thinking.

Source for standard: NGA & CCSSO, 2010.

Figure 1.3: Listing knowledge items for a priority standard.

Generating knowledge items is a rather concrete exercise, although it can take a while. In our work with teams, the process can take anywhere from ten to fifteen minutes per standard for adequate discussion without getting too carried away. This is especially true if individual teachers are not necessarily familiar with the content. For example, teachers who move to teach a new grade, are just entering the profession, or are teaching new material will need to devote more time to this component. Very often, however, these focused conversations and collaborative exercises reveal new insights about knowledge items and implicit skills that even veteran teachers hadn't considered. Teams do not initially rank the items, which can help make the practice easier. Working collaboratively in your PLC on this process is therefore essential so all members of a team are clear about the foundational knowledge that leads to deeper, conceptual understanding.

EXERCISE
Identify Knowledge Items

Work as a collaborative team to identify knowledge items aligned to your unwrapped standards. When ready, add these items, aligned to each unwrapped standard, to your PREP template. Your team might generate a list, reference a page number from a source (for example, a page in a textbook with engaging ways to begin a story, a diagram, or a list of vocabulary), or create a graphic organizer.

Be aware that sometimes a standard is lean and does not include all that it should in order to address it thoroughly. These knowledge items are therefore implied. For example, the standard "Use dialogue and description to develop experiences and events" requires teams to keep probing and repeatedly complete this sentence frame: *I want students to know . . .* (W.4.3b; NGA & CCSSO, 2010). For example, *I want students to know that dialogue should serve a purpose, such as moving the plot forward or showing characters' reactions. I want students to know types of dialogue or speaker tags—beginning, middle, end, or no tag.*

Use the following questions to guide this exercise.

★ What should students know relative to a priority standard targeted for this lesson?

★ What knowledge items do we expect students to know that are explicitly stated?

★ Which knowledge items are implicit and require us to make inferences?

Determine Skills

Teams now review their annotation of unwrapped standards and knowledge items (in list form or on a graphic representation) to identify skills—what students actually *do*. Education consultant H. Lynn Erickson (2002) defines *skills* as the "specific competencies required for complex process performance. Skills need to be taught directly and practiced in context" (p. 166). Therefore, it is incumbent on teachers to explicitly teach skills through authentic, real-world learning experiences.

Students in preK through first grade require different learning experiences than those implemented in older elementary classrooms. As Gaye Gronlund (2013) explains in her book *Planning for Play, Observation, and Learning in Preschool and Kindergarten*, young children are active learners, and "watching demonstrations or listening to lectures is not their primary mode for taking in new information" (p. 13). Rather, prekindergartners, kindergarteners, and first graders need to actively explore, experiment, and try out new skills for themselves. Often, playful learning—a key component to the development of quality early childhood education—provides teachers with an ideal, authentic context for integrating explicit literacy instruction. For example, a teacher might engage students in writing scripts for a puppet show, crafting song lyrics, or playing word games based on a new phonics skill.

In addition, by peeking into students' make-believe worlds and carefully observing their performance with a targeted skill, teachers can assess students' proficiency levels and determine next instruction steps. Authentic assessment opportunities such as these are better suited to the developmental level and experiences of young students. Since prekindergarten students are not good test takers, traditional paper-and-pencil assessments do not always generate reliable data. Instead, young learners need opportunities to demonstrate competence in more appropriate ways, such as "teachers' observations of children, clinical interviews, collections of children's work samples, and their performance on authentic activities" (NAEYC, 2009a, p. 22).

The unwrapped, annotated priority standards serve as a guide to determine skills. Standards, like skills, include verbs. However, some of the verbs used in the content standards are not necessarily observable but rather vaguely measurable mental verbs, such as *understand* and *know*. Instead, teams should vie for using measurable action verbs like *define, analyze,* or *compare*. For example, in this grade band, students can *define* a science concept or term, such as *evaporation*, through drawing, labeling, or orally explaining. During shared reading, students can *analyze* a fictional character's traits by referring to key details in the story and orally explaining how the character reacts to them. To *compare* in mathematics, students can sort a group of items, such as blocks of different shapes and color, according to their characteristics and then orally explain their reasoning behind the categories they create. Therefore, teams need to study the annotated standards and knowledge items to fashion skills that are sufficient to cover the intent of the standard as well as concrete enough to measure student aptitude. Once identified and defined, these skills are often referred to as *learning targets*—"smaller increments of learning . . .

that will create a step-by-step path leading to that standard" (Bailey & Jakicic, 2017, p. 21). Throughout this book, you'll notice references to both learning targets (the skills embedded in the standards) and standards (overall learning goals).

With a collective understanding around what students need to know (knowledge) and be able to do (skills), teachers can design instruction that addresses these skills explicitly. It is imperative that educators pay attention to each standard's verb and full context so that the rigor of instruction matches the expectation for students. For example, consider the first bullet in the PREP template's Skills column. Students need to be able to ask questions about key details in a text. That means it is a priority that instruction leads students to be able to *ask* questions that lead to clarification of what they have read, rather than asking questions unrelated or tangential to the text at hand. Likewise, assessment will need to match the exact skill that is being measured. In this case, students cannot simply select a multiple-choice answer to demonstrate that they know how to ask. Essentially, they would be selecting questions that have already been spelled out in a multiple-choice format. Rather, the assessment should be open-ended, giving students the opportunity to show they can meet the rigor of the skill.

Figure 1.4 highlights the skills identified for the friendship and acceptance unit.

Unit Priority Standard	Knowledge	Skills (Learning Targets)
RL.K.1 With prompting and support, ask and answer questions about key details in a text.	• Readers understand the difference between a question and statement. • Questions can ask *who, what, when, where, why,* and *how.* • Readers ask questions of the author to help understand a text more deeply. • Readers use background knowledge and clues from the text to help understand a text more deeply. • Readers show understanding of key details by explaining their thinking.	• Ask questions to clarify understanding of a text. • Answer questions about a character, setting, or event in a story, drawing on key details in the text.

Source for standard: NGA & CCSSO, 2010.

Figure 1.4: Listing skills for a priority standard.

EXERCISE
Determine Skills

Using the unwrapped, annotated standards and the knowledge items, collaborative teams work on determining skills and enter them on their work-in-progress PREP template. For examples of skills to use as a guide, refer back to figure 1.1 (pages 14–16).

Use the following questions to guide this exercise.

★ What cognitive process can students demonstrate to show they can apply what they've learned?

★ What measurable action verbs can our team align to each unwrapped standard?

★ Do the skills have transfer value rather than being anchored to specific content?

After unwrapping priority standards, identifying knowledge items, and determining skills, collaborative teams are primed to consider the level of intended rigor for each learning target. This will help them later, when developing assessments. To ensure students have the benefit of a rich learning experience, teams conscientiously assign depth of knowledge to the skills.

Assign Levels of Rigor (DOK) for Learning Targets

Teams now return to the unwrapped skills that serve as learning targets to examine complexity. This scrutiny can lead to powerful discussions regarding the learning targets' intended rigor; this discussion helps teachers match the challenge level in their instruction and assessments. We use Norman Webb's (1997, 1999) Depth of Knowledge, a thinking taxonomy, to identify the level of rigor in our examples.

DOK is a scale of cognitive demand composed of the following four levels (Webb, 1997, 1999).

1. **Recall:** Level 1 requires rote recall of information of facts, definitions, terms, or simple procedures. The student either knows the answer or does not.

2. **Skills and concepts:** Level 2 requires engagement of mental processing or decision making beyond recall or reproduction. Items falling into this

category often have more than one step, such as organizing and comparing data.

3. **Strategic thinking:** Level 3 requires higher-level thinking than levels 1 and 2 and could include activities or contexts that have more than one possible solution, thereby requiring justification or support for the argument or process.

4. **Extended thinking:** Level 4 requires high cognitive demand in which students are synthesizing ideas across content areas or situations and generalizing that information to solve new problems. Many responses falling into this category will require extensive time as they imply that students will be completing multiple steps, as in a multivariant investigation and analysis.

Webb's DOK differs from other taxonomies by looking beyond the verb used in the learning target and examining the context in which skills are to be performed and the depth of thinking required. Although the verb choice helps indicate the complexity, teachers must consider the full context of the standard since the verb does not always give the complete picture of rigorous expectations. For example, teachers can devise any of these learning targets using the verb *identify*, but each carries a different level of expectation: *Identify* a character in the story. *Identify* the traits of a character. *Identify* a change in a character's perspective. Asking students to identify a character from a story requires nothing more than basic recall—DOK level 1. To identify a character's traits, students must make a decision based on a story's facts—DOK level 2. Identifying a change in a character's perspective involves the higher-level thinking of DOK level 3, since students must formulate an argument and justify their claims with support.

What DOK level did we assign to the first learning target for RL.K.1: "With prompting and support, ask and answer questions about key details in a text" (NGA & CCSSO, 2010)? Figure 1.5 (page 36), an excerpt from the full PREP template, shows that we assigned the learning target *Ask questions to clarify understanding of a text* a DOK level 2, because it requires students to draw on the characters, events, and details of a story in order to formulate their own clarifying questions about the text.

Knowing if the learning target is a DOK level 2 or higher, and that more is then expected than simple recall of information, teams should discuss the type of assessment that will best indicate whether students are meeting this expectation at the intended level of rigor. If students are expected to *apply* their knowledge that

Unwrapped Unit Priority Standard (Words that appear in capital letters in this template are key verbs in the teaching unit; underlined words are key nouns and noun phrases.)	Knowledge Items	Skills (Learning Targets and DOK Levels)
RL.K.1 With prompting and support, ASK and ANSWER questions about key details in a text.	• Readers understand the difference between a question and statement. • Questions can ask *who, what, when, where, why,* and *how.* • Readers ask questions of the author to help understand a text more deeply. • Readers use background knowledge and clues from the text to help understand a text more deeply. • Readers show understanding of key details by explaining their thinking.	• Ask questions to clarify understanding of a text. (DOK 2) • Answer questions about a character, setting, or event in a story, drawing on key details in the text. (DOK 2)

Source for standard: NGA & CCSSO, 2010.

Figure 1.5: Listing DOK levels for a priority standard.

questions can ask *who, what, when, where, why,* and *how* and that readers ask the author questions to understand a text, then the assessment questions also need to go beyond simple recall of terms. Assessment will be discussed further in chapter 2 (page 39).

When considering the level of expectations of learning targets, be careful not to change a target's intended rigor for students with special needs, students learning English, or those simply struggling with the content or skills. One exception is for students with severe disabilities who may not be able to function independently as an adult. Each of these students should be considered separately to determine an instructional plan that is as rigorous as possible.

For all students, it is more effective to determine how instructional scaffolds and supports could be employed to ensure that students can meet the intended rigor as opposed to beginning instruction at a grade level lower than the student's age-appropriate placement. This decision demonstrates the commitment to supporting students in truly closing the learning gap because it means we continue to focus on all students' progress toward grade-appropriate learning targets. Work with your team on the following exercise to identify DOK levels so you can afford learning that challenges students appropriately. Access to rigorous standards for all students is discussed further in chapter 9 (page 239).

At this point in the PREP template completion, add DOK levels, indicating the cognitive demand for each of the learning targets.

EXERCISE

Assign Levels of Rigor for Learning Targets

Refer to figure 1.1 (pages 14–16) for support in assigning DOK levels for your learning targets.

Use the following questions to guide this exercise.

★ Has our team considered the full context of the standard rather than relying on the verb alone, which sometimes gives an incomplete picture of rigor?

★ What is the complexity of each skill embedded in the full standard?

★ Have we keenly reviewed our learning targets to be sure we are not consistently aiming too low or even too high?

Summary

In a PLC, critical question one—*What is it we want our students to learn?*—incorporates several components that begin with and derive from standards. Together the standards drive effective curriculum design, and each component in the six-step pre-unit protocol has a role and purpose. The *knowledge* items represent foundational information that is specific to content material, the *skills* reflect what students are expected to do, and *depth of knowledge* ensures appropriate rigor. As collaborative teams complete the PREP template, they assure their students the quality-driven and rigorous curriculum they so rightly deserve.

In the next chapter, we explore how the PREP work integrates with assessments, which consequently guides instruction for students. We also discuss the different types of assessment and the learning progression necessary to prepare students for performing well on a given assessment. Additionally, we share rubrics for assessing mastery and as an instructional tool, examine collaborative scoring, and discuss how to productively use the information gleaned from student work to further achievement. Keep exploring with us as we connect coherent and robust instruction in literacy to useful assessments for our students in preK through first grade.

CHAPTER 2

Review Assessment Types and Formats

In chapter 1, we took a deep dive into the first critical question of a PLC to establish precisely what students need to know and be able to do by the end of a unit. In doing so, collaborative teams follow the proposed six-step PREP to secure common learning expectations for every student in every classroom, solidifying a foundation from which all subsequent unit planning evolves. By establishing clarity on the priority standards to be assessed *and* the specific knowledge and skills students must acquire to show proficiency, teachers set the groundwork for the second critical question of a PLC: "How will we know if each student has learned it?" (DuFour et al., 2016, p. 59).

Assessment is particularly important in making instructional decisions in the primary grades due to the diverse levels of knowledge and skills students possess. For some students, this initial classroom setting is their first experience with literacy, while others have been immersed at home or elsewhere. We have worked with students who come into the classroom with little knowledge of how to write their name or how to hold a book, as opposed to those who already know how to read. For this reason, assessment is imperative for the primary classroom teacher to determine levels of knowledge, as well as next steps for each learner.

To provide the tools and guidance to eventually design assessments, this chapter focuses on assessment types and formats, highlighting the unique features of teaching literacy. As a natural extension of these topics, the next two chapters center on identifying classroom and common assessments and rubric design.

Assessment Types and Formats

Throughout an instructional cycle, teachers administer both common and individual classroom assessments to collect data on student progress that drive instruction. Teacher teams design or find common assessments, or revise existing ones, that give students opportunities (yes, many!) to demonstrate their learning in myriad ways. Although the convenience of prepackaged assessments entices teachers, it is necessary for them to review, and sometimes revamp, those assessments to make sure they evaluate precisely the right skills. Whether creating assessments for the first time or planning to administer prepared assessments from a purchased literacy program, teachers must ensure that each assessment clearly measures students' understanding of the priority standards. Whichever assessments are administered, they should reveal who has yet to demonstrate proficiency, and therefore which students require additional support to progress toward mastery, as well as those who need extended opportunities for further challenge.

What follows is an explanation of assessment types along with examples of formats and methods. For a more in-depth examination, conduct your own search to collect information that will augment the discussion that follows. The Illinois Assessment of Readiness Digital Item Library (https://il.digitalitemlibrary.com) hosts a variety of examples categorized by evidence statements. Teacher teams utilize this bank of questions to determine ways to assess learning targets. Although these libraries are designed to display sample questions starting with grade 3, they can be extremely helpful to teachers who educate preschoolers, kindergartners, and first graders so they can gain a sense of rigor in standards. We also list a variety of useful resources in The Assessment Journey section (page 53). Some sources might have slightly different definitions, so reach an agreement as a team. Always be mindful that an assessment must match exactly what you intend to assess so it can inform your teaching and maximize student growth.

Assessment Types

In truth, *assessment*—a term used pervasively in education—can cause confusion with its varied terminology. In essence, teachers "assess to gather information about student learning and either use that information *formatively* to advance learning or use it *summatively* to verify that it has occurred" (Schimmer, 2019). Collaborative teams judiciously choose an appropriate assessment, and even a combination of them, for different purposes based on what will best measure learning targets.

Educational researcher and theorist Robert J. Marzano (2010) identifies three examples of assessments to collect formative scores over time: (1) unobtrusive, (2) obtrusive, and (3) student generated. Obtrusive and student-generated assessments can be couched under more formal assessment formats, such as selected-response and constructed-response items, discussed later in this section and which textbooks and other sources have aplenty. We'll first explain formative and summative assessments.

Formative Assessments

Formative assessments are assessments *for* learning (Stiggins, 2005). Some are unobtrusive and some are obtrusive. They check for understanding and allow students the opportunity to practice skills and strategies in order to eventually master them. In other words, they guide and inform a teacher's instructional plan daily and weekly:

> An assessment functions formatively to the extent that evidence about student achievement is elicited, interpreted, and used by teachers, learners, or their peers *to make decisions about next steps in instruction that are likely to be better, or better founded*, than the decisions they would have made in absence of that evidence. (Wiliam, 2011, p. 43; emphasis added)

Formative assessments, when done well, provide meaningful information about how individual students are progressing throughout an instructional unit. This allows teachers to intervene with students who need a differentiated approach by providing scaffolded support and corrective instruction to those who are almost there, and even extending the learning of already proficient students.

Summative Assessments

In order to check in on student learning, teams collect a variety of formal and informal data from formative and also from *summative* assessments, which are assessments *of* learning (Stiggins, 2005). Traditionally, teachers issue summative assessments at the conclusion of a unit to ascertain what students learned as a culmination of a comprehensive unit of instruction (or course); such assessments were considered evaluative only. Summative assessments are typically scored and used as evidence of student achievement as well as determinants of the next instructional steps or even placement in particular classes; they are obtrusive-type assessments. However, the definition has been broadened to indicate that teachers can assign them to assess mastery of targeted learning objectives at different points in a unit. In this way, some summative assessments can even be considered formative, which is predicated on the way teachers use the assessment data. For example:

> Summative assessment can occur at the end of a unit when all of the learning objectives have been taught, at the end of several lessons that form a subset of meaning in the unit, or even at the end of a single lesson if the lesson

objective has been fully met and students have had adequate opportunity to achieve mastery. Using summative assessments at the end of a lesson or set of lessons helps teachers ensure that students have developed the foundation on which subsequent lessons will build. Summative assessment takes its name from its purpose of "summing up" what students have learned at a logical point in time. (Tomlinson & Moon, 2013, p. 92)

Think of the journey through a unit of instruction as a road trip, from an initial starting point to a desired end point. As teachers travel through their instructional unit from point A to point B, formative assessments are the quick pit stops taken along the way to check in on student learning, while the summative assessments can represent both the longer rest stops (perhaps for lunch!) as well as the final destination. The latter provides evidence of what students have mastered during chunks of instruction plus how far they have traveled at the culmination of a unit of study. Figure 2.1 illustrates an assessment road trip.

With all of this said, we suggest teams use data derived from assessments identified as summative (such as an end-of-unit assessment) to guide instructional decisions about priority standards. Student learning does not abruptly end at unit completion; therefore, teachers should continue to address the learners' needs as data indicate.

Unobtrusive Assessments

Unobtrusive assessments occur while students participate in the learning process and tend to be informal. Marzano (2010) explains that "in contrast to obtrusive assessments, unobtrusive assessments do not interrupt the flow of instruction. In fact, students might not even be aware that they are being assessed" (p. 24). During unobtrusive assessment, teachers watch and listen for specific indicators of student learning, such as the kinds and quality of responses plus the level of engagement. For example, a teacher circulates around the room listening in on small-group discussions or observes students as they complete a quick-write or a graphic organizer (a visual representation of your ideas).

Education researchers Gretchen Owocki and Yetta Goodman (2002) emphasize the need for *kidwatching* in the classroom as a way to gather valuable data on students' strengths and areas for growth:

The primary goals of kidwatching are to support and gain insight into children's learning by (1) intensely observing and documenting what they know

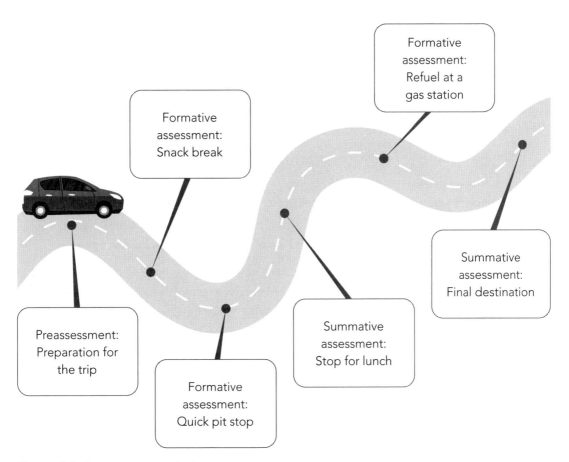

Figure 2.1: Assessment road trip.

and can do; (2) documenting their ways of constructing and expressing knowledge, and (3) planning curriculum and instruction that are tailored to individual strengths and needs. (p. x)

Kidwatching leads to informed decision making. As they kidwatch daily, teachers lean in and listen closely to a student as he reads with his partner, take note when a student struggles with a reading skill during independent practice, or conference with a student to gather valuable input from the student's perspective. The more information teachers have on students, the better they can assist those students during small-group instruction.

As needed, teachers approach students to redirect those who are off topic, pose questions to propel students to arrive at a new insight, or clear up any misconceptions. Additionally, teachers intentionally scan the room during instruction to be sure students actively listen, record key information, or exhibit on-task behavior. If not, they adjust on the spot. For instance, a kindergarten teacher may use a cooperative learning structure such as a Rally Coach (Kagan & Kagan, 2009) to gather data on a student's understanding of medial vowel sounds. While students work with a partner to identify the missing vowel sound, the teacher observes students who are demonstrating full understanding of the learning target, as well as those who may need more support.

Using a checklist or a recordkeeping form like the one in figure 2.2, teachers might opt to track students' contributions so they can attend to gaps in the following days. Checklists are specifically designed for recordkeeping; therefore, teachers must be acquainted with the rubric and know what is expected for mastery prior to conducting the assessment.

Individual teachers informally and unobtrusively assess as part of their daily classroom instruction to check for understanding. Since a collection of assessments provide teachers with salient information to ascertain students' levels of proficiency on essential standards, teachers also use more formal methods to determine how well students can demonstrate a skill.

Obtrusive Assessments

When teachers assign *obtrusive* assessments, they interrupt classroom instruction and issue a task for students to complete or perform, including a quiz, essay, or other artifact. However, there are a host of other obtrusive methods of assessments at varying degrees of engagement. Remember to match any assessment to the purpose and complexity of the measured standards. Consider the literacy examples in which students can do the following.

- Retell a story using a voice recorder.
- Complete a graphic organizer that captures the main topic and key details of a text.
- Write an original setting for a story they will create.
- Draw a picture and write a sentence explaining a fact about the topic.
- Use a dot stamper to identify how many syllables are in a word.
- Fill in the missing sounds in a consonant-vowel-consonant word.

Obtrusive assessments can be both formal and informal. The previous examples depict more formal options in that students produce something they submit to teachers for careful review and oral or written feedback (like constructed

Concept or Skill: Determine whether a sentence is a statement or a question.				
Student Name	**Demonstrates mastery and can apply the concept or skill in an advanced way (4)**	**Demonstrates mastery of the concept or skill (3)**	**Has some understanding of the concept or skill (2)**	**Demonstrates limited understanding of the concept or skill (1)**
John D.			Can explain the difference between statements and questions but can't correctly identify examples of them ✓	
Suzy S.		✓		
Darel J.	✓			
Aditi V.			Inconsistently identifies examples of questions and statements ✓+	

Figure 2.2: Unobtrusive student data recording form—Example.

Visit go.SolutionTree.com/literacy for a free reproducible version of this figure.

responses). Teachers might also issue quick, informal check-ins to indicate next instructional steps. For example, teachers can ask students to turn in an exit slip on the way out of class or before a transition period, respond to questions on whiteboards, or signal with thumbs-up or thumbs-down to prompts (like selected responses). For additional ideas suitable to multiple content areas, see figure 2.3. Some entries can serve as formative or summative depending on how the teacher assigns them and uses the data.

A	B	C	D
All-about book Alphabet book	Book cover Brochure Bulletin board	Cartoons Checklist Comic book	Descriptive writing (of setting, character, individual, event, and so on) Dictionary with pictures
E	**F**	**G**	**H**
Exit ticket Explanatory paragraph	Fable Fairy tale Fantasy story	Graphic organizer Greeting card	Handbook Historical fiction How-to steps
I	**J–K**	**L**	**M**
Informational paragraph Interview (questions or complete script) Invitation	Journal entry	Label Legend Letter	Magazine article or layout Memoir Menu Multimedia project Mural
N	**O**	**P**	**Q–R**
Narrative Nature log Newspaper article or layout	Opinion piece Outline	Pamphlet Personal narrative Poem Portfolio Poster	Questions and answers Reader's theater Research report or project

S	T–U	V	W–Z
Scrapbook (annotated) Short story Song lyric Storyboard Summary	T-chart Timeline Travelogue	Venn diagram	Written response

Source: Adapted from Glass & Marzano, 2018, p. 74.

Figure 2.3: Writing assessment options A to Z.

*Visit **go.SolutionTree.com/literacy** for a free reproducible version of this figure.*

Choose judiciously to ensure that the item generates student responses that inform whether, and to what degree, students have the knowledge and skills indicated in a standard. To achieve this (and avoid merely selecting activities that appear fun and yield little proof of mastery), create a clear standards-based task and provide students with options from figure 2.3. All-about books, for instance, are appropriate after reading an informational text about planets, while reader's theater would serve as a suitable match after students have read a fiction story that includes narrative elements such as characters and events. Teachers might assign a task in which students identify the key ideas from an informational text: *After reading about how caterpillars change into butterflies, make a poster, brochure, or cartoon to show others what you have learned. Use your pictures and words to share the key details from the text.*

Student-Generated Assessments

Student-generated assessments involve students choosing ways they can demonstrate what they learn. Teachers can lead a brainstorming session in which they ask students to generate a list of options to show their understanding of a particular topic. Or, teachers can provide students with choices to support them in this endeavor and use ideas from other formative assessments. For example, a lesson focusing on retelling major events in a story might have students choose to retell the story using an app such as Puppet Pals. Others might create a reader's theater highlighting characters and major events, creating a script for peers to read aloud. And still, there are those who prefer to create a mini book with words and illustrations. This type of formative assessment promotes student agency and engagement, boosting engagement as they determine the best way to provide evidence of learning (Ryan & Deci, 2009).

Fluency Checks

Frequent checks on reading fluency are critical to the classroom assessment continuum. In emphasizing the distinct tie between fluency and comprehension, education scholars John J. Pikulski and David J. Chard (2005) synthesize the definitions of *fluency* proposed by the National Institute of Child Health and Human Development's National Reading Panel (2000) and Theodore L. Harris and Richard E. Hodges (1995) to offer this definition:

> Reading fluency refers to rapid, efficient, accurate word recognition skills that permit a reader to construct the meaning of text. Fluency is also manifested in accurate, rapid, expressive oral reading and is applied during, and makes possible, silent reading comprehension. (Pikulski & Chard, 2005, p. 510)

To make meaning of complex curricular materials used throughout instruction and assessment, and to reach mastery of rigorous reading standards, fluent reading is essential. Additionally, as students transition to more independent and silent reading during the early elementary years, reading with accuracy and automaticity becomes even more critical. When a student's "cognitive capacity is drained by the processing of decoding words, little or no capacity is available for the attention-demanding process of constructing and responding to the meaning of a text" (Rochman, 2017, p. 22). By assessing and monitoring a student's fluency frequently throughout the school year, teachers keep a close eye on the student's reading progress and use the formative data to design reading instruction and corrective instruction.

Performance Assessments

Performance assessments are more complex than other obtrusive assessments, spanning a few days or over a week, measuring multiple learning outcomes and promoting critical thinking. Teachers gather extensive evidence not only about a product or performance that students complete, but also about the process used to achieve the finished piece, which is scored using a rubric. Students find this type of assessment highly engaging, as it allows them to apply knowledge and skills representative of what's happening in the real world (Ryan & Deci, 2009). They can work collaboratively but ultimately generate individual products.

According to Stanford Center for Assessment, Learning and Equity (SCALE, n.d.), performance assessments require students to think, produce, and demonstrate learning through work authentic to the discipline or real world and incorporate four key principles.

1. A performance assessment targets and improves knowledge and higher-order-thinking skills that advance students' literacy skills so, ultimately, students can apply what they learn to a novel situation (a hallmark of other assessments, as well). Additionally, it is an assessment *for* and *of* learning (Stiggins, 2005).

2. As students work on the assessment, they participate in myriad activities which in and of themselves present learning opportunities. Teachers can collect information about the effectiveness of their teaching and can adjust, as needed, while students engage in the various tasks.

3. A performance assessment is intrinsically linked to curriculum and instruction, rather than issued as an independent experience at the end of a unit.

4. The process students engage in while producing their products presents a learning-by-doing situation.

Performance assessments will certainly be designed differently for prekindergartners, kindergartners, and first graders, yet they need not be overlooked. At the heart of the performance assessment, students synthesize multiple targets across multiple content areas. An example of this higher-order thinking might call on students to complete a research project in which they determine what animals make good pets as part of the science unit on plants and animals. Within this assessment, students would research to determine important details about animals, survey classmates about the animals of their choice, and write an opinion paragraph about which pet they should ultimately choose. Assessments such as these require higher-level critical thinking from learners.

Running Records

To investigate the distinct reading strengths and needs of individual students, teachers will also conduct running records toward the end of kindergarten and throughout first grade. *Running records*—individually administered assessments used to monitor a student's reading progress—serve as an ongoing measure of a student's oral reading capabilities. These assessments provide teachers with valuable formative, diagnostic data from which to make instructional decisions regarding reading instruction. Literacy researcher Marie M. Clay (2013) emphasizes the necessity in making the data actionable, asserting that "records are taken to guide teaching" and "what teachers record can challenge them to think with greater clarity about the progress of beginning readers" (p. 52).

With ongoing running records like the one in figure 2.4 (page 51), teachers monitor reading factors that affect comprehension, such as the student's strategy use, rate, accuracy, errors, and ability to self-monitor. During one timed minute, teachers record the reader's miscues or errors above the words as he or she reads. Text read by students is added to the template in figure 2.4. Teachers will mark errors and record notes about the reader's behaviors (such as *uses picture clues*, *self-monitors*, *rereads*, and *repeats words or phrases*). Before reading, the teacher briefly introduces the text and sets the timer for sixty seconds. Timing reveals the student's ability to read at an appropriate rate (not too fast or too slow). While the student reads aloud, the teacher makes a check mark in the column that corresponds with the student's error. Errors are distinguished by two categories: (1) true errors, marked as E, and (2) errors made and then corrected by the reader, marked as SC. The latter reveals that a reader is self-monitoring while reading, which is imperative to true comprehension. The teacher marks the following when such errors occur: M (meaning) when the student uses cues (*puppy* versus *dog*), S (structure) when the student uses syntax to discern the right word (*jumped* versus *jumping*), and V (visual) when the student uses the way a word looks to discern (*horse* instead of *hose*; Clay, 2005). The teacher also writes any important observations. Later, you may choose to code them (or not) using miscue analysis. From there, the "analysis of running records should have a major impact on the teaching decisions the teacher makes while responding to and helping extend the beginning reader's literacy learning" (Fried, 2013, p. 5).

Fluency is critical to students understanding the complex resources they encounter during instruction, practice, and assessment. Mastering reading standards requires fluency. Measuring accuracy and automaticity matter because those skills are required of students during independent reading. Running records allow teachers to design and target differentiated instruction.

Assessment Formats

In addition to determining which *type* of assessment best fits the language of the learning standards and learning progression (in chapter 3, page 61), teams also analyze skills in each standard to decide which assessment *format* will allow students to demonstrate proficiency. Teams construct selected response and constructed response assessments after careful and thorough understanding of critical question one: What do we want students to know and be able to do (DuFour et al., 2016)?

	Total		E			SC		
	E	SC	M	S	V	M	S	V
Start timer. (60 seconds) Stop timer.								
Total								

Total time: 60 seconds

Accuracy: _____ ÷ _____ = _____ %
    Number of words read correctly   Total words read

Rate: (_____ − _____) ÷ _____ × 60 = _____ word count per minute
   Total words read   Total errors   Time read in seconds

Student name: _____ Date: _____

Book title: _____

Level _____, Words

Book introduction:

Figure 2.4: Running record template.

*Visit **go.SolutionTree.com/literacy** for a free reproducible version of this figure.*

Selected Responses

Sometimes teachers format an assessment by posing multiple-choice, matching, fill-in-the-blank, and true-or-false prompts that ask students to select an answer from a provided list. *Selected responses*, a method used as an obtrusive assessment since teachers interrupt instruction to administer them, allow students to display knowledge of factual information, main ideas, and basic skills that involve one correct answer. Students can take these assessments quickly, and teachers can easily score them and obtain a broad overview of foundational information students know and don't know. Selected response assessments remove subjectivity; only one correct answer is expected. For instance, students demonstrate understanding of character traits by choosing from a list rather than generating their own response when asked to describe a character. Teams offer one correct response, as well as other nonexamples, which provides clarity and removes subjectivity when analyzing data.

However, with this assessment, sometimes students can guess at the answer, and they aren't designed for students to demonstrate higher-level understanding. Therefore, teachers can couple a selected response with other methods to obtain a full impression of students' capabilities.

Students can complete formal selected-response items with pencil and paper and submit them for teachers to assess. Additionally, teachers can engage students informally by posing a question and asking students to respond on small whiteboards or using hand signals (thumbs or fingers). For thumb signals, teachers present a prompt, and students display thumbs-up to indicate *yes* or *true*, or thumbs-down for *no* or *false*. For finger signals, teachers provide a key to show what each number—one, two, three, or even four fingers—means, and students respond accordingly for each prompt. For either type of response, students make a fist to signify "I am unsure" or "I don't know."

As a subsequent assessment option, students can identify whether a sentence is a question or a statement using finger signals. Since literacy skills should not be taught in isolation, these examples originate from a complex text at the center of instruction, *Chester's Way* by Kevin Henkes (1988). Teachers may easily generate an arbitrary list of statements and questions unrelated to text—however, we suggest using authentic, complex text that complements the unit theme (friendship and acceptance in this case). Figure 2.5 shows the simplicity of a selected response.

One finger = *This is a question.*
Two fingers = *This is a statement.*
A fist = *I am not sure.*

A. What are some activities or games that Chester and Wilson enjoy playing with each other?

B. Chester's mom calls Chester and Wilson "two peas in a pod" (Henkes, 1988, p. 8).

C. How is Lilly's way of doing things different than Chester's?

D. How did Chester and Wilson respond when Lilly asked them to play?

E. Chester and Wilson were scared when older boys circled them on their bikes.

F. What do you predict will happen when Victor moves into the neighborhood?

Figure 2.5: Selected-response active participation—Example.

Constructed Responses

Broadly speaking, aside from students choosing a clear-cut answer to an objective prompt, which is indicative of a selected response, *constructed-response* items require students to respond to more open-ended tasks. As the name denotes, this format requires students to construct either a relatively short or expanded response without the aid of suggestions or choices like in selected-response items. Students might produce a one- or two-sentence answer, or produce a graphic organizer, a descriptive setting or character, a summary, or an outline as mentioned in the Obtrusive Assessments section (page 44).

Constructed response assessments typically take one or maybe two class periods. Sometimes students examine some kind of stimulus as the basis for their response, such as reading a text, studying a graphic, watching a short video, or listening to an audio recording. Their responses reveal how well they can apply knowledge and skills, in general, as well as construct meaning and demonstrate understanding from the stimulus. Unlike selected-response items that teachers can expeditiously score and ascertain a right or wrong answer, teachers need more time to score students' constructed responses because they are more subjective and require agreement about interpretation of the rubric used for scoring purposes. Students who struggle with writing may have trouble accurately demonstrating what they have learned. Therefore, it is important for teachers to consider all learners when creating or choosing constructed response assessments. We write more about responding to students who struggle in chapter 5 (page 121).

The Assessment Journey

Notice, in figure 2.6 (page 54), how our district adapted the notion of *summative* to reflect an iterative process. Rather than call the end-of-unit assessment a *summative assessment*, we elected to use *formative assessment* to indicate that the information teachers glean from the culminating assessment can formatively further students' learning. Therefore, assessment is viewed as a continuum—a recurrent cycle of instructing and assessing.

In figure 2.6, the horizontal timeline from the circle on the far left to the one on the far right represents assessments in one cycle, or unit of instruction. Each circle reflects a different type of assessment that teachers administer throughout the unit to monitor individual and whole-class student progress both formally and informally. Although the diagram includes four circles, the instructional cycle certainly isn't limited to just that number of assessments. Specifically, the second

PLC critical question one:
What is it we want our students to learn?

*Team should engage in the pre-unit exploration protocol (PREP) before beginning the unit of instruction.

PLC critical question two:
How will we know if each student has learned it?

Assessment Continuum and Data Analysis: Repeating Cycle for Units of Instruction

Optional preassessment with data conversation

→ Data-driven instruction →

Formative classroom assessments

→ Data-driven instruction →

During-unit common formative assessments with data conversation

→ Data-driven instruction →

End-of-unit common formative assessment with data conversation

Preassessment
- Administered at least one to two weeks in advance
- Used to determine what students already know to tailor the instructional unit plan and differentiate to meet specific student needs
- May or may not be common

Formative Classroom Assessments
- Administered daily
- Used to make decisions in the moment or day to day (checklists, observations, conferences, and so on)
- May or may not be common

During-Unit Common Formative Assessments
- Administered during the unit of instruction within a defined window
- Used to check in on student progress toward mastery of essential learning outcomes
- Are common at the team or district level

End-of-Unit Common Formative Assessment
- Administered at the end of a unit of instruction within a defined window
- Used to assess students' current level of mastery after a significant amount of instruction
- Is common at the district level

PLC critical question three:
How will we respond when some students don't learn it?

PLC critical question four:
How can we extend the learning for students who have demonstrated proficiency?

Source: Adapted from Kildeer Countryside Community Consolidated School District 96, Buffalo Grove, Illinois. 2018. Used with permission.

Figure 2.6: Example of assessment continuum and data analysis.

circle indicates several formative classroom assessments—obtrusive, unobtrusive, and student generated—such as exit slips, observational data, student conference data, quick writes, journal entries, graphic organizers, or other artifacts. In fact, a true depiction of a particular unit continuum may have six, eight, or even ten (or more) assessment circles on the timeline. When teachers check in on student learning, they accumulate and examine data to monitor progress and respond in effective ways to continually promote student growth.

Between the circles on the continuum, the data teachers collect from each prior assessment drives daily standards-based instruction. From data, teachers can identify which students need additional support and which students are ready to extend their learning. They then proceed by making informed instructional decisions, such as reteaching, introducing new information, scaffolding, increasing the rigor of tasks, or giving students additional opportunities to practice skills.

This continuous cycle of assessing and instructing ensures that each student receives precisely what he or she needs to progress toward mastery. Even the end-of-unit assessment is used formatively, as mentioned earlier, since teachers' work to support every student in mastering the grade-level standards is never complete. Teachers may have taught the unit over the course of several weeks; however, if some students have not demonstrated mastery, teachers still find ways to provide differentiated support—hence the nature of a true cyclical assessment continuum.

For a more in-depth treatment, consider reading any of the following additional resources on designing quality-driven selected- and constructed-response items. You might participate in a professional book study with team members and conduct a jigsaw activity. After or while reading a particular book, come together to discuss highlights with each other.

- *Design in Five: Essential Phases to Create Engaging Assessment Practice* by Nicole Dimich (2015)

- *Simplifying Common Assessment: A Guide for Professional Learning Communities at Work* by Kim Bailey and Chris Jakicic (2017)

- *Common Formative Assessments 2.0: How Teacher Teams Intentionally Align Standards, Instruction, and Assessment* by Larry Ainsworth and Donald Viegut (2015)

- *Designing and Assessing Educational Objectives: Applying the New Taxonomy* by Robert J. Marzano and John S. Kendall (2008)

- *Teacher-Made Assessments: How to Connect Curriculum, Instruction, and Student Learning* by Christopher Gareis and Leslie Grant (2015)

Literacy Assessment Considerations and Suggestions

While assessment is a steady and frequent factor in any effective instructional unit, each content area has different instructional demands to facilitate all student learning. In mathematics, for example, a teacher may collect responses to a word problem. Social studies teachers can assess students' understanding of needs and wants through graphic organizers, while a physical education teacher might utilize observational data on the gross-motor skills demonstrated in class. Literacy, too, has its own unique considerations in the area of assessment. Types of text and time for scoring are two specific considerations.

Types of Text

Early literacy teachers must consider the types of texts students encounter for assessment purposes, since younger students access information and narrative content through both their own independent reading and teacher read-alouds. Specifically, in states that have adopted the CCSS, "students should be guided into thoughtful reading of even the simplest texts used with beginning readers," and in addition, students need to encounter "complex texts to build knowledge through read-alouds," exposing students to more sophisticated vocabulary and content than they could read on their own (Coleman & Pimentel, 2012b, p. 5).

Therefore, in preK through first grade, some assessment items will require students to demonstrate their ability to independently read and comprehend grade-level text, whereas other assessment items may measure students' listening comprehension of complex teacher read-alouds. Whether it is accessed through individual reading or with a teacher read-aloud, complex text from a range of literary and informational sources offers students a wealth of knowledge, content, and vocabulary to "develop proficient readers with the capacity to comprehend texts across a range of types and disciplines" (Coleman & Pimentel, 2012b, p. 3).

Students respond to a text using a combination of drawing, dictating, and writing to demonstrate understanding of the content they read. For example, teachers can formulate a task in which students write an informational paper showing their understanding of the main topic of a nonfiction text. Or, teachers can ask students to share their opinions or write a narrative about an event that happened in their lives. Even in the primary grades, including our preK learners, some assessments demand an extended length of time for completion as students learn and experience the steps of the writing process. While preK learners may not be expected to engage in all steps of the writing process, they would be fully expected to draw, write, or dictate to show their understanding of a text they have listened to. For example, a preK teacher who reads *Bad Apple: A Tale of Friendship* (Hemingway, 2012) might ask students to draw a picture of the two most important characters in the story. Other times, students are asked to respond in an on-demand situation in a compact period of time.

It's true that tasks that align with the complex processes of reading and writing typically take longer to complete than those that don't require using these core literacy skills. To meet the rigor of the standards, students must employ a number of skills and strategies, often simultaneously, across literary strands. For instance, to retell a story, students first need to identify the characters, setting, and major events in the story before they can sequence the plot items into chronological order. Grasping and implementing the reading strategies that aid in comprehension can understandably be time intensive. Add on a writing task for students to demonstrate their understanding of the reading, with grammar and conventions intact, and the amount of skills being assessed compounds.

Time for Scoring

Another assessment reality in literacy is the time it takes for teachers to score students' writing. Additionally, the subjective nature of scoring certain skills—asking and answering questions about a text, for example—can present a challenge. Susan M. Brookhart (2013) refers to these types of items as *high-inference*, which require assessors to make a decision and draw a conclusion about how to interpret a criteria description.

To address this type of subjectivity, precisely scaled rubrics with descriptions for each level of proficiency provide specific information not only for the teacher but for the student and parents as well. In addition, participating in a collaborative-scoring process with grade-level teammates and establishing common anchor papers—examples of student responses at each level of performance—will lead to more accuracy and consistency when assessing and reporting on literacy tasks. See chapter 4 (page 93) for a detailed discussion of rubrics, collective scoring, and anchor papers.

To demonstrate proficiency in the multifaceted areas of literacy, students need continuous practice reading and writing. In turn, teachers must be purposeful in conducting myriad assessments tied to standards that yield the information necessary to improve students' practice. Although it may take more time to score students' products in literacy, teachers can maximize time so they can assess and provide necessary feedback expeditiously. Jennifer Serravallo (2014) suggests teachers move from student to student to offer immediate feedback and provide support needed on the spot. During individual student conferences, teachers provide such feedback. The following types of critique might be provided (Serravallo, 2017).

- ▸ **Provide a compliment:** The teacher shares something the writer does well.

- ▸ **Give a directive:** The teacher gives the direction for the writer to try something.

- ▸ **Provide redirection:** The teacher names what a student is doing and gives direction to do something different.

- ▸ **Ask a question:** The teacher asks the writer to consider trying something different.

- ▸ **Provide a sentence starter:** The teacher presents the writer with the language necessary to communicate ideas.

It is not uncommon, for example, for a student to love to draw rainbows. This is something familiar and a safe way for a student to express him- or herself. In a *coaching conference* the teacher would begin by complimenting the very colorful drawing this young author has created. At this point, the teacher would then provide the appropriate reminder of the learning target; *authors and illustrators work together to tell a story.* By providing redirection the teacher would point out that this writer's story is about when she lost a tooth and needs to make sure the details in her illustration and the details in her story work together to tell the story. The teacher would then direct the student to make a change to this and move on to another student for a *coaching conference.* By quickly conferring with students, teachers expand their ability to address student needs in a timely manner.

EXERCISE
Purposes and Types of Assessment

Teams can brainstorm formative and summative literacy assessments that they might issue for their targeted unit. After reading about learning progressions in the upcoming chapter, teams return to the following questions and use them to identify various assessments to discuss with team members. For now, though, teachers should have a heightened awareness of the types of assessments to add to what they already conduct and have a healthy list of options.

Use the following questions to guide this exercise.

★ What types of unobtrusive assessments can I conduct in my classroom?

★ What formative and summative assessments can we administer to give an accurate picture of what students can do?

★ What types of formal and informal data can we collect during instruction?

★ What does our journey of assessment look like, and what adjustments might we make to optimize data collection?

Summary

With unwrapped priority standards, knowledge items, key skills, and levels of rigor determined via the PREP process, teacher teams are well-positioned to begin determining which assessments they will conduct. For each learning target, they can start to decide which types of assessments are ideal for appraising students' proficiency. With an understanding of assessment options in place, teams can turn their attention to how they will teach the standards they've identified as priority.

In the next chapter, teams create a learning progression to map out the stepping-stones of knowledge and skills that students must acquire on their journey toward mastery of both content-area and literacy standards. What will students need to learn first? How will teachers build on that knowledge? And what data will they collect along the way to determine if students learned the knowledge and skills necessary to eventually demonstrate proficiency? Continue reading to grasp the importance of learning progressions and how they steer effective instruction and assessment.

CHAPTER 3

Develop a Learning Progression to Guide Instruction and Assessment

During the PREP articulated in chapter 1 (page 11), teams unwrap priority standards to gain clarity around the standards and determine the specific learning targets (skills) that need to be taught, so they can answer PLC critical question two: "How will we know if each student has learned it?" (DuFour et al., 2016, p. 59).

As teams use Webb's (1997, 1999) DOK levels to distinguish learning targets, they might naturally begin organizing the knowledge items and learning targets into an instructional sequence. This work sets the stage for creating a *learning progression*, which W. James Popham (2011) defines as:

> a sequenced set of subskills and bodies of knowledge (*building blocks*) a teacher believes students must master en route to mastering a demanding cognitive skill of significant curricular importance (a *target curricular aim*) . . . [a] formal, thought-through outline of the *key content of instruction*—what's pivotal to be taught and mastered, and in what sequence. As such, it's a foundation for sound instruction and effective planning. It's also the backbone of a sensible, *planned* approach to formative assessment. (p. 10)

By working together to sequence knowledge items and skills into a clearly articulated continuum of learning, teams essentially map out the step-by-step journey students will take toward proficiency. With rigor in mind, teachers list the order they will eventually teach them—from rudimentary to more complex—working up the proverbial ladder to mastery. In developing learning progressions, which are each guided by one or more complimentary priority standards, teachers catalog and design target-aligned assessments for students to demonstrate understanding of knowledge and skills. Their compiled list of myriad assessments from chapter 2 (page 39) will complete and fortify the learning progression. Then they plan high-quality instruction to move students forward in their learning.

This chapter provides a template your team can use to develop literacy-focused learning progressions. It then outlines a six-step process, using a literacy-based example, that helps teams learn how to establish the foundational knowledge and skills the priority standard requires. Finally, the chapter concludes with a section on how to set an instructional timeline for teaching learning progressions and assessing students' level of mastery in a unit.

Teachers, and sometimes even collaborative teams, often neglect or overlook learning progressions, an essential step in instruction and assessment design. Despite a PLC's collaborative culture, teacher teams often dedicate time to unwrap their standards, but jump to assessment writing without working together to determine the continuum of how learning develops as students strive to master a specific target. However, learning progressions help teachers design assessments that emphasize literacy, pinpoint students' performance, and choreograph their instruction at each step toward meeting a standard. Doing this sets the stage for differentiated instruction.

For those students who are missing essential building blocks, including those who have low proficiency with essential literacy skills, teachers may need to backtrack along the continuum and reteach a concept or offer remediation on a particular skill. In other instances, students might already possess the knowledge and skills needed to advance further on the continuum, prompting teachers to increase the pace of instruction and provide extended learning opportunities for a target. In both situations, assessments guided by the learning progression provide data that allow teachers to appropriately match their instruction to their learners' specific needs (Heritage, 2008).

Learning Progression Steps

In developing a learning progression and cataloging assessments, teachers navigate the instructional moves they will take and identify ways students can demonstrate their learning. The following sections explain our six-step learning progression process, which incorporates assessment decisions. The section discussing the last step provides resources to ascertain text complexity and choose appropriate texts.

1. Select a priority standard.

2. Sequence the learning targets (skills).

3. Sequence the knowledge items.

4. Determine all assessments.

5. Identify and design common formative assessments.

6. Discuss options for texts.

Teams can use the learning progression example in figure 3.1 (page 64) to design a learning progression that drives assessment choices and recommended texts and resources. This is a completed example for a kindergarten priority standard. Teams might elect to add or delete more rows than are included in this template. Additionally, notice the option for either Learning Target (Skill) or Knowledge Item in rows, indicating that each learning progression is distinct—customized for the one each team designs. The arrow in the template reflects an upward trajectory, since it mimics the graduated order in which teachers present instruction.

Please note that on this example, the team chose to highlight the learning targets (skills) so that they stand out among the knowledge items. Although knowledge items represent important steps along the progression, they play a supporting role to the skills. As stated in chapter 1, the *knowledge* items represent foundational information that students need to perform the *skills*—what students are expected to do. See the reproducible "Learning Progression and Assessments Template" (pages 261–262) for a blank template.

Ultimately, teams design a learning progression for each identified priority standard. They might choose to include supporting standards as well. For our example, we will detail only *one* learning progression of the six priority standards that exist for this kindergarten unit. Keep reading to learn the thinking behind this kindergarten team's construction of the featured learning progression in figure 3.1, including ideas for assessments as a guide for completing a learning progression with your team.

Select a Priority Standard

When the kindergarten team discussed the priority standard about asking and answering questions in a text, they acknowledged that it comprises many skills

Priority standard: "With prompting and support, ask and answer questions about key details in a text." (RL.K.1)

Learning Progression Steps	Learning Progression Components	Assessments	Possible Texts and Resources
Step 8	**Priority standard RL.K.1:** "With prompting and support, ask and answer questions about key details in a text."	*Common summative formal: Constructed response** Students will ask questions about the characters, settings, or events in a story and then answer one of the questions by drawing on specific details in the text.	*Chrysanthemum* (Henkes, 1991)
Step 7	**Learning target (skill):** Answer questions about a character, setting, or event in a story, drawing on specific details in the text.	*Common formative informal: Constructed response** Teachers ask students to use a combination of drawing, dictating, and writing to explain how a character changes in a text.	*Peter's Chair* (Keats, 1967) *Big Al* (Clements & Yoshi, 1991)
Step 6	**Knowledge item:** Readers show an understanding of key details in a text by explaining their thinking.	**Classroom formative informal: Constructed response** Students engage in a close reading of a text and respond to text-dependent questions.	*Bad Apple: A Tale of Friendship* (Hemingway, 2012) *The Recess Queen* (O'Neill & Huliska-Beith, 2002)
Step 5	**Knowledge item:** Readers use background knowledge and clues from the text to help understand its key details.		
Step 4	**Learning target (skill):** Ask questions to clarify understanding of a text.	*Common formative formal: Constructed response** After listening to a read-aloud, students will meet with the teacher to share questions they generated about key details in the text.	*Leo the Late Bloomer* (Kraus & Aruego, 1971) *The Girl and the Bicycle* (Pett, 2014)
Step 3	**Knowledge item:** Questions can ask *who, what, when, where, why,* and *how*.	**Unobtrusive formative informal: Teacher observation** Students will engage in a small-group round-robin sharing of questions they generated about a text while the teacher observes.	*Corduroy* (Freeman, 1968) *Ribbit!* (Folgueira & Bernatene, 2013)
Step 2	**Knowledge item:** Readers ask questions of the author to help understand a text more deeply.		
Step 1	**Knowledge item:** Know the difference between a question and statement.	**Unique formative informal preassessment: Teacher observation** From a list, identify examples of statements and questions.	*Chester's Way* (Henkes, 1988) *Hooway for Wodney Wat* (Lester & Munsinger, 1999)

*Grade-level teams analyze and discuss data collected from common formative and summative assessments.

Source for standard: NGA & CCSSO, 2010.

Figure 3.1: Learning progression template—Kindergarten example.

*Visit **go.SolutionTree.com/literacy** for a free reproducible version of this figure.*

and works in concert with other reading standards that ultimately lead toward students comprehending a text's key ideas and details. The team will eventually develop several learning progressions, each focused on a priority standard in early literacy skill areas.

Since a learning progression builds in sophistication to meet the curricular outcome of one or more priority (likely some supporting) standards, teams record their selected standard or standards in the top row of the template to represent the overarching goal. They record it again on the top rung of the learning progression ladder (the last step in students' learning) because an eventual end-of-unit (summative) assessment must align to it. Figure 3.2 illustrates using gray shading. We will continue to expand on this figure over the rest of this chapter.

Priority standard: "With prompting and support, ask and answer questions about key details in a text." (RL.K.1)				
	Learning Progression Steps	**Learning Progression Components**	**Assessments**	**Possible Texts and Resources**
	Step ___	**Priority standard RL.K.1:** "With prompting and support, ask and answer questions about key details in a text."		

Source for standard: NGA & CCSSO, 2010.

Figure 3.2: Learning progression in progress.

Sequence the Learning Targets (Skills)

When the collaborative team unpacked the priority standard, teachers identified two specific skills that now serve as learning targets: (1) ask questions to clarify understanding of a text and (2) answer questions about a character, setting, or event in a story, drawing on key details in the text (NGA & CCSSO, 2010).

To determine how to sequence learning targets, teams engage in *backward planning* or *backward analysis*, a process that starts with the end goal in mind then determines the steps necessary to reach it (Wiggins & McTighe, 2005). Previously, the kindergarten team assigned DOK level 2 to each of their learning targets. Teachers might be inclined to sequence learning targets based on the rigor of these skills by putting DOK 1 targets in the bottommost row and then graduating sequentially to more complex depths of knowledge, although this isn't always the case. Ultimately, they would apply a combination of all skills—along with addressing knowledge items—to aid students in asking and answering questions about the key details in a text, a DOK level 3 task.

In our kindergarten example, although both learning targets require the same depth of knowledge, the team decided that students must first learn to ask their own clarifying questions about a text before they can draw on the characters, events, and details of a story to answer questions presented to them. Therefore, the team determined that students do two things: (1) initially learn how to ask questions about a text and (2) draw on textual evidence to answer questions.

Based on this analysis, the team placed those learning targets on the metaphorical ladder in teaching order, mindful that they build in a hierarchical fashion from the bottom up. Since learning targets represent skills crucial to mastering the priority standard, these rows are lightly shaded on the learning progression to indicate their significance, as shown in figure 3.3.

At this point in the process, the learning progression captured on the sample template reflects a work in progress since the team has yet to add knowledge items, which are essential to assisting students to grasp skills. Until all items have been entered onto the template, teachers will not know the exact configuration or number of learning progression steps. As teams work through the remaining steps and dig into knowledge, they might decide to shuffle the order of what they input in light of any new thinking or ideas. The key is collaboration and discussion to arrive at a plan that supports your students and the teaching style of the team members.

Constructing the progression electronically assists with manipulating the entries to reorganize or add and delete rows, as needed. For this reason, it is wise to hold off on numbering the steps of the learning progression until team members agree with the sequence of all the learning targets and knowledge items.

Sequence the Knowledge Items

As a reminder, knowledge comprises facts, dates, people, places, examples, and vocabulary and terms, including concept words. Knowledge items are what students should know (expressed as nouns) so that they can perform the skills (learning targets) we want them to do. Popham (2008) states that every identified building block "should be so unarguably important that a student's status regarding every building block must be and will be verified via formal or informal assessment" (p. 37). Because knowledge items indicate important steps on students' learning journey, teachers refer again to the PREP template and discuss how to

	Learning Progression Steps	Learning Progression Components	Assessments	Possible Texts and Resources
	Step ____	**Priority standard RL.K.1:** "With prompting and support, ask and answer questions about key details in a text."		
	Step ____	**Learning target (skill):** Answer questions about a character, setting, or event in a story, drawing on specific details in the text.		
	Step ____	**Learning target (skill) or knowledge:**		
	Step ____	**Learning target (skill) or knowledge:**		
	Step ____	**Learning target (skill):** Ask questions to clarify understanding of a text.		
	Step ____	**Learning target (skill) or knowledge:**		
	Step ____	**Learning target (skill) or knowledge:**		
	Step ____	**Learning target (skill) or knowledge:**		

Priority standard: "With prompting and support, ask and answer questions about key details in a text." (RL.K.1)

Source for standard: NGA & CCSSO, 2010.

Figure 3.3: Learning progression in progress—Learning targets.

sequence them in a way that will enable students to achieve the learning targets. As a reminder, those knowledge items for standard RL.K.1 follow.

▸ Readers understand the difference between a question and statement.

▸ Questions can ask *who, what, when, where, why,* and *how.*

▸ Readers ask questions of the author to help understand a text more deeply.

▸ Readers use background knowledge and clues from the text to help understand a text more deeply.

▸ Readers show understanding of details by explaining their thinking.

Discussions around the knowledge items led the collaborative team to further probe their thinking: How should knowledge items be sequenced to enable students to achieve the learning targets? What must we explicitly teach and in what order must we teach it? By answering these questions, the team agreed that the first step on the learning progression would be for students to know the difference between a question and statement. Once students can differentiate a question from a statement, teachers can focus their instruction on helping students understand *why* readers ask questions. The team, therefore, input the following knowledge item next (what would become step 2) on the learning progression: readers ask questions of the author to help understand a text more deeply.

With these understandings in place, students are ready to learn how to craft a good question, so the team added to the learning progression the next logical knowledge item: questions can ask *who*, *what*, *when*, *where*, *why*, and *how*. With these three knowledge building blocks added in sequential order from the bottom up, the learning target—ask questions to clarify understanding of a text—becomes the fourth step of the learning progression.

To reach the next learning target listed on the progression—answer questions about a character, setting, or event in a story, drawing on specific details in the text—the kindergarten team agreed that students must initially know how to use both their background knowledge and clues from the text to help them understand its key details. Students can then show their understanding of these key details by explaining their thinking. For instance, after determining a character's trait in a read-aloud book, a student might support her inference by explaining, "I know the character is nice because she gave her friend a hug." Once the team agreed on this sequence, the team members added the remaining knowledge items to the learning progression, shown highlighted in figure 3.4, and numbered the steps.

The sequenced learning progression establishes a thoughtfully articulated and logical plan for tackling the next stage of the learning progression: assessment design. Note, however, that since a learning progression reflects the work of a particular team engaged in this process, another team implementing these same standards might decide to fashion the unit in a different way. With so many options

Priority standard: "With prompting and support, ask and answer questions about key details in a text." (RL.K.1)

	Learning Progression Steps	Learning Progression Components
	Step 8	**Priority standard RL.K.1:** "With prompting and support, ask and answer questions about key details in a text."
	Step 7	**Learning target (skill):** Answer questions about a character, setting, or event in a story, drawing on specific details in the text.
	Step 6	**Knowledge:** Readers show an understanding of key details in a text by explaining their thinking.
	Step 5	**Knowledge:** Readers use background knowledge and clues from the text to help understand its key details.
	Step 4	**Learning target (skill):** Ask questions to clarify understanding of a text.
	Step 3	**Knowledge:** Questions can ask *who, what, when, where, why,* and *how.*
	Step 2	**Knowledge:** Readers ask questions of the author to help understand a text more deeply.
	Step 1	**Knowledge:** Readers know the difference between a question and statement.

Source for standard: NGA & CCSSO, 2010.

Figure 3.4: Learning progression in progress—Knowledge items.

for and approaches to instruction, teachers might wonder, "How will we know that we got it right? Is our sequence for instruction correct?" According to W. James Popham (2007), with few exceptions, "there is no single, universally accepted and absolutely correct learning progression underlying any given high-level curricular aim" (p. 83). Popham (2007) argues that separate teams of committed educators can unwrap the exact same standard and come up with diverse learning progressions, and that is perfectly fine. Collaborative teams taking the time to think deeply about learning, discuss the targets' nuances and where and when to emphasize literacy skills, and carefully sequence a learning progression will benefit student learning far more than individual teachers making their own off-the-cuff decisions.

Determine All Assessments

Teams must now identify the assessments for each step on the ladder. As detailed in chapter 2 (page 39), teachers use a variety of formative assessments to collect data on student progress that drive instruction forward. They administer many of these check-ins through classroom formative assessments as they ask students, for example, to complete exit slips, quick writes, or graphic organizers. They also unobtrusively formatively assess by observing and listening to students as they participate in a group activity, engage in discussion with a partner, or contribute to a class discussion. Teams now determine assessments for each step on the ladder so students can show evidence of what they have learned. As a resource, team members return to the brainstormed list of formative and summative assessments that they generated as a result of the exercise in chapter 2 (pages 58–59).

Teacher teams ask themselves the following questions.

- ▶ "What types and formats of assessments can we use?"
- ▶ "What evidence will each assessment yield that will reveal whether or not students are achieving mastery?"

For classroom assessments, individual teachers have the freedom to choose how they want their students to meet a particular skill or knowledge item. It might be that team members plan together and do, in fact, issue the same one, but it is not mandatory. Even if your team is designing a progression for a specific standard, it is not a given that your team will come to the same consensus about assessments that ours did. Even within a single collaborative team, teachers may opt to choose for their classroom how they want students to meet a particular skill or knowledge item. It might be that, as the team plans together, each member does issue all the same assessments, but it is not mandatory in all cases. Teams also make decisions with regard to how long they spend on a particular step since students in some classrooms might progress at a faster or slower pace than another. This exemplifies the flexibility—or loose aspect—of PLC culture (DuFour et al., 2016). The critical, non-negotiable factor, though, is that all members of a team are prepared to issue the common assessments in a day or two of each other and arrive at the data analysis meeting prepared to discuss scores.

At critical steps along the ladder, teams collaborate to design common formative assessments, as well as an end-of-unit common summative assessment. Typically, these common assessments will be more formal, consisting of selected-response items, constructed-response items, a combination of both, or sometimes a performance assessment. Teachers always administer these assessments in the same manner and in relatively the same time period of a day or two as the rest of the team, as mentioned.

Based on the data from these various assessments, teams make myriad informed decisions about how to move students through the learning progression, such as helping each other determine what to reteach, what extensions to offer, how to scaffold instruction for struggling learners and provide additional support, when to provide response to intervention, and how to increase the rigor for those needing further challenge. Step 5 in building a learning progression—identify and design common formative assessments—provides a more in-depth discussion of common formative and summative assessments. (See chapter 5, page 121, for a thorough discussion about data analysis.)

To design valid assessments for each step of a learning progression, teams will need to consider the level of rigor (DOK) for the intended learning target and choose an assessment method that matches the cognitive demand of the learning. They take into account the items and design pertinent assessments to measure students' takeaway of factual information, as well. For example, say teachers only use the selected-response multiple choice and true-false formats to assess the *Answer questions about a character, setting, or event in a story, drawing on key details in the text* learning target, which is assigned DOK 2 in this book's example. Would that format be sufficient for a teacher to ascertain with confidence that students could think deeply about the key details in a story and use them to support their thinking? Probably not. An assessment can only be valid if it measures what it is intended to measure; therefore, teachers align the rigor of the learning target with the assessment format.

Selected-response items could uncover whether students know the answer to a text-dependent question; however, the constructed-response format can more aptly assess to what degree students can draw on the events, characters, and plot elements of a story to support their answer. The selected-response format would be too narrow and miss the mark in giving students a proper avenue with which to demonstrate their understanding of a more rigorous task required of this particular learning target. A combination of selected- and constructed-response items, or a constructed-response task alone, would allow students to paint a more exacting picture of their capabilities.

Reliable assessments mean that teachers can trust that the results indicate which students have and have not reached proficiency based on the learning target the assessment item is meant to gauge. Bailey and Jakicic (2017) explain two ways of contributing to the reliability of assessments: (1) always including a sufficient number of questions for each learning target and (2) writing the question or task in language accessible to students so they clearly understand what they are asked to do. If students are hampered by the directions, that can skew the results. Researchers Christopher Gareis and Leslie Grant (2008) assert that "at least three to four selected-response questions per learning target will eliminate lucky guessing" (as cited in

Bailey & Jakicic, 2017, p. 70). For constructed-response questions, one well-written question should instill confidence in a team that it can decide on next steps.

To determine where students in a classroom and across the grade level might experience hurdles, teachers can assume the role of the student and take the assessment that they created. The entire team should engage in this work and bring the work to a team meeting to discuss what they noticed. By simulating what students will do to demonstrate mastery, teachers can fully understand and appreciate the expectations for them. In this regard, looking at the assessment implies more than a glance or preview. Instead, by acting like a student and participating in the assessment, teachers uncover mistakes or unclearly written tasks or directions. Additionally, this exercise pinpoints where students might struggle the most so teachers can align their instruction accordingly.

Considering this field presents a vast amount of information, we have just scratched the surface. For this reason, consider reading additional resources on designing quality-driven selected- and constructed-response items. You might organize a professional book study with team members and conduct a jigsaw activity. After or while reading a particular book, come together to discuss highlights with each other.

Identify and Design Common Formative Assessments

With a list of assessments determined, the collaborative team reviews it and identifies which become the common formative assessments and end-of-unit common summative assessment that all grade-level teachers will administer at agreed-on steps in the learning progression. Although formative assessments given by individual teachers can provide timely feedback and valuable data to both teachers and students, this data alone "cannot become a catalyst for improvement" (DuFour, DuFour, Eaker, & Many, 2010, p. 184).

In order for teachers to use the data to spur students toward growth and achievement, there must be a basis for comparison. Therefore, teams collaboratively take the following steps for grading calibration.

1. Develop common assessments.

2. Collect students' work.

3. Analyze students' work together against a common rubric.

When determining which assessments to use or create along the learning progression, teams might ask themselves, "From our list, which will be common formative assessments that we create and administer as a team?"

Teams should carefully consider which steps along the learning progression will require the focus and attention of a common formative assessment and which can be individually assessed by teachers. Most likely, teams will develop common formative assessments to measure student progress on critical learning targets rather than on knowledge items, which can often be measured using informal teacher check-ins. Teachers judiciously identify assessments as common ones based on those learning targets that are more complex and often difficult for students to learn. In addition, they consider the realistic conditions of how frequently teams can meet and the amount of time available, since data analysis and collective reflection take dedicated, uninterrupted time together as a professional learning community. Once the team settles on which steps in the learning progression to commonly assess, they also commit to consistent administration in terms of format and time, and schedule a team meeting in which they will analyze and discuss the data.

Teachers of students who struggled with a particular learning target can seek assistance and suggestions from those whose students excelled in this particular area. In addition, common formative assessment data conversations help teachers determine which students need additional support and who would benefit from extra challenges. Once identified, teachers can share instructional strategies, lesson ideas, and best practices to meet these students' needs. Refer back to figure 3.1 (page 64) to see the assessments assigned to each step of the learning progression, as well as the common formative assessments identified in steps 4 and 7.

Although this chart makes it look as though all teachers on the team are expected to administer the exact same assessment, that is not the case. As a reminder, aside from the collective commitment to the common assessments in steps 4, 7, and 8, the ideas recorded in the template serve as a possibility for teachers to use in their classrooms. Teams often find a record of assessment ideas generated during team discussions to be highly beneficial as teachers often reflect in isolation and need to remember conversations. While they may choose alternate assessment methods for steps in the learning progression that do not denote a common formative assessment, they take caution to ensure all assessments match the level of rigor of the standard or learning target. The following sections highlight the team's discussion points to provide a glimpse into their thought process and collective decision making around assessment design at each step in the learning progression, as follows.

- **Step 1: Knowledge item**—Know the difference between a question and statement.

- **Steps 2 and 3: Knowledge items**—Readers ask questions of the author to help understand a text more deeply, and questions can ask *who, what, when, where, why,* and *how.*

▸ **Step 4: Learning target (skill)**—Ask questions to clarify understanding of a text.

▸ **Steps 5 and 6: Knowledge items**—Readers use background knowledge and clues from the text to help understand its key details, and readers show an understanding of key details in a text by explaining their thinking.

▸ **Step 7: Learning target (skill)**—Answer questions about a character, setting, or event in a story, drawing on specific details in the text.

▸ **Step 8: Priority standard**—With prompting and support, ask and answer questions about key details in a text.

Knowledge Item: Know the Difference Between a Question and Statement

With each step of the progression as a touchstone for assessment, we begin with the bottom rung: *know the difference between a question and statement*. The team decided that this basic knowledge item, which requires a low level of cognitive demand, can be easily assessed using a quick selected-response activity. While brainstorming ideas on how to collect this data, a teacher suggested gathering students on the carpet and asking them to determine whether a sentence is a statement or a question. Once the teacher shares the sentence, students hold up one finger to indicate *This is a question*, two fingers to indicate *This is a statement*, and a fist to indicate *I am not sure*. While students signal their responses, the teacher takes quick notes on which students get it and which need more support. For timely data collection management, a teacher might find it easiest to put check marks by names on a student roster that respond incorrectly as generally there will likely be fewer incorrect responses than correct.

Although step 1 is a knowledge item—a key concept that students must know before continuing their learning journey—the teacher assesses it as a skill. To demonstrate their understanding of the difference between questions and statements, students must show what they know by signaling. Though knowledge is what we want students to know, it is assessed when students do something to demonstrate that knowledge.

Knowledge Items: Readers Ask Questions of the Author to Help Understand a Text More Deeply, and Questions Can Ask Who, What, When, Where, Why, and How

When steps along the learning progression can blend together into one assessment opportunity, teachers should take advantage of these opportunities. The more efficiently and effectively data can be collected, the more responsive instruction and intervention will be. When making assessment decisions for steps 2 and 3 of the learning progression, the kindergarten team saw an opportunity to merge these knowledge items and assess them both together. The knowledge items of *readers ask questions of the author to help understand a text more deeply* and *questions can ask* who, what, when, where, why, *and* how are so closely related that an observation of a small-group round-robin brainstorming session could give teachers the information needed to gauge students' understanding of both. If assessments are well designed, they can tell us whether our students have learned multiple learning targets, and if they can see the connections among those targets and use them in a meaningful way (Bailey et al., 2014).

Learning Target (Skill): Ask Questions to Clarify Understanding of a Text

Although the first three steps of the learning progression represent key building blocks of student knowledge, the team decided these steps did not necessitate a team-developed and team-analyzed common formative assessment. With informal classroom assessments, teachers can individually collect data, gauge student learning, and calibrate instruction to position students for instruction and assessment of the learning target at step 4 (ask questions to clarify understanding of a text). Since this learning target is critical to students' overall mastery of the priority standard, the team agreed to create and administer a common formative assessment.

When choosing which type of assessment to use, teachers decided a constructed response in which students conference with the teacher to orally share questions generated about a read-aloud text would give all students, including those who are still learning to write, an opportunity to share their learning. In addition, the constructed-response method of assessment allows students to appropriately demonstrate the mental processing involved in crafting their own questions about a text. When the team identified this common formative assessment, the teachers discussed plans for how they would administer the assessment in each of their classrooms, develop a common analytic rubric, prepare students' data, and meet for data analysis. On the learning progression example (figure 3.1, page 64), teachers labeled the assessment at step 4 as a common formative assessment.

Knowledge Items: Readers Use Background Knowledge and Clues From the Text to Help Understand Its Key Details, and Readers Show an Understanding of Key Details in a Text by Explaining Their Thinking

Moving up the learning progression, you'll notice the kindergarten team decided to use one assessment to determine students' understanding of both step 5 (readers use background knowledge and clues from the text to help understand its key details) and step 6 (readers show understanding of key details in a text by explaining their thinking). Since these knowledge items require a higher level of mental processing (DOK 2) in which students must identify major events in the story, organize their thoughts, and interpret information, the kindergarten team chose a constructed-response assessment format by engaging students in a close reading of a text. As students closely read the text and respond to text-dependent questions, teachers can take anecdotal notes of student responses, keeping track of which students have a handle on the learning.

Learning Target (Skill): Answer Questions About a Character, Setting, or Event in a Story, Drawing on Specific Details in the Text

As the team continued to brainstorm assessment ideas, you'll notice at step 7 they chose to create a common formative assessment to determine students' understanding of a critical learning target (answer questions about a character, setting, or event in a story, drawing on specific details in the text). As you recall from chapter 1 (page 11), the team agreed that this learning target is DOK level 2 due to the complexity of thinking required for students to interpret the text and support their ideas. Therefore, the team decided a short constructed response would be an appropriate assessment method for demonstrating this level of thinking. To facilitate the needs of all learners, teachers will ask students to use a combination of drawing, dictating, and writing to explain how a character changes in a text. The team analyzes the results of this common formative assessment, creating an opportunity to respond to student needs before reaching the final step of the progression.

Priority Standard: With Prompting and Support, Ask and Answer Questions About Key Details in a Text

Finally, with the building blocks of knowledge and skills strategically mounted in place, students embark on the final rung of the ladder in step 8. Here, they demonstrate their understanding of the full standard RL.K.1—"With prompting and support, ask and answer questions about key details in a text"—and partake in a formal summative assessment that necessitates a well-constructed and detailed response highlighting the student's proficiency of the overall learning outcome (NGA & CCSSO, 2010). The collaborative team designed a common summative assessment that would allow students to tap into all the knowledge and skills they had accumulated throughout the learning progression by responding to the following prompt: students will ask questions about the characters, settings, or events in a story and then answer one of these questions drawing on specific details in the text. As with common formative assessments, teams design the prompt, discuss how to administer it, and create a common rubric for assessment and instruction.

Throughout each step of a learning progression, teachers check in on student progress several times, using the formative data to differentiate lessons, reteach a concept, or move students further ahead. It not only provides a framework for gathering formative data, but also guides student preparation for a summative assessment. Essentially, by the time students reach the end of a learning progression, they should have the background knowledge, skills, and experience necessary to take on a summative assessment and demonstrate a comprehensive understanding of the full standard.

On this sample kindergarten learning progression, the team used a variety of formative assessments to check in on student progress. However, data do little good if teachers don't use them to develop a plan of action. When data from these formative assessments indicate that students already have prior knowledge of a concept, teachers move them up to the next step on the progression, letting them forge ahead onto new learning experiences. If other students need more time to work through a skill, teachers slow their pace or try a different approach to instruction.

As mentioned earlier in the chapter, although we refer to an assessment as *summative*, our work to support every student in mastering the grade-level standards is never complete. We may have taught a unit over the course of several weeks, but if every student has not demonstrated mastery, we still find ways to provide differentiated support. Throughout a school year, teachers may also choose to continue working with the same standards by applying them to more rigorous texts or teaching them in combination with other standards to create new learning experiences. Summative assessments provide evidence of what students have mastered at the culmination of a unit of study, but teachers still use this data to determine next steps for every student.

EXERCISE
Develop a Learning Progression and Assessment Plan

Teams can sequence the unwrapped learning targets and knowledge items from their PREP template into a learning progression by starting at the simplest concepts and working up to the most complex skills. Each step on the learning progression acts as a touchstone for formative assessments and an opportunity for teams to discuss the best type and format of assessment.

Use the following questions to guide this exercise.

★ What priority standard is the basis for the learning progression we will first build?

★ How can we sequence the skills and knowledge items?

★ What types and formats of assessments will we conduct, and does each coincide with the item or skill's required DOK?

★ As a team, what common formative assessments will we issue?

Discuss Options for Texts

As Wiley Blevins (2017) explains, "One type of text cannot meet all the reading demands of young readers" (p. 155). Therefore, a variety of texts is necessary for teaching and assessing literacy in preK through first grade. At this age, students not only learn to read grade-level text on their own, but they also build their vocabularies and background knowledge through texts read aloud to them (Coleman & Pimentel, 2012b). Teachers will need to carefully consider options for both grade-level text and for read-aloud text, since each plays a critical role in these classrooms. The following sections discuss the unique criteria for determining the complexity of read-aloud texts and grade-level texts.

Read-Aloud Text

As noted in the CCSS, children in the upper-elementary grades are expected to read texts independently and respond to them in writing. However:

> Children in the early grades (particularly K–2) should participate in rich, structured conversations with an adult in response to the written texts that are read aloud, orally comparing and contrasting as well as analyzing and synthesizing, in the manner called for by the *Standards*. (NGA & CCSSO, 2010, p. 33)

By engaging students in a read-aloud of a story or informational text, teachers grant students access to content and information they might not otherwise be able to read and comprehend on their own (NGA & CCSSO, n.d.). For this reason, teachers will need to read aloud both fiction and content-rich nonfiction texts that build students' knowledge and vocabulary, laying a foundation for independent reading and comprehending complex grade-level texts.

Students should experience rich, engaging text throughout instruction; therefore, teachers should pay particular attention to choosing read-aloud text at the appropriate complexity level. Whereas a DOK level categorizes skills by the complexity of thinking required to accomplish them, text complexity refers to a text's challenge level based on its quantitative and qualitative features and reader factors.

For read-aloud text used in an assessment, careful consideration is paramount as it may yield very different results when analyzing data and ultimately determining proficiency and mastery of learning targets. For example, a student might be able to apply a skill when listening to simpler text; however, when applied to a text in a more complex level, the student may actually struggle to demonstrate proficiency independently.

When determining read-aloud texts to use for assessment (and instructional) purposes, teams must think about a text's quantitative and qualitative features, as well as the student population and task in a given classroom.

> ▸ *Quantitative features* include determining what can be counted, like word length and frequency, sentence length, number of syllables, text cohesion, and other calculable properties. Schools typically use computer software to generate quantitative measures (such as Lexile, Flesch-Kincaid, and so forth).

> ▸ *Qualitative features* include the language used, the complexity of the shared ideas, and other attributes of the text, such as its structure, style, and levels of meaning.

> ▸ *Student population and task* refers to a classroom's particular composition—specifically cognitive abilities, motivation, knowledge, and experiences—and the task students in that classroom are asked to complete. Teachers must use their professional judgment and expertise, coupled with what they know about their students, when attending to this area of text complexity.

Using just one of these three criteria will render measurement incomplete and perhaps invalid. For example, John Steinbeck's (1939) *The Grapes of Wrath* measures quantitatively at a grade band of 2 to 3, yet clearly the qualitative and reader considerations dictate that this text is only appropriate for a much higher grade level.

Grade-Level Text

Although many texts should be devoted to read-alouds, preK–1 students will also need opportunities to read grade-level texts on their own. Teams should also take into consideration that students must be able to comprehend texts of steadily increasing complexity as they progress through grade levels. By the time they grad-uate, students must be able to read and comprehend independently and proficiently the kinds of complex texts commonly found in college and the workplace. However, for the purpose of determining the complexity of grade-level texts, the CCSS warns that "texts for kindergarten and grade 1 may not be appropriate for quantitative analysis, as they often contain difficult-to-assess features designed to aid early read-ers in acquiring written language" (NGA & CCSSO, n.d., p. 8). Instead, preK through first-grade teachers must pay particular attention to the element of *student population and task*. Since many young readers at this stage are still developing their understanding of the alphabet, phonological awareness, and phonics skills, they are not ready to tackle the demands of regular texts. Wiley Blevins (2017) suggests providing young readers *controlled text*, "in which a high proportion of the words are decodable based on the sound-spelling relationships previously taught" (p. 151). Through repeated reading practice with these decodable texts, students directly con-nect newly acquired phonics skills to the actual reading of text.

At this time, as they decide the progression of learning for students, teams may also want to consider which stories or texts, both read-aloud and grade-level texts, would best suit the demands of the assessed knowledge and skills. Since the sample kindergarten reading standard requires students to ask questions about the key details in a text, the team purposefully selected stories that have rich details, a variety of characters, and memorable settings. Texts always should also be rich in content and provide opportunities to hold students' attention, promote higher-order (and lower-level DOK) thinking, and have relevance in their lives.

In addition to teacher selection of texts, students from prekindergarten through first grade need opportunities to choose their own texts for independent reading time—both during and outside of school. Students need access to a wide range of reading materials on a variety of topics and genres that will help build their knowl-edge, interest, and overall joy of reading (Coleman & Pimentel, 2012b). During independent reading time, students might delve into a decodable text or "read" the pictures of a favorite book. Allowing choice boosts student engagement and feelings of autonomy, leading to a lifelong love of reading.

Realistically in a three-week unit, teachers would select between one and three texts for a whole-group setting, and between one and three texts for a small-group setting, always keeping in mind the goal of content-rich text that promotes higher-order thinking. As teams generate suggestions about the types of texts and tasks to use when assessing along their learning progressions, they can refer back to the learning progression example (figure 3.1, page 64) and use it as a tool for jotting down and visually displaying any notes on their ideas. There you can see the suggested texts listed for the example unit.

To support teams' selecting appropriately challenging text, members can try the following and then check any contenders using the three-part complexity model (quantitative, qualitative, and student population and task).

▸ Solicit suggestions from other school districts, colleagues, bookstore owners, and local librarians.

▸ Search the internet for titles of award-winning books.

▸ Refer to the online resources in table 3.1, which are recommended in *Complex Text Decoded: How to Design Lessons and Use Strategies That Target Authentic Texts* (Glass, 2015).

Table 3.1: Text-Finding Resources

California Department of Education **www.cde.ca.gov/ci/cr/rl**
This resource provides recommendations for preK–12 literature across content areas. A customized search tool helps users find texts to suit their criteria. For example, search for the following. • Classifications such as alphabet books, concept books, graphic novels, picture books, photo essays, and wordless books • Awards such as Caldecott, California Young Reader Medal Program, Golden Kite Author and Illustrator Award, National Book Award, and Nobel Prize • Cultural designations such as African, Filipino, Korean, Middle Eastern, and Native American • Genres such as drama, fantasy, humor, tall tale, nonfiction, and speech
Appendix B of the Common Core State Standards **www.corestandards.org/assets/Appendix_B.pdf**
Appendix B of the CCSS compiles complex text suggestions for grade-level bands across content areas and categorizes them by text type such as stories, poetry, and informational texts. Some entries are titles only. Others are excerpts taken from whole works, so educators can find and expose students to the original text sources. In addition, this source includes sample performance tasks that educators might issue.
National Council of Teachers of English (NCTE) Awards **www.ncte.org/awards**
NCTE grants these awards each year. The links cited include other awards for outstanding books at all levels and content areas. • **Orbis Pictus Award:** This award promotes and recognizes excellence in the writing of nonfiction for students across content areas. Although one title is awarded each year, up to five honor books are also recognized and eight additional recommended books can be named.

continued ⟶

- **NCTE Charlotte Huck Award for Outstanding Fiction for Children:** This award promotes and recognizes excellence in fiction writing for students. The evaluative criteria focus on titles that have the potential to transform students' lives by inviting compassion, imagination, and wonder.

International Literacy Association's Choices Reading Lists
www.literacyworldwide.org/get-resources/reading-lists

Each resource provides literary titles with annotated lists.

- **Children's Choices (K–6):** This list consists of one hundred favorite book titles chosen by approximately ten thousand children. It is not solely compiled for teachers, librarians, and bookstore owners; it is also geared to parents, grandparents, guardians, and caregivers. This list is a project of a joint committee supported by International Literacy Association and the Children's Book Council.

- **Teachers' Choices (K–8):** The approximately thirty books on this list have been identified as outstanding trade books that teams of teachers, librarians, and reading specialists consider exceptional for curriculum use and enjoyable for readers ages five to fifteen.

Source: Adapted from Glass, 2015.

For more information on ways to consider appealing to students' cultures, as well as ideas for bringing them into the classroom, see chapter 9 (page 239).

EXERCISE
Consider Options for Complex Text

Teachers must be aware of what, in particular, qualifies a text to be complex. Review the three-part complexity model explained in this chapter and the reproducibles "Read-Aloud Text Complexity: Qualitative Measures Rubric—Literature" and "Read-Aloud Text Complexity: Qualitative Measures Rubric—Informational Texts" (pages 265–268) to ascertain the complexity level of any text under consideration for classroom instruction.

Use the following questions to guide this exercise.

★ What plans can our team make to select appropriately challenging complex texts?

★ Can we use the text as a mentor text to exemplify any of the learning targets?

★ Has our team considered culturally responsive texts (chapter 9, page 239)?

★ What texts do we already use, and how do they evaluate?

Learning Progression Timelines

After completing the learning progression for each priority standard and selecting or designing assessments as indicated in this chapter, teams begin planning a unit's execution. In doing so, they generate a team calendar that guarantees that students are afforded opportunities to learn and practice the standards, demonstrate their knowledge, and receive additional support. On the calendar, teams pinpoint dates for instruction and assessment of *all* priority and nonpriority standards from the PREP template and develop an attainable timeline. Additionally, they reserve time for intervention—teaching for students who have yet to master standards—and providing extension for those who have achieved mastery.

The kindergarten team also used its District 96 assessment continuum (figure 2.6, page 54) as a resource while creating the unit calendar (figure 3.5, pages 84–86). However, while planning instruction, they clearly acknowledged that if a majority of students struggled at any point during the learning progression while teachers conducted the lessons, the team would reevaluate this original timeline to accommodate students' needs.

We are often asked, "How many common formative assessments should a team create and administer?" There is not a magic number or correct answer. When teams make decisions regarding when and how to issue assessments, teams are encouraged to create and administer common formative assessments based on the following.

▸ The unit's length

▸ Number of priority standards addressed

▸ The standards' complexity

▸ The overall calendar

Assessing a small number of standards enables teachers to respond quickly and, intuitively, the more assessments a team administers, the more data the team collects. With data aplenty, teachers can respond more often and more precisely to student needs. For this reason, dates for the assessment (both formal and informal), as well as dates for corrective teaching and extension, should be planned ahead in the unit. Use your professional judgment and be realistic about when to administer common formative assessments; they require consistent administration and a team data-inquiry conversation. You will want to plan this around your team meeting schedule and allow for ample time for each teacher to assess student work to be prepared for the team data-inquiry conversation.

Unit 1: Friendship and Acceptance (Three weeks)				
Time Frame: August and September (Six weeks)				
LP = Learning progression Today's Date: August 20 (Two weeks prior to unit)				
Monday, 8/20	**Tuesday, 8/21**	**Wednesday, 8/22**	**Thursday, 8/23**	**Friday, 8/24**
Team meeting: PREP for Unit 1	Instruction for beginning-of-year unit takes place while team engages in PREP for upcoming 9/3 friendship and acceptance unit.			
Monday, 8/27	**Tuesday, 8/28**	**Wednesday, 8/29**	**Thursday, 8/30**	**Friday, 8/31**
Team meeting: PREP for Unit 1	Instruction for beginning-of-year unit takes place while team engages in PREP for upcoming 9/3 friendship and acceptance unit.			**Preassessment RF.K.1d**
Monday, 9/3	**Tuesday, 9/4**	**Wednesday, 9/5**	**Thursday, 9/6**	**Friday, 9/7**
Day one: **Team meeting:** Data-inquiry process, preassessment of RF.K.1d **Instruct priority standards:** RL.K.1 (LP1) RL.K.3 (LP1) W.K.3 (LP1 and 2) **Instruct nonpriority standards:** RF.K.1a RF.K.1b RF.K.1c RL.K.10	Day two: **Instruct priority standards:** W.K.3 (LP3) RF.K.1d (whole group or small group determined by data) **Instruct nonpriority standards:** RL.K.2 RL.K.10	Day three: **Instruct priority standards:** RL.K.1 (LP2 and 3) RL.K.3 (LP2) W.K.3 (LP3) **Instruct nonpriority standards:** RF.K.1a RF.K.1b RF.K.1c RL.K.10	Day four: **Instruct priority standards:** W.K.3 (LP3) RF.K.1d (small-group instruction) **Instruct nonpriority standards:** RL.K.4 L.K.1b L.K.2a RL.K.10	Day five: **Instruct priority standards:** RL.K.1 (LP4) RL.K.3 (LP3 and 4) W.K.3 (LP4 and 5) RF.K.1d (small-group instruction) **Instruct nonpriority standards:** RL.K.2 RL.K.10

Assessment:	Assessment:	Assessment:	Assessment:	Assessment:
Informal teacher observation of	Formal one-to-one assessment	Informal teacher observation of	Informal teacher observation of	Common formal formative assessment: Short constructed response of
RL.K.1 (LP1) RL.K.3 (LP1) W.K.3 (LP1 and 2)	RF.K.1d and preassessment RF.K.3a	RL.K.1 (LP2 and 3) RL.K.3 (LP2) W.K.3 (LP3)	RL.K.1 (LP2 and 3) RL.K.3 (LP2) W.K.3 (LP3) Formal one-to-one assessment: RF.K.1d and preassessment RF.K.3a	RL.K.1 (LP4) RL.K.3 (LP3 and 4) W.K.3 (LP4 and 5)
Monday, 9/10	**Tuesday, 9/11**	**Wednesday, 9/12**	**Thursday, 9/13**	**Frida, 9/14**
Day six: **Team meeting:** Data-inquiry process **Instruct priority standards:** RL.K.1 (LP5 and 6) RL.K.3 (LP5) W.K.3 (LP6) RF.K.1d (whole group or small group determined by data) RF.K.3a (whole group or small group determined by data) **Instruct nonpriority standards:** RL.K.4 RL.K.5 RL.K.10	**Day seven:** **Instruct priority standards:** W.K.3 (LP7) **Instruct nonpriority standards:** RL.K.5 RL.K.7 L.K.1b L.K.2a RL.K.10	**Day eight:** Flexible day **Instruct priority standards:** Corrective instruction or extension based on all previous assessments (whole group or small group determined by data)	**Day nine:** **Instruct priority standards:** W.K.3 (LP8) **Instruct nonpriority standards:** RL.K.2 RL.K.9 RL.K.10	**Day ten:** **Instruct priority standards:** RL.K.1 (LP7) RL.K.3 (LP6 and 7) W.K.3 (LP9) RF.K.3a (whole group or small group determined by data) **Instruct nonpriority standards:** RL.K.10
Assessment: Formative, informal: Short constructed response of RL.K.1 (LP5 and 6) RL.K.3 (LP5)	Assessment: No created assessment today. Teachers gather unobtrusive, observable data. This will not be assessed.	Assessment: No created assessment today. Teachers gather unobtrusive, observable data.	Assessment: No created assessment today. Teachers gather unobtrusive, observable data.	Assessment: Common formal formative: Short constructed response of RL.K.1 (LP7) RL.K.3 (LP6 and 7) W.K.3 (LP9)

Figure 3.5: Team calendar for a unit—Example.

continued →

Monday, 9/17	Tuesday, 9/18	Wednesday, 9/19	Thursday, 9/20	Friday, 9/21
Day eleven: **Team meeting:** PREP for unit 2 **Instruct priority standards:** W.K.3 (LP10) **Instruct nonpriority standards:** RL.K.7 RL.K.10	**Day twelve:** **Instruct priority standards:** W.K.3 (LP10) **Instruct nonpriority standards:** RL.K.9 RL.K.10	**Day thirteen:** Flexible day **Instruct priority standards:** Corrective instruction or extension based on all previous assessments	**Day fourteen:** End-of-unit, common summative assessment for all priority standards (day one of two)	**Day fifteen:** End-of-unit, common summative assessment for all priority standards (day two of two)
Assessment: No created assessment today. Teachers gather unobtrusive, observable data.	**Assessment:** No created assessment today. Teachers gather unobtrusive, observable data.	**Assessment:** No created assessment today. Teachers gather unobtrusive, observable data.	**Assessment:** Short constructed response of RL.K.1 (LP8) RL.K.3 (LP8) W.K.3 (LP11)	**Assessment:** Short constructed response of RL.K.1 (LP8) RL.K.3 (LP8) W.K.3 (LP11)
Monday, 9/24	**Tuesday, 9/25**	**Wednesday, 9/26**	**Thursday, 9/27**	**Friday, 9/28**
Team meeting: PREP for unit 2 *and* Data-inquiry process; common summative assessment from unit 1; bring data to team meeting	Instruction for unit 2 begins. Instruction (corrective or extension) of priority standards for unit 1 begins.			

Source for standards: NGA & CCSSO, 2010.

*Visit **go.SolutionTree.com/literacy** for a free reproducible version of this figure.*

Figure 3.5 illustrates the kindergarten team calendar complete with an indication of learning progression steps for all priority standards, all nonpriority standards, and assessments that guide instruction. This calendar is available for the entire team to access and utilize throughout the unit. As they are teaching, they make notes about possible calendar adjustments and discuss suggestions for revisions at a team meeting.

In the calendar, you will see each priority standard reflected along with the step of the learning progression that will be instructed for that day. For example, RL.K.1 stands for Reading Literature Kindergarten Standard 1 (NGA & CCSSO, 2010), and LP1 stands for learning progression step 1. Nonpriority standards and assessments are also noted.

These are the steps this team took, and which your team might also take.

1. Begin constructing unit calendars by inserting any days off school or other important events, like field trips.

2. Note team meetings to appropriately pace common formative assessments and data-inquiry conversations. The team that created this example meets formally once a week on Mondays during collaborative team time provided in their schedule. However, they informally touch base frequently and almost daily.

3. Indicate when to administer a preassessment prior to the unit to plan instruction.

4. Fill in standards and assessments based on learning progressions in a realistic time frame for the unit.

The calendar catalogues all priority and nonpriority standards from the unit along with aligned assessments, team meetings, and plans for responsive instruction. The common assessments, as outlined on the calendar, help teachers pace instruction and find common discussion points to learn from one another. This collaborative process, during which teams analyze and discuss student data, results in both coordinating and calibrating the curriculum as teachers move through the unit. It is imperative that teachers also collect classroom data that may or may not be common with teammates, including unobtrusive, informal assessment data.

In designing the calendar, teachers are mindful that all students learn the material but not always through whole-class instruction on a consistent basis. While planning the unit calendar, they address individual needs through other avenues, including small groups and one-to-one assessments and corrective instruction or extension.

Opportunities to press pause on instruction to gather a sense of where learners are in proficiency are embedded within the calendar, labeled *flexible days*. It is possible all learners will not comprehend targets immediately; therefore, during the data-inquiry team meetings, teachers will determine next steps for students at all levels of proficiency. A few learners may require more support with priority standards. Thus, teachers will engage in corrective instruction in small groups. Alternatively, students may demonstrate understanding early in the unit, leading teams to determine appropriate ways to extend learning.

Completing the PREP template explained in chapter 1 (page 11) occurs one to two weeks prior to the start of a unit. That allows teachers to gain clarity and prepare for instruction. As they map assessments, collaborative teams take the following into consideration.

- Unit standards sequence
- Pace
- Repeated learning progression steps
- Time constraints
- Common formative assessments scheduling
- Corrective teaching and extension
- Team meetings

Unit Standards Sequence

Because several priority and nonpriority standards typically exist in a single unit, teams put careful thought into how to map all the learning taking place. On the sample calendar in figure 3.5 (pages 84–86), the team began with priority standard RL.K.1 because the skills embedded in it are necessary to adequately reach proficiency of priority standard RL.K.3. The team chose to collect data quickly on the standard to glean information about which students might struggle with subsequent priority standards. These data will also help teachers plan future whole-group and small-group lessons. RL.K.1 will persist as a focus while instructing the other priority standards since students will use the skill of asking and answering questions about a story to fully master RL.K.3. The team believed this also paired nicely with nonpriority standard RL.K.7: "With prompting and support, describe the relationship between illustrations and the story in which they appear (e.g., what moment in a story an illustration depicts)" (NGA & CCSSO, 2010). The students would engage in many close reads during instruction, and teachers could naturally embed the skill of relating illustrations to text.

Pace

On the calendar, notice that the team immediately begins instructing the writing priority standard W.K.3 ("Use a combination of drawing, dictating, and writing to narrate a single event or several loosely linked events, tell about the events in the order in which they occurred, and provide a reaction to what happened"; NGA & CCSSO, 2010) at the beginning of the unit as writing instruction is a daily staple of literacy instruction. This standard becomes the prime focus of whole- and small-group writing instruction throughout the three-week unit. During week two, teachers also collect unobtrusive data on standard W.K.1b during small-group instruction or individual conferencing. Though this standard is not currently listed as a priority, the team plans to prioritize it in subsequent units. Therefore, the data collected during the initial stages of instruction for it also serve as preassessment data for future lessons. Instruction aligned to both the priority and nonpriority writing standards continues throughout the unit calendar.

Repeated Learning Progression Steps

In the calendar, notice that steps of the learning progression, for both reading and writing standards, are sometimes repeated. For example, step 2 and step 3 of the learning progression for standard RL.K.1 are planned for day three and day four. Two reasons might compel a team to repeat steps: (1) preassessment data indicate that more than one lesson would be necessary or (2) the step's complexity is notably high. For the learning progression steps that take two days (or more) to teach, the assessment is listed on the second day, since that is when teachers will assess the standard.

Time Constraints

Further considerations revolve around time, including the time it typically takes for students to complete standards-aligned classwork and assessments. For example, teachers keep in mind the rate at which a kindergarten student could produce written stories that include drawings, as well as time for dictation. They also understand that the timeline for each step of the learning progression should be swift but not so swift that it is unproductive.

Common Formative Assessments Scheduling

The team scheduled their first common formative assessment on the fifth day of the unit. This assessment is designed to check in on the students' proficiency of step 4 of the learning progression for reading standard RL.K.1. The team will analyze and discuss these data at the scheduled team literacy meeting the following week, which is also indicated on the calendar. During the team's data-inquiry conversation, next steps for instruction based on the data from the common formative assessment are emphasized.

The team's next common formative assessment occurs on day ten. For this check-in point, the team created a common formative assessment that evaluates a step of the learning progression for two different standards at once: RL.K.1 and RL.K.3. Teachers maximized assessment time by having students demonstrate their proficiency of both skills simultaneously. They carefully crafted the assessment items so that precise data could be gleaned to measure each skill distinctly. From there, instruction continues for both priority and nonpriority standards until the common summative assessment is issued on days fourteen and fifteen, addressing all priority standards from the unit.

Common formative assessments for other priority standards would be included in this calendar. However, for this unit calendar, only assessments specifically tied to the sample learning progression have been included. The common summative assessment also needs to be calibrated and taken to a team meeting for data analysis to ensure for corrective instruction in the subsequent unit calendar.

Corrective Teaching and Extension

You'll see days on the calendar on which no priority standards are instructed. The team felt it necessary to leave small windows of time for additional corrective teaching or extension. *Corrective teaching* speaks to PLC question three, as it serves students who have yet to master a standard. *Extension*, which relates to question four, refers to those who have successfully mastered a standard. Chapter 5 (page 121) addresses interventions, as well as extensions.

Throughout the entirety of the unit, team members are responsive to the data collected from both their daily classroom assessments and common formative assessments by meeting the identified needs of students during whole-group instruction, small-group instruction, or individual conferencing. Concurrently, teachers continue to instruct on other standards in the learning progression unless they determine that most students have not mastered the standard. If this is the case, teacher teams look critically at their instruction and examine their teaching to provide alternative strategies for reteaching their whole class and helping all students succeed.

Just because a standard is taught does not necessarily mean that students have learned it. Flexible days, staggered in the calendar, provide opportunities to reteach or refine the learning of all priority and nonpriority standards. Additionally, it helps account for any necessary calendar adjustments due to emergency closings, unexpected assemblies, or other unforeseen events. After a few days of corrective teaching and extension, teams strive to adhere to the agreed-on date on the calendar so they do not impact subsequent units.

Team Meetings

Teachers need time to participate in a team data-inquiry meeting (chapter 5) in response to common data. You will read more about collaborative scoring sessions in chapter 4 (page 93). The purpose of those meetings is different from the data-inquiry meetings. Both are highly important in the PLC process. Over time, you will see how these collaborative sessions will also help inform your data-inquiry meetings. Along with these team data-inquiry meetings, teams take time to prepare the unit. These meetings are consistently placed in the calendar. During a data-inquiry meeting, teams analyze student results to accomplish three goals: (1) identify specific trends, observations, or outcomes, (2) interpret the results and determine what led to the results, and (3) develop an intervention plan to address the trends or patterns in the data they have collected. To help guide their analysis and discussions, teams ask themselves the following questions.

▸ "What strengths do students demonstrate that reflect proficiency?"

▸ "What weaknesses do the data reflect?"

▸ "What instructional strategies help proficient students master the learning target?"

▸ "Why might some students struggle with these concepts or skills?"

▸ "What will your learning team do next to address the trends or patterns in the data that you've collected?"

EXERCISE
Map Out Assessment Dates

At this junction, team members work together to produce a team calendar. In doing so, they can use the suggestions in the bullets below to assist them in this exercise.

Use the following questions to guide this exercise.

★ What are ways that teachers on the team might divvy up some of these tasks prior to attending the team meeting? For example, some teachers can research preassessments to share with the team, others can draft ideas for the assessment tasks, and still others can research a tool or format for the team calendar to share with the team.

★ Who will be responsible for creating a calendar template that the team can populate in discussion together, and where will this document live for all to access?

★ In which order should we address priority and nonpriority standards so they can build on one another in instruction?

★ How can we pace instruction so that data-inquiry meetings are accounted for and our teaching remains responsive?

Summary

It is critical that teacher teams carefully design a learning progression that sequences the step-by-step instructional moves teachers take to teach the skills and knowledge necessary for students to attain mastery of priority standards in any given unit. This crucial aspect of curriculum design also provides teachers and teams with guidance in developing assessments, gathering evidence of student performance, and adjusting instruction to meet students' specific needs.

When teams develop the learning progression, they also take into account the various texts students will experience as the vehicle to meet expectations. Such works can also serve as reading and writing mentor texts. Since choosing complex read-aloud texts can prove challenging, teachers implement a three-part model to help them select the appropriate texts. It involves examining a text's quantitative and qualitative aspects, as well as considering students' characteristics and the tasks they are asked to perform.

Once teams build a learning progression and determine assessments, they fashion a team calendar. On it, they record dates for instruction, assessments, interventions, and data analysis. Individual teachers can duplicate the team calendar and record their classroom assessments on it, as well, to be sure to intentionally map out all that is required to assist all students toward mastery of priority standards.

After teams map out instruction and assessment dates, teams look at the next chapter, which supports teams in understanding and designing rubrics and student checklists and using them as instructional tools. Additionally, teams will learn a process for consistently scoring student work so all teachers assess uniformly.

CHAPTER 4

Develop Collective Understanding of Mastery Expectations

With a solid learning progression in place, teacher teams have positioned themselves to deliver a guaranteed and viable curriculum and rigorous learning journey for every student. Thus far, teams have mapped the steps students will take in acquiring the knowledge and skills needed to reach overall mastery of the standards and ensured those standards include a literacy emphasis ("How will we know if each student has learned it?"; DuFour et al., 2016, p. 59), and determined how to assess students along the way. However, a commitment to collaboration as a professional learning community doesn't end there.

Though a teacher may know what *type* of data to collect from students to measure their progress, he or she cannot ensure that all students will be evaluated similarly and held to the same learning expectations unless there is a collective understanding of what it actually means for a student to master each standard. How will we know when a student has mastered a learning standard? How will we measure student proficiency levels? Collective understanding, imperative in this process, ensures teams work together to hold students to consistent expectations of mastery. Teacher A may expect students to identify internal and external character traits when describing characters, while Teacher B looks for students to merely identify external characteristics. These inconsistent expectations allow teams to become disjointed in instructional practice, as Teacher A is approaching standards in a very different manner from Teacher B.

Despite the necessity of discussing and scoring student work together, a lack of collaboration around the scoring of student work is a common pitfall of many teams. They do great work to prepare for instruction but often evaluate student performance in isolation and realize that teachers just down the hallway lack clarity on what mastery looks like, or further, accidentally happen into a conversation that unveils a notable difference in the evaluation of student performance. Upholding a commitment to collaboration avoids this common setback. Together, collaborative teams carve out time to solidify consistent expectations in specific ways, including creating rubrics and student checklists and engaging in collaborative scoring sessions, which we will discuss in this chapter.

Students use checklists that name items required for an assignment as a guide to ensure they are including the designated items in their performance tasks or written responses. For example, kindergarten writers are expected to include capital letters at the beginning of each sentence, as well as punctuation at the end of a sentence. A checklist serves as a reminder to writers of what is essential.

Whether providing students with a rubric, checklist, or both, it is important that learning expectations are transparent for students so they know what it takes to produce quality products. With ongoing use throughout instruction, explicit modeling on how to use rubrics and checklists, and reinforcement by the teacher, these tools become instrumental in the learning process.

Rubrics

Teachers of any grade likely come across a medley of rubrics—also called *rating scales* or *scoring guides*—of all sizes and purposes. Ideally, a *rubric* is "a coherent set of criteria for students' work that includes descriptions of levels of performance quality on the criteria" and is important because it lets students know "the qualities their work should have" (Brookhart, 2013, pp. 4–5).

Though the benefits of rubrics are evident, there are many ways to construct and apply them. There are holistic and analytic rubrics and common analytic rubrics, and if constructed and used well, common analytic rubrics benefit both teachers and students. Author Kathy Tuchman Glass (2017) describes *holistic* rubrics this way:

A holistic rubric might include a broad entry about the use of proper writing conventions instead of specifying which particular convention is the focus (such as proper use of subject-verb agreement or quotation marks in dialogue). Usually, holistic-scoring systems are used with an on-demand prompt for a school, district, or state summative assessment. . . . Although these rubrics do reflect students' strengths and weaknesses, they often provide a single score without feedback to identify specific areas that need attention or demonstrate where a student shows mastery. (p. 60)

An example is conventions in a kindergarten rubric being generalized, such as *Some mistakes in punctuation, spelling, and capitalization.*

Analytic rubrics are educative. They devote each criteria item to a specific skill that students need to master and provide teachers, as well as students, with feedback for improvement. In this regard, analytic rubrics are a highly effective tool for classroom instructional purposes and for scoring both formative and summative assessments. Therefore, in a PLC, teams most often use common analytic rubrics that are aligned to a learning standard since they provide the most useful information to glean strengths and weaknesses in students' performance to move their learning forward.

Task-specific rubrics detail criteria specific to a particular assignment, such as these items for a science writing task: *accurately details the characteristics of plants, thoroughly reveals the differences between two animals*, or *correctly explains the similarities in plants and animals.* This type of rubric assesses knowledge pertaining to a specific topic or task pertaining to a particular unit of study; it measures performance for a particular point in time and can likely only be applied to a single assignment. Due to its temporary application to one assignment or one unit, the feedback provided to the student doesn't typically allow for the tracking or monitoring of long-term goals. The student knows how he performed on this particular assignment but has limited information about how to improve his skills for the next unit of study. Given these limitations, we focus our efforts in this chapter on analytic rubrics, specifically common analytic rubrics.

Common Analytic Rubrics

Common analytic rubrics fit the bill of addressing the first question of a PLC—What do we want students to know and be able to do? (DuFour et al., 2016)—to measure knowledge and skills. Therefore, teams create this type of rubric to assess student performance based on criteria that align to the standards or expectations of student performance. Any time certain skills are assessed in and across content areas and units of study, the same analytic rubric can be used.

Using comparative data, students can observe their progress, identify skills to work on, and even set personal growth goals. Teachers have several data points from which to assess students' proficiency, check their progress over time, and thoughtfully plan instruction and interventions. Additionally, rubrics set the learning expectations for students so that success criteria are transparent. Such rubrics serve as instructional tools—essentially a how-to guide for discerning the requirements needed to attain proficiency. This helps students advocate for their own learning.

Regardless of an analytic rubric's visual format, it encompasses the following common components.

- **Scoring criteria:** What standards-based skills and learning targets will be assessed? Some discrete line item criteria might include *generate questions about a text, use details to describe a setting,* or *differentiate between fact and opinion.*

- **Performance levels:** Levels can be represented on a three- to six-point scale. Typically, teams use the same number system as reflected in the school or district report card. Should the rubric use exclusively numbers or terms, or use a combination of both? The point system can be coupled with these or other terms: *advanced, proficient, developing,* and *basic; extends, mastery, developing,* and *not mastering;* or *advanced, proficient, partially proficient,* and *novice.* Avoid evaluative terms like *excellent, good,* or *fair.* Therefore, on a four-point scale the line item for figurative language constitutes an advanced level of eight possible points. (That said, though, if teachers are expressly targeting a conventions skill, such as using capital letters or end punctuation, then writing mechanics become a featured skill worthy of the same point value.)

- **Criteria descriptors:** What description can accompany the scoring criteria for each level of performance? For the criterion item *create a narrative story with sequenced events through a combination of drawing, dictating, and writing,* the descriptions might include the following.

  - *Level 4*—Narrative includes two or more logically sequenced and relevant details.

  - *Level 3*—Narrative includes a single event or several loosely related events.

  - *Level 2*—Narrative includes sequencing that is out of order.

  - *Level 1*—Narrative includes marks or nonrepresentational pictures linked to a story or event.

These descriptors illustrate the justification behind a particular score and indicate to students what they can do to improve and move closer to mastery.

The rubric in figure 4.1 (page 98) addresses a group of reading standards from the unit on friendship and acceptance. This rubric is more holistic because it addresses standards that include multiple learning targets. *Ask* and *answer* questions about key details in a text, as well as identify *character*, *setting*, and *major events*, are examples of a standard that would be scored holistically because students must demonstrate full understanding of all targets in a standard to be considered proficient.

In this rubric, students are evaluated on their overall proficiency of two of the overarching learning standards. Teachers may find this more useful as the culminating rubric at the end of the unit, or at an interim checkpoint where students are measured on their overall proficiency. It provides information on a student's ability to meet the full range of knowledge and skills embedded in each standard.

The analytic rubric in figure 4.2 (page 99), on the other hand, addresses two of the learning targets: specific skills that were gleaned from the full standard during the unwrapping process (page 26) and arranged into the learning progression (page 62). This rubric is helpful when assessing and collecting data specific to those targets or verbs that are embedded in the overall standard. In our experience, when standards are unwrapped, altering the coding of the targets becomes helpful. The standard "With prompting and support, ask and answer questions about key details in a text" is unwrapped into two learning targets (RL.K.1; NGA & CCSSO, 2010).

1. **RL.K.1 (A):** With prompting and support, ask questions about key details in a text (steps 1–4 of the learning progression).

2. **RL.K.1 (B):** With prompting and support, answer questions about key details in a text (steps 5–7 of the learning progression).

For teachers and students, this type of rubric offers more explicit feedback since the scoring criteria and criteria descriptors are broken down by skill rather than by the full, overarching standard. It becomes a useful tool for teachers and students during the learning process and allows teachers to collect more precise data to pinpoint individual learning needs and next steps for instruction.

Common analytic rubric development and testing are explained in the following sections.

Common Analytic Rubric Development

When teachers collaboratively design a common analytic rubric, teams clarify and agree on expectations for proficiency levels, and may opt, at higher grade levels, to include half points. The goal is to create a rubric that can be used repeatedly

Levels of Performance

Scoring Criteria	4.0 Extends	3.5	3.0 Mastery	2.5	2.0 Developing Mastery	1.5	1.0 Not Mastering
RL.K.1: With prompting and support, ask and answer questions about key details in a text. Text should be in the kindergarten end-of-year proficiency band or beyond.	Uses the strongest key details from the text to demonstrate a deeper understanding of the text by: Consistently asking questions about key details in a text, including those that are literal and non-literal Consistently answering questions about key details in a text, including those that are literal and non-literal Consistently asking and answering questions that begin with who, what, where, when, why, and how Doing these things independently with no prompting or support		Uses key details from the text to demonstrate a full understanding of the text by: Consistently asking questions about key details in a text Consistently answering questions correctly about key details in a text Consistently asking and answering questions that begin with who, what, where, when, why, and how Doing these things with prompts or support		Uses key details from the text to demonstrate a limited understanding of the text by: Inconsistently asking questions about the key details in a text Inconsistently answering questions about the key details in a text Inconsistently asking and answering questions that begin with who, what, where, when, why, and how Doing these things with frequent or leading prompts or support		Demonstrates a limited understanding or no understanding of the text by: Being unable to ask questions about the key details in a text Being unable to answer questions about the key details in a text Doing these things with many scaffolds or much support
RL.K.3: With prompting and support, identify characters, settings, and major events in a story. Text should be in the kindergarten end-of-year proficiency band or beyond.	Uses the strongest key details from the text to demonstrate a deeper understanding of the text by: Consistently describing the character and character's reactions, responses, or feelings through inferring Consistently describing the setting and its most important details or why the setting is important to the story Doing these things without prompting and support		Uses key details from the text to demonstrate a full understanding of the text by: Consistently identifying the characters in a story Consistently identifying the settings in a story Consistently identifying the major events (big event, problem, or solution) in a story Doing these things without prompting and support		Uses key details from the text to demonstrate a limited understanding of the text by: Inconsistently identifying characters in a story Inconsistently identifying settings in a story Inconsistently identifying major events in a story		Demonstrates a limited understanding or no understanding of the text by: Being unable to identify characters in a story Being unable to identify the settings in a story Being unable to identify the major events in a story

Criteria Descriptors

Source for standards: NGA & CCSSO, 2010.

Figure 4.1: Rubric for standards RL.K.1 and RL.K.3.

Visit go.SolutionTree.com/literacy for a free reproducible version of this figure.

Scoring Criteria	4 Extends	3 Mastery	2 Developing Mastery	1 Not Mastering
RL.K.1 (A): With prompting and support, ask questions about key details in a text. Text should be in the kindergarten end-of-year proficiency band or beyond.	Uses the *strongest* key details from the text to demonstrate a *deeper understanding* by: Consistently asking questions about key details in a text, including those that are literal *and non-literal* Consistently asking questions that begin with *who, what, where, when, why, and how* Doing these things independently with no prompting or support	Uses key details from the text to demonstrate a *full understanding* by: Consistently asking questions about key details in a text Consistently asking questions that begin with *who, what, where, when, why, and how* Doing these things with prompts or support	Uses key details from the text to demonstrate a *limited understanding* by: Inconsistently asking questions about the key details in a text Inconsistently asking questions that begin with *who, what, where, when, why, and how* Doing these things with frequent or leading prompts or support	Demonstrates a *limited understanding or no understanding* by: Being unable to ask questions about the key details in a text Doing this with many scaffolds or much support
RL.K.1 (B): With prompting and support, answer questions about key details in a text. Text should be in the kindergarten end-of-year proficiency band or beyond.	Consistently answering questions about key details in a text, including those that are literal *and non-literal* Consistently answering questions that begin with *who, what, where, when, why, and how* Consistently identifying the most important major events (big event, connected events, or problem or solution; amount depends on the story) in a text Doing these things independently with no prompting or support	Consistently answering questions correctly about the key details in a text Consistently answering questions that begin with *who, what, where, when, why, and how* Doing these things with prompts or support	Inconsistently answering questions about the key details in a text Inconsistently answering questions that begin with *who, what, where, when, why, and how* Doing these things with frequent or leading prompts or support	Being unable to answer questions about key details in a text Doing this with many scaffolds or much support

Source for standard: NGA & CCSSO, 2010.

Figure 4.2: Rubric for learning targets for standards RL.K.1 (A) and RL.K.1 (B).

in multiple assessment situations for students to demonstrate understanding of particular standards throughout the year. Providing various opportunities for students to show to what degree they can master standards allows for practice and the assurance of proficiency. For example, if the target skills revolve around asking and answering questions about key details in a text, teachers can read various complex text across content areas while utilizing the same common rubric to measure student understanding of this skill.

For rubrics to guide teachers in measuring students' performance and achievement fairly and accurately, teams participate in collaborative scoring sessions discussed later in this chapter. As you read about these steps, review these general guidelines for rubric generation, referring to figure 4.1 (page 98) while participating in an exercise to develop or revise existing rubrics.

1. Determine performance levels and terminology.

2. List the scoring criteria.

3. Craft the descriptors.

Determining Performance Levels and Terminology

The point scale typically mirrors the grade reporting system in a school or district. Our experience helped us realize that using a letter system (E for extends, for instance) was difficult for parents to understand. Furthermore, to retain consistency between elementary and middle school scales, we decided on a number system (4, 3, 2, 1) to establish common language when reporting. The same applies to the terms coupled with each score, such as *extends, mastery, developing mastery,* and *not mastering.* Some schools may need to revise their rubrics to adopt these growth indicators rather than judgmental language like *excellent* or *poor,* or insert terms, if desired, where they currently aren't included. For suggestions, consult curriculum products or standardized testing for ideas on the proficiency labels atop rubric columns. Enter these levels across the top row of a rubric, as shown in figure 4.1.

Listing the Scoring Criteria

For a standard-aligned rubric, the learning targets are the elements to be measured, so list them on the left side of the rubric to indicate the scoring criteria. Group a small set of aligned criteria and ensure that each line item is dedicated to a skill to avoid overlap, which would only create confusion when scoring. In figure 4.1, the focus is on understanding answering questions and narrative elements, so the learning targets align to this topic of study. When students complete a summative assessment demonstrating their overall understanding of fictional elements, teachers will use a comprehensive rubric with more criteria items. For the common formative assessment, teams—as well as teachers in their classrooms—chunk the discrete standards in a manageable group of learning targets. Refer to figures 4.1 and 4.2 to compare differences in these types of rubrics.

Crafting the Descriptors

With assessment criteria and levels of proficiency in place, teams devise the descriptors for the performance criteria at each level. For each scoring criterion, teams collaborate to write a description that matches each level of performance. Rubric designers begin in one of two ways.

1. In one approach, they begin with the *mastery*—or what some refer to as *proficient*—column which represents the grade-level expectations and aligns with the standard. They build up or down from there.

2. Others begin with the *extends* or *advanced* column, describing what student work looks like when a student moves beyond grade-level mastery expectations to work that is more advanced and sophisticated. From this point, the rubric designers describe performance levels moving down.

Teams new to this process are likely to choose option 1 as they build their capacity to clarify what is expected as most fundamental, seeking anchor papers to guide their work. Once teams are well versed in the practice of collaborative scoring, discussions will naturally begin to focus on exemplary, advanced work samples.

Typically in the primary grades, the language in the criteria descriptors is often generic enough to be applied to oral or written work. The goal is to create a rubric suitable for multiple assessment situations, such as in a small-group discussion, conferences, or while completing a task or written response. This leads to efficiency in collecting data about student performance.

The *Mastery* column signifies the goal for all students as it reflects the grade-level expectation articulated in the standards. That text follows.

▸ Consistently asking questions about key details in a text

▸ Consistently answering questions correctly about key details in a text

▸ Consistently asking and answering questions that begin with *who, what, where, when, why*, and *how*

▸ Doing these things with prompts or support

During the process of creating a rubric, teams will often need to determine the meaning of certain terms or phrases used in the language of the standard. For example, the standard RL.K.1 in figure 4.1 includes the phrase, *with prompting and support* (NGA & CCSSO, 2010). In other words, the teacher can provide students prompting and support to help them ask and answer questions about key details. But what does this *prompting and support* actually look like when applied in a kindergarten setting? One teacher's level of prompting and support might be quite different than that of another. Different interpretations of the language of the standard can lead to different learning experiences for students and scoring practices for teachers, interfering in our goal of delivering a guaranteed curriculum to all students.

Therefore, the Kildeer teacher team decided to clearly define *prompting and support* and list on the rubric suggested phrases or questions teachers could use to assist students with this standard, as indicated in the following possible prompts and supports.

- ▸ "Can you tell me what happened at the beginning of the story? What happened after that? What happened at the end of the story?"

- ▸ "Can you find the part that tells where the story takes place (picture or words)?"

- ▸ "Who was in the story? Can you find (picture or words) this character?"

- ▸ "Look at the picture. Can you tell me what is happening in the story? How does the picture help you?"

- ▸ "What is the same about the characters in the two stories? What is different?"

- ▸ "How did the characters solve the problem in the two stories? Did they solve the problem in the same way?"

- ▸ "Tell me more."

- ▸ "Why?"

- ▸ "Explain."

- ▸ "How else?"

- ▸ "What's another way?"

Once collaborative teams have worked out the details and language for mastery, they can move onto the *Extends* criteria, which are to the left of the *Mastery* column.

- ▶ Consistently asking questions about key details in a text, including those that are literal and non-literal

- ▶ Consistently answering questions about key details in a text, including those that are literal and non-literal

- ▶ Consistently asking and answering questions that begin with *who, what, where, when, why,* and *how*

- ▶ Doing these things independently with no prompting or support

The *Extends* column serves a distinct purpose since in a professional learning community, a teacher's obligation is to push or encourage students who already demonstrate understanding of the standard. Providing students with a descriptor dedicated to extending performance for those who have already mastered a standard upholds this commitment. As teachers provide instruction, some students may grasp a concept quickly. In this case, it is important to differentiate instruction, leading those students in the next step.

Developing Mastery identifies what the initial stages of proficiency look like for a student.

- ▶ Inconsistently asking questions about the key details in a text

- ▶ Inconsistently answering questions about the key details in a text

- ▶ Inconsistently asking and answering questions that begin with *who, what, where, when, why,* and *how*

- ▶ Doing these things with frequent or leading prompts or support

Typically, early in the instructional cycle, many students will be at the developing mastery level as it demonstrates partial understanding of the standard, progressing toward mastery. Often, students who are developing mastery may also require prompting and support from the teacher, as they are not yet independently demonstrating proficiency.

The *Not Mastering* column reflects students still unable to demonstrate even partial understanding of the standards, despite adult guidance and prompting. The following indicators identify a student who demonstrates a limited understanding or no understanding of the text. The student is not mastering the standards.

- ▶ Being unable to ask questions about the key details in a text

- ▶ Being unable to answer questions about the key details in a text

- ▶ Doing these things with many scaffolds or much support

The descriptions tend to be far from proficient and typically indicate deficits as student responses are inaccurate or missing. This student still needs additional differentiated opportunities to learn and master the material.

Common Analytic Rubric Testing

Once completed, teams should test the rubric by analyzing and scoring actual student work or teacher-created exemplar pieces collectively. The goal is to ensure sufficient clarity in the language among all team members so that the rubric can be effectively implemented. Rubrics often need tweaking and revision once teachers use it for scoring in a real setting. However, teachers should simulate using the rubric to identify mistakes or items that may arise as teams sit to analyze student work.

With the rubric complete, consider ways to effectively use it as an instructional tool for students.

EXERCISE
Develop a Rubric

Using the guidelines, work collaboratively as a team to design a grade-level common analytic rubric. Then, try the rubric prior to scoring students' work.

Use the following questions to guide this exercise.

★ What point system will our team use on the rubric?

★ What are the scoring criteria items?

★ Is there an existing rubric that we can adjust to ensure that it includes the essential elements?

Rubrics as an Instructional Tool

Intentionally utilizing rubrics during instruction can allow students to assume responsibility for their learning and contribute to achievement. We recommend that teachers create student-friendly rubrics to use with students. Short sentences or phrases that get to the very heart of the target—*I named my topic* or *I used end marks*—empower writers to hold themselves accountable. Such rubrics have allowed students in the very early years to work with peers as they share work during a writer's workshop. When rubrics are in place, peers praise, coach, and specify feedback because both students are clear about expectations.

To capitalize on using the rubric as an instructional tool for improvement, teams can review the following suggestions together and determine how to implement them.

▸ Set goals and track progress.

▸ Articulate expectations of a task.

▸ Discern between samples showing mastery and those not showing mastery.

▸ Self-assess.

▸ Conduct peer feedback.

▸ Solicit teacher feedback.

Set Goals and Track Progress

Rubrics can equip students with the information necessary to make strides in their learning by setting goals over time and tracking their own progress. Students, teachers, and parents can review a student's past performance and celebrate growth throughout a unit, semester, or school year. By using the rubric as an instructional tool, teachers on a team provide students with consistent feedback and growth opportunities throughout instruction and prior to assessing a summative assessment. Student-friendly rubrics allow learners to communicate and hold each other accountable for expectations of mastery. Retelling stories, a substantial venture for most young learners, encompasses multiple learning targets within one standard. Self-monitoring with tools like figure 4.3 (page 106) enables students to be in charge of their learning and advocate for themselves so they can move forward in their learning.

Articulate Expectations of a Task

Rubrics also make the success criteria transparent to students so they are aware of the expectations of assignments they complete. Education author W. James Popham (2008) claims it is:

Absolutely requisite that students understand the evaluative criteria by which the quality of their performances will subsequently be judged. How can students make decisions about the effectiveness of their progress in mastering a particular curricular outcome if they don't know the factors by which their performance is to be evaluated? (pp. 79–80)

	Yes, I have it!	I am working on this.	My partner agrees.
I told the setting.			
I named important characters.			
I named the problem.			
I included the characters' feelings.			
I kept the events in order. 1 → 2 → 3			
I used transition words. FIRST THEN NEXT LATELY			
I told the solution.			

Figure 4.3: Retelling checklist—A self-monitoring tool.

*Visit **go.SolutionTree.com/literacy** for a free reproducible version of this figure.*

Making criteria forefront in students' minds early in the unit via a rubric sets the stage for success as they progress with a keen focus on expected outcomes. Experts agree that students engaged in learning understand what they're doing is important and want to take responsibility for their own learning (Julia Thompson, as cited in Ferlazzo, 2014). Primary learners use formative assessments, such as a quick interview with the teacher about letter names and sounds, to set goals and monitor progress. This process ensures a sense of ownership in their learning. A kindergarten student might create a bar graph tracking fluency, or more specifically, use a tool like the one in figure 4.4 (page 108), identifying the letters with which he or she still needs to demonstrate proficiency.

Discern Between Samples Showing Mastery and Those Not Showing Mastery

During instruction, teachers should ask students to compare strong and weak student samples based on particular target areas. For instance, in a lesson focusing on asking questions about key details in the text, teachers share—with students—student responses that represent solid examples of well-constructed questions that are related to text as well as questions unrelated or lacking in textual support.

Successful readers ask questions and pursue answers to these questions, but the metacognitive demands make this strategy one of the most difficult to address instructionally. Strong examples in this target include questions such as *I wonder why Chrysanthemum isn't asking a teacher for help* as opposed to *I wonder why Chrysanthemum wears dresses* (Henkes, 1991). Both represent questions a kindergartner might ask—however, the latter demonstrates surface-level questioning related to external characteristics. Sentence stems like the following offer an appropriate scaffold.

- ▸ "I wonder _____."
- ▸ "I'm confused by _____."
- ▸ "What does _____ mean?"
- ▸ "Why did _____?"

To determine strong versus weak examples, students sort examples and non-examples under the headings Good Questions and Better Questions and use the rubric to guide decisions. This exercise of using the rubric to assess writing allows students to discover what qualities comprise optimal performance. Matching criteria with concrete examples helps students understand how the rubric supports their growth.

Target	4 Extends	3 Mastery	2 Developing Mastery	1 Not Mastering
RF.K.1d: Recognize and name all upper- and lowercase letters of the alphabet.	Not applicable	Student **consistently** demonstrates application of the skill independently. Demonstrated by: • Accurately naming both uppercase and lowercase letters (all letters) • Automatically naming both uppercase and lowercase letters (all letters)	Student demonstrates skill **with** adult support and prompting. Demonstrated by: • Inconsistently naming both uppercase and lowercase letters (half the letters) • Inconsistently showing automaticity when naming both uppercase and lowercase letters (half the letters)	Student **inconsistently** demonstrates skill even with adult support and prompting. Demonstrated by: • Being unable to name uppercase or lowercase letters (five or fewer letters) • Not showing automaticity when naming letters • Requiring high support and many scaffolds

I am reviewing the letters of the alphabet. My teacher has circled the ones I need help with. Please help me with these at home.

Aa	Bb	Cc	Dd	Ee	Ff	Gg
Hh	Ii	Jj	Kk	Ll	Mm	Nn
Oo	Pp	Qq	Rr	Ss	Tt	Uu
Vv	Ww	Xx	Yy	Zz		

Source for standard: NGA & CCSSO, 2010.

Source: © 2019 by Kildeer Countryside School District 96. Used with permission.

Figure 4.4: Tracking letter-naming proficiency.

*Visit **go.SolutionTree.com/literacy** for a free reproducible version of this figure.*

Self-Assess

After students complete the task of sorting examples and nonexamples, they can use the rubric to assess their own efforts and uncover areas that need attention. They can then make adjustments during the learning process before taking a summative assessment. To conduct self-assessment, teachers familiarize students with the rubric elements and format, plus model how students can use rubrics optimally. As is the case with all learning opportunities, teachers are gathering unobtrusive data. Using a checklist, as explained previously, teachers observe to determine who demonstrates proficiency and who may need a bit more support.

Conduct Peer Feedback

Rubrics serve as a tool for classmates to provide feedback to each other. When doing so, teachers must model for students how to engage in the task of peer review for the express purpose of providing constructive feedback and ensuring reliable input to steer revision. Teachers focus on specific line items of the rubric for this exercise. When students share their work with each other, it supports them in applying what they learn to improve their own work.

Solicit Teacher Feedback

As a revision tool during the learning process, rubrics allow teachers to note areas in which students need to stretch or make improvements, such as, "What a detailed job you've done describing what you did in your story. What you need to do next is add how you *felt*—what you *said or did*. That way you include a reaction to the events." Then offer strategies. Additionally, they are beneficial tools in a small-group setting or when conferring with students to provide feedback. Together, the teacher and the student can identify strengths and areas for growth directly on the rubric, which then becomes a tangible takeaway from the conversation and a guide for independent practice.

For rubrics to be effective instructional tools, their language must be accessible for students. Very early learners are just beginning to grasp the importance of what is expected and ways to communicate understanding. Typically, teams are likely to create a student version of the rubric. A student-accessible version of the same rubric breaks down the expectations of the standard in student-friendly language. When creating student-friendly rubrics, teams must take caution when drafting the newly worded performance descriptors to ensure the rigor mirrors the original intention at each level of proficiency.

In many cases, teams may choose to utilize much of the same academic language with students and conduct lessons to introduce the academic vocabulary and format in the rubric. This is another reason it is important to go over a rubric with students at the start of each unit. Teams will also isolate and chunk specific line items to denote focus lessons, and then refer to these specific items as they formatively assess.

Student Checklists

Whereas a rubric defines the quality of each scoring criterion, a *student checklist* itemizes the required learning goals in an assignment. For learners at this age, checklists are companion pieces that do not differ wildly from the rubric. Teachers may use the terms interchangeably with preK through first-grade students as they refer to items on the rubric and the checklist to conduct lessons, making connections between learning experiences and expectations.

Unlike rubrics, checklists are not used for scoring or reporting purposes; rather, the list serves as a guide and self-checking tool for students as they work to complete a written response or other task. For example, when creating a checklist for writing a summary of a story, refer to the descriptors in the rubric and include line items such as *I name my topic* and *I include big ideas from the story.* Figure 4.5 shows an example of checklist items for an informational-explanatory writing assignment.

I am including a topic sentence.	☺	😐	☹
I am including big ideas from the story.	☺	😐	☹
I am using capital letters to start a sentence and the word *I*.	☺	😐	☹
I am using punctuation at the end of a sentence. . ! ?	☺	😐	☹

Figure 4.5: Student checklist for a writing assignment.

*Visit **go.SolutionTree.com/literacy** for a free reproducible version of this figure.*

With a definitive checklist in place, both teacher and student maintain a parallel vision of expectation for the end product. Rather than an afterthought, students use checklists in real time as they write or complete a multistep task; therefore, they are written with first-person pronouns and present-tense verbs. Writers as young as kindergarten are able to notice and name topic sentences within texts they read. Teachers model and ultimately expect these students to compose paragraphs with a sentence that names the topic.

To promote more autonomy, students may also begin creating their own checklists prior to writing or creating a class assignment based on a rubric. Crafting their own list of expectations promotes critical thinking as students determine the necessary requirements needed to complete a complex task consistent with the expectations laid out by the grade-level team.

When teams create a checklist, they should initially present them to students in an engaging way to generate ownership and familiarity with items. Consider the following exercise, which teachers on a team can conduct. It serves a dual purpose: exposing students to elements of the writing that they will produce and setting up the expectations for their writing task (Glass, 2017).

1. Display for the class an exemplary writing sample connected to the science unit on animals that is representative of what students will ultimately produce, such as a paragraph about animals from Australia.

2. Distribute the teacher-prepared checklist. Students compare this checklist with the exemplary writing sample. Help students notice the connection between the student-friendly checklist and the exemplar.

3. Pair students and have them share with each other their own personal writing and compare it with the checklist. Partner A begins by sharing his or her work as partner B listens, all the while paying attention to items on the checklist. Partner B coaches or celebrates the work of partner A. Partners switch roles, using the checklist to guide their conversation.

Visit **go.SolutionTree.com/literacy** to access a free reproducible version of this exercise. After some practice with teacher-generated checklists, students may co-create their own checklists prior to writing or creating a class assignment based on a rubric. Doing so promotes critical thinking as students decide on the requirements necessary to complete a complex task consistent with the expectations laid out by the grade-level team.

EXERCISE
Create Student Checklists

Once the rubric is complete, teams work collaboratively to design an accompanying student checklist for a common formative assessment. Write items in first-person point of view and with present-tense verbs so students use it as a guide while they address the performance task. Make sure the language is accessible to students.

Use the following questions to guide this exercise.

★ Are items on the checklist aligned to standards?

★ Is each item written in first-person point of view?

★ Is the assessment task written at the top?

★ When might students have a future opportunity to create their own checklist?

Collaborative Scoring

When teams convene to engage in a collaborative scoring session, they collectively score student work for the purpose of calibrating scoring practices and establishing a standard rating. Together, teams score the same assessment task using an agreed-on analytic rubric. Additionally, they ensure ahead of time that the task is administered consistently; otherwise, results may be skewed. For example, if one teacher provides a graphic organizer for students to plan their writing and other teachers do not, this will likely impact student performance.

By participating in this collaborative-scoring process frequently throughout an instructional cycle, teachers establish and maintain a shared understanding of the rubric, consistency in their evaluation of student work, and common expectations of mastery for all students in every grade-level classroom. Even teachers who are without grade-level or content-alike teammates can participate in the collaborative-scoring process with colleagues from another grade level, as it is just as important to vertically align student expectations from one grade to the next.

Use figure 4.6 as a team checklist for the collaborative-scoring process to ensure your team's scoring practices are aligned.

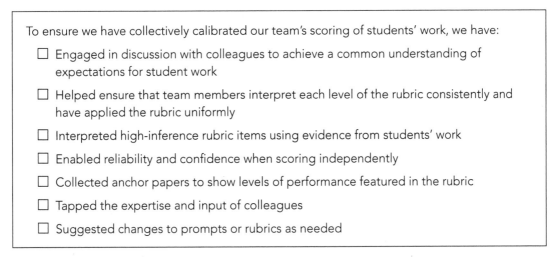

To ensure we have collectively calibrated our team's scoring of students' work, we have:

☐ Engaged in discussion with colleagues to achieve a common understanding of expectations for student work

☐ Helped ensure that team members interpret each level of the rubric consistently and have applied the rubric uniformly

☐ Interpreted high-inference rubric items using evidence from students' work

☐ Enabled reliability and confidence when scoring independently

☐ Collected anchor papers to show levels of performance featured in the rubric

☐ Tapped the expertise and input of colleagues

☐ Suggested changes to prompts or rubrics as needed

Figure 4.6: Checklist to calibrate the team-scoring process.

*Visit **go.SolutionTree.com/literacy** for a free reproducible version of this figure.*

The Collaborative-Scoring Process

To close any evaluation gaps, teacher teams participate in a collaborative-scoring process to align their scoring practices. During this designated team time, the goal is to reach consensus about student examples of proficiency for each criterion to ensure consistent scoring. To support this endeavor, teams of teachers collect *anchor papers*—examples of student writing at various performance levels—to accompany a rubric.

When teams convene to engage in a collaborative scoring session, they collectively score student work that is common among all grade-level classes *and* conducted in a common manner to allow for meaningful discussions around comparative student experiences.

Written or recorded (if orally presented) work would be best in this process so all collaborators can engage with the samples. Our recommendation is to score student work collaboratively as frequently as time allows, guaranteeing it happens for every standard at least once. The process takes the following seven steps.

1. Collect anchor assignments.

2. Select student samples prior to meeting as a team.

3. Review the task and common rubric.

4. Score the first assignment.

5. Discuss scores and arrive at a consensus.

6. Repeat the process, collect anchor papers, and take notes.

7. Score the full set.

The following sections discuss each step.

Collect Anchor Assignments

While participating in the collaborative-scoring process, teams decide upon and collect anchor papers—concrete examples from students' writing of each element on the rubric at all proficiency levels. Since items on a writing rubric contain highly subjective items that teachers often interpret differently, anchor papers serve as a best representation of what each score means for all criterion items and become designated examples by which other student work is compared. Anchor assignments serve as benchmarks for assessing written work, which contributes to reliability when teachers independently score their students' writing. The assignments also aid parent conferences so family members and guardians are aware of how to interpret rubric scores.

Additionally, teachers use the inventory of anchor papers categorized by performance levels for instructional purposes. When teachers conduct lessons using anchor papers, students can capably determine where their writing meets the standard and where they need to focus their attention for improvement. Specifically, students critique and score anchors against the rubric, which compels them to identify strengths and weaknesses pertinent to targeted writing skills. Teachers also model how to use these sample papers to self-assess and give peer feedback so they can apply these strategies on their own.

Anchors that reflect high-quality characteristics that meet or exceed criterion items on the rubric are deemed *exemplars*. Along with comparing strong versus weak examples of writing, teachers should design lessons that give students the opportunity to read, analyze, and emulate exemplary models in particular so they can apply elements of good writing to their own work (Graham & Perin, 2007).

Select Student Samples Prior to Meeting as a Team

Prior to meeting as a team, teachers review their students' papers. They preselect samples that represent a variety of achievement levels holistically, constituting broad levels of a proficiency, even though the team will ultimately score each line item on the analytic rubric. Specifically, each teacher collects two or three papers at each level to share with colleagues.

▸ Samples that are *not mastering* expectations

▸ Samples that are *developing mastery*

▸ Samples that exhibit *mastery* of overall grade-level expectations

▸ Samples that *extend* beyond grade level

Teachers can affix sticky notes to label each pile. Additionally, they conceal students' names to avoid bias and preserve anonymity. Classroom teachers, though, should devise a system for identifying these papers after collaborative scoring for intervention purposes, such as writing numbers or letters on each paper then generating a class list to match the code to each student.

Every team member (unless otherwise specified) makes enough copies of each sample assessment for every teacher on the team or sends electronic copies of these preselected papers in advance of the meeting. Team members should then bring the following to the collaborative scoring session.

▸ Copies of preselected samples to share with team members, unless electronic versions were sent prior to the meeting

▸ Entire class set of papers in case there is time to score more than the preselected ones, or if other samples are needed during discussion

▸ A copy of the common rubric used to score the assessment

▸ Note-taking tools to collect information about student performance

▸ Electronic devices if viewing and scoring papers digitally

Review the Task and Common Rubric

To begin the collaborative-scoring process with the team, together all teachers review the writing prompt or task that students completed, along with the accompanying rubric used for scoring. With a clear understanding of the assessment, teams discuss any high-inference or subjective items on the rubric to clarify expectations.

During scoring, discussion will likely be required to reach consensus; however, at this point, teachers may clarify unclear criterion items. For example, in the standard W.K.3: "Use a combination of drawing, dictating, and writing to narrate a single event or several loosely linked events in sequential order," the kindergarten team expressly looked for students to use characters when writing events in a sequential order, but questions arose from some teammates (NGA & CCSSO, 2010).

▸ Will students score a 1 if they only have drawing and dictating, but are able to explain how characters contribute to the story's sequence?

▸ What about students who use phrases and whole sentences to dictate the story, rather than specific one-word events?

> ▸ What if a student includes several different characters in the story—is this student extending beyond grade-level expectations?

Determining what teachers expect before scoring begins sets everyone off on the same path toward accurate and consistent scoring of student work.

Score the First Assignment

In large groups, the team can select a facilitator. The facilitator (or any teacher if no facilitator is needed) asks for an assignment identified as assignment A from one of the teachers and reads it aloud. Or, teachers can read it silently, since everyone should have a hard or electronic copy. Individually, everyone scores each criterion item on the team's common rubric while taking notes about what they notice from the descriptors that match the performance on the student's paper.

Discuss Scores and Arrive at a Consensus

When ready, the facilitator asks each teacher to share his or her scores for each line item one at a time. In large groups, facilitators can record and tally these scores for all to see. If all teachers agree on a score for a criterion item, move onto the next one and repeat the process.

The facilitator leads a discussion only for discrepancies on scoring. In these situations, teachers share their impressions of each line item, citing distinct performance indicators from the rubric with textual evidence from the student's work. The team engages in conversation until they reach consensus on a definitive score for the item in question.

Dialogue about student proficiency and expectations of mastery is a necessary and valuable part of the process, and as it develops, teachers often find themselves rethinking, refining, and aligning their understanding of student mastery with their teammates. If differences of opinion occur, teams should use the rubric language to guide their evaluations. In particular, team members may have various expectations about character description and may elect to examine additional student examples to compare and further calibrate their scoring practices.

Repeat the Process, Collect Anchor Papers, and Take Notes

Teachers repeat this process several times for each of the remaining student papers, always mindful that the goal is to reach consensus as well as determine which examples qualify as anchors. As they score, some teams naturally discuss possible candidates for anchors at different levels of proficiency. These are the papers teachers use when they individually score their class sets of papers after the session. In our experience, this process requires teams to dedicate more than just one team meeting. The role of facilitator is extremely important as teams work to accomplish this process in a timely manner.

Whether it is during or after the collaborative process of scoring all preselected papers, teachers need to take notes about how they can use the anchors during instruction and collect these papers to share with the team. As mentioned, teachers create learning opportunities for students to examine strong and weak samples and notice the elements that account for these differences. They may also have students study *exemplars*—those papers that are excellent examples—and focus on what makes them stellar so they can emulate the skills the student writer exhibits. Therefore, teachers should leave a calibration session with plans for incorporating anchors into their instructional program.

While participating in this collaborative process, teachers will also find themselves reflecting on the reliability and validity of the assessment and might ask themselves the following questions.

▸ "Did the assessment tool provide adequate evidence to determine if a student mastered the standard?"

▸ "Were the questions worded clearly enough to elicit detailed and accurate student responses?"

▸ "Was the assessment formatted in a student-friendly manner?"

As teachers consider these factors, they may make a collective decision to adjust the assessment tool for future use, or they may decide as a team to collect additional formative data to gain a clearer snapshot of students' abilities.

Either way, participating in the collaborative-scoring process allows teams to develop shared expectations for student achievement and refine assessments to make them as efficient and informative as possible. Although this process focuses on collaborative scoring of written work, teams can also adapt it for reading or performance tasks in all disciplines. For instance, when teams assess comprehension, teachers can record students reading excerpts. Using an analytic rubric they have customized for this task, the teacher team members can participate in a modified version of the collaborative-scoring process this section articulates.

Score the Full Set

Once teachers collect anchors during collaborative scoring and have clarity about aligning student work to levels of proficiency on the rubric, they score the full set of their students' papers. Afterward, they record their students' strengths and areas for growth to guide future instruction. Additionally, they input all of their students' scores onto a spreadsheet or other data-collection tool, and then reconvene as a group to discuss findings across the grade level and at the classroom level. Read Collective Data Inquiry (page 122) in the upcoming chapter for a thorough set of steps for effectively using the data from common formative assessments.

EXERCISE
Score Collaboratively

Once teams issue the common formative assessment, teachers engage in collaborative scoring so they can then independently score their students' papers with consistency against the agreed-on rubric. They then enter the class set of scores onto a data-collection tool in preparation for a team meeting in which they further analyze the scores.

Use the following questions to guide this exercise.

★ Are all team members aware of the calibration session protocol? If not, how can the points in this section be communicated to everyone? For example, after issuing the common formative assessment, what are the logistical plans for meeting together?

★ Are we appointing a facilitator?

★ Will teachers share the various levels of student work in hard copy or electronically?

★ After the session, what are the plans for collecting and sharing anchor papers?

★ How will we give feedback to students based on the findings?

★ How will we change our instruction as a result of input from colleagues?

Summary

Assessments play a critical role in the progression of learning in all classrooms. To further augment their value, collaborative teams can design effective rubrics and collaboratively score student work to ensure accuracy and consistency when measuring learning. Our commitment to student growth doesn't end there, though. As teachers in a PLC, we analyze and respond to the data we collect to determine specific needs for every student.

In chapter 5, the link between data and intervention takes center stage. What do our data tell us about our students' learning needs? What scaffolds, supports, and other learning opportunities do students need to reach proficiency? How will we appropriately challenge students who are already mastering the material? Consideration of these questions will help to sharpen the already fine-tuned focus teachers place on student learning and achievement.

CHAPTER 5

Respond to Data to Ensure All Students Learn: Response to Intervention

As members of a PLC, teachers attend to critical questions three and four—"How will we respond when some students do not learn it?" and "How will we extend the learning for students who have demonstrated proficiency?" (DuFour et al., 2016, p. 59). To lay a strong foundation for all students to achieve competency in reading comprehension and writing skills, we must provide struggling readers with intentional interventions targeted at their specific literacy needs. In addition, for those students who show proficiency or are already moving beyond it, teachers provide extensions. To accomplish this goal, teachers employ RTI, a three-tiered intervention system that pinpoints the intensity of instruction needed to support students at different levels, starting with core instruction (Buffum, Mattos, & Malone, 2018). Facilitating a successful RTI process requires teachers to measure students' skills and use data to determine which types of targeted teaching to employ, and do so in a timely manner. Since the fundamental tenet of the PLC process is the belief that all students can and will learn, educators engage in intervention, which signifies responsive teaching. As explained in chapter 3 in the Learning Progression Timelines section (page 83), we define *intervention* as the opportunity to remediate skill gaps for students as well as extend learning for those who have already acquired skills.

According to David Coleman and Susan Pimentel (2012b), "The first three years of instruction (K–2) are the most critical for preventing students from falling behind and preventing reading failure" (p. 3). In preK through second grade, the students who tend to struggle with literacy begin school lacking a strong foundation in speaking and reading. These students often experience difficulty and frustration while learning to read in the early grades and while reading to learn in later grades. Sadly, research shows that students struggling to read by the end of first grade will remain poor readers throughout elementary school (Coleman & Pimentel, 2012b). In an effort to close achievement gaps for students and make a profound and long-lasting impact on their development, educators in a PLC work together to provide high-quality, timely, and systematic interventions targeting students' specific needs—literacy in this case. The team data-inquiry process—a team meeting expressly dedicated to analyzing students' common assessment results— proves essential to literacy intervention.

Therefore, we begin this topic by explaining how to implement and prepare for collective data inquiry and clarifying guidelines for proactively responding to the data. Later in the chapter, we explain the implication of intervention during the discussion of response to intervention when teachers must achieve clarity about determining next steps in learning for students.

Collective Data Inquiry

When teachers systematically collect data, analyze the results, and respond to the ever-shifting instructional needs of students, these actions powerfully contribute to growth. The research of Ronald Gallimore, Bradley A. Ermeling, William M. Saunders, and Claude Goldenberg (2009) finds that when collaborative teams implement an inquiry-focused protocol to address issues with instruction, student achievement significantly increases. This only occurs when teams persevere to work on a learning problem until it is solved and realize the correlation between how they teach and positive student gains. Therefore, it is critical that teams participate in collaborative data inquiry to examine assessment results and use this information as an opportunity to steer instruction intentionally to push student learning even further. Teams look at data and figure out what they themselves can do differently.

As Jenni Donohoo and Steven Katz (2017) contend, collaborative inquiry helps build teachers' sense of *collective efficacy*: "the belief that, together, they can positively influence student learning over and above other factors and make an educational difference in the lives of students" (p. 21). When teachers can attribute student success to their instructional practices rather than to outside factors, they shift from the assumption "I planned and taught the lesson, but they didn't get it," to beliefs such as "You haven't taught it until they've learned it" (Gallimore et al.,

2009, p. 553). In general, teachers capitalize on the expertise of team members to learn about instructional experiences using scaffolds and other strategies that can lead to the success of many students.

To begin, a team prepares for each data-inquiry meeting and uses student data during it.

Prepare for a Data-Inquiry Meeting

As discussed in chapter 3 (page 61), teams set the stage for their upcoming data-inquiry meetings by using their learning progressions to map out the dates for core instruction, assessment, and intervention onto their team calendar. To ensure your team is prepared for a data-inquiry meeting, teachers must complete the tasks shown in figure 5.1.

☐ Identify the assessment or assessments to be discussed.

☐ Ensure each team member administers and scores all his or her students' assessments in a logical and feasible time frame. (All team members should administer the assessment in their classrooms within a defined and agreed-on window of time; generally, teachers each conduct the assessment within a day or two of their teammates.)

☐ Guarantee all team members have access to the team data-collection tool and are proficient in using it.

☐ Verify all team members enter data (students' results) onto the data-collection tool prior to the meeting. (Teams must be invested in using data-inquiry meeting time to analyze students' results rather than input scores or grade papers. Therefore, to help keep all teammates prepared and on track, we recommend sending out an e-mail reminder a few days before the meeting emphasizing that each teacher enter data before the scheduled meeting.)

☐ Remind teammates to bring the actual assessments (the task and students' work) to the data-inquiry meeting so teachers can refer to them in conversation. To help provide a more complete picture of student progress, teams should also be prepared to augment their results with alternate forms of data, both formal and informal, gathered during other learning experiences based on the same targets as the common assessment. Teachers can take this additional data into account when planning for interventions and extensions.

Figure 5.1: Data-inquiry meeting preparation checklist.

*Visit **go.SolutionTree.com/literacy** for a free reproducible version of this figure.*

Use Student Data in a Data-Inquiry Meeting

To help teachers manage, process, and discuss their results, author Tom W. Many (2009) recommends committing to a set of guidelines, or rules, for using data.

Based on his suggestions, we developed three criteria to assist teachers during the data-inquiry process.

1. The data are accessible, easy to manage, and purposefully arranged.

2. The data are publicly discussed.

3. The data are action oriented.

When a teacher team ensures its data meet these criteria, it will increase the inquiry meeting's productivity and utility. The following sections elaborate on each of these criteria.

The Data Are Accessible, Easy to Manage, and Purposefully Arranged

Teams choose and devise a data-collection tool (such as a print or computer-generated table, chart, graph, or spreadsheet) for sharing and displaying student results. By serving as a representation of data, it is sometimes called a *data wall*—a figurative reference if (for example) teachers view data on a computer spreadsheet, or literal if displayed on a wall. Austin Buffum, Mike Mattos, and Janet Malone (2018) recommend formatting the team's data-collection tool to include both individual student results and classroom results for each of the assessment's targets and accompanying scoring criteria.

This tool must make data easy to manage and access during the meeting, or the inquiry process becomes cumbersome, hindering teachers from engaging in the analysis process. Teachers must also purposefully arrange data in a format that is complete, accurate, and straightforward (Many, 2009). If not, the team might spend the majority of its meeting organizing data rather than engaging in the meeting's most critical purpose—collaboratively determining the next steps in instruction for student learning.

Teams must grant all members—including other professionals who support the students, such as special education teachers, related services providers, teachers of English learners, principals, and assistant principals—access to the tool. These educators may already be a part of your teacher team and participate in decision making, but collaborative teams in a PLC can vary depending on the needs of the school. So, inviting invested educators who may not be part of your team to examine the data guarantees that they can responsively support students through their lens.

As discussed in chapter 4 (page 93), teams collaboratively design an analytic rubric that reflects the scoring criteria for the common formative assessment. In the kindergarten sample unit on friendship and acceptance, step 4 of the learning progression includes the assessment (refer back to figure 3.1, page 64) which addresses this one significant skill: *With prompting and support, students ask questions about key details in a text.* Figure 5.2 shows a portion of our data wall, which includes the kindergarten team's assessment and the criteria from its team analytic rubric for the administered assessment. Formatting the data-collection tool this way helped clearly display each student's proficiency level for the scoring criteria, highlighting the specific strengths and weaknesses in learning.

Learning Target: With prompting and support, students ask questions about key details in a text.			
Common Formative Assessment Task: After listening to a read-aloud, students will meet with the teacher to share their questions about key details in the text.			
Student	**Teacher**	**Scoring Criteria** Asks questions that begin with *who, what, when, where, why,* or *how*	**Scoring Criteria** Asks questions about the key details in a text
Carlos	Teacher A	3 (Mastery)	3 (Mastery)
Suzy	Teacher A	2 (Developing Mastery)	1 (Not Mastering)
Latisha	Teacher A	3 (Mastery)	2 (Developing Mastery)
John	Teacher B	3 (Mastery)	2 (Developing Mastery)
Rohan	Teacher B	1 (Not Mastering)	1 (Not Mastering)
Anna	Teacher B	2 (Developing Mastery)	2 (Developing Mastery)
Ritika	Teacher C	2 (Developing Mastery)	2 (Developing Mastery)
Kyle	Teacher C	1 (Not Mastering)	1 (Not Mastering)
Ramon	Teacher C	3 (Mastery)	4 (Extends)

Source: Adapted from Buffum et al., 2018.

Figure 5.2: Team data collection—Example.

Visit go.SolutionTree.com/literacy for a free reproducible version of this figure.

Accessible, manageable, and purposefully arranged data help teachers maintain focus on student results and limit potential distractions from a faulty or complicated presentation format.

EXERCISE
Design a Data-Collection Tool

With your collaborative team, review an upcoming common formative assessment and its common analytic rubric to guide you in designing a data-collection tool that allows for easy access and management of your team's data.

Use the following questions to guide this exercise.

★ What type of data-collection tool will we devise (for example, a sticky note chart, table, or Excel spreadsheet)?

★ How will we display our data?

★ How will all team members and other educators in our school access the data-collection tool?

★ What scoring criteria will we include?

The Data Are Publicly Discussed

Teams embark on the process of publicly discussing students' results during their team meeting after all teachers have entered their data on the tool. To help teammates cultivate a safe, supportive environment for data inquiry, education consultant Joellen Killion (2008) suggests developing data-discussion norms that "keep the focus on issues rather than people, engage people in an appreciative inquiry approach rather than a deficit approach to a situation, and result in a plan of action that energizes and motivates people" (p. 7). According to DuFour et al. (2008), norms represent commitments that "help team members clarify expectations regarding how they will work together to achieve their shared goals" (p. 471).

Figure 5.3 has examples of ways to guide a team meeting conversation when developing data-discussion norms. Teams use the following three steps.

1. In the Data-Analysis Goals column, teams jot down the overall goals for their data discussions.

2. In the Avoid This column, teachers brainstorm and record behaviors that might prevent them from reaching each goal. For instance, to achieve the desired goal of keeping the focus on issues rather than people, team

Data-Analysis Goals	Avoid This	Try This (Norms)
Keep the focus on issues rather than people.		
Engage people in an appreciative inquiry approach rather than a deficit approach to a situation.		
Develop a plan of action that energizes and motivates people.		

Source: Adapted from Killion, 2008.

Figure 5.3: Creating data-discussion norms.

Visit **go.SolutionTree.com/literacy** for a free reproducible version of this figure.

members might decide that *blaming each other, criticizing a teacher's instructional strategies,* or *refusing to share their data with a teammate* are behaviors to be avoided.

3. In the Try This (Norms) column, team members rewrite the list of Avoid This behaviors into productive actions members might try to attain the desired goal. These alternatives can become the norms. In this instance, teachers might suggest changing *criticizing a teacher's instructional strategies* to *reflect on the effectiveness of a teaching strategy.*

By turning negatives into positives, teams establish a clear and affirming list of commitment statements all teammates will be inclined to adopt (DuFour et al., 2016).

In addition to norms, which include communication guidelines reflected in the Try This (Norms) column, teams use *protocols*—procedures—for examining student data. Teachers examine the strengths and weaknesses in their instruction and include time frames for meetings. To determine how long to convene, teachers take into account the assessment's length and the number of criteria to ascertain. In preK through first grade, a team data discussion of a literacy-based common formative assessment typically takes between forty-five minutes and an hour.

In Kildeer Countryside School District 96, team members analyze data using the Here's what. So what? Now what? protocol, identifying data trends, determining what led to the results, and ultimately developing an intervention plan to responsively teach particular students by providing corrective instruction or extension.

Here's what. means that teachers focus on the strengths and weaknesses that the data and student work reveal. After looking critically at how students perform, they ask *So what?* to interpret the results and uncover what led some students to succeed and others to miss the mark. Since all teachers strive to gain better results, they endeavor to learn from each other. This part of the meeting relies on collegial openness and support as teammates share ideas and respond to the following kinds of questions.

- "Does a teammate have ideas that will enhance instruction for students who are still unclear?"

- "Is there a scaffold another teacher used in class that seemed to provide just the right amount of support? How about an extension opportunity that helped push students' thinking?"

- "Can a teammate suggest a graphic organizer to record, in writing or pictures, the key ideas of a text, a visual display or chart showing the steps of a reading strategy, or a hands-on cooperative learning structure that yielded positive results?"

Teachers also examine what might have derailed learning or produced less-than-desirable results. They might ask the following questions to probe for insights.

- "Did instruction truly align with the priority standards?"

- "Was literacy instruction proactive, and did teachers notice when students were struggling with a new reading strategy?"

- "Did lessons follow the gradual release of responsibility model (page 148) to slowly and deliberately hand over the responsibility of comprehension to students when they were ready?"

Finally, *Now what?* helps teams determine concrete intervention plans. This section of the protocol is inspired by Buffum and his colleagues (2018) in *Taking Action: A Handbook for RTI at Work™*. When one of our teams approached this part of the data discussion, they realized that struggling students need a differentiated approach because some need more assistance than others. Therefore, our team dedicated the first two columns in the Creating Data-Discussion Norms chart (figure 5.3) to students who scored in the Not Mastering and Developing Mastery categories on the rubric (figures 4.1, page 98, and 4.2, page 99). Our conversation then turned to those who scored in the Mastery and Extends levels. By virtue of attaining the learning target, these students benefit from an extension opportunity for challenge, although teachers may need to differentiate learning based on students' current understanding.

The organizer shown in figure 5.4 features a template with guiding questions—modeled after Kildeer's protocol—that teams can use to capture the notes from their data discussion. Since teams participate in a continuous cycle of assessment and acting on the data that teams analyze, they can also use this tool for both common formative *and* summative assessments. Typically, during these discussions, one team member records the notes using a digital copy of the template that is accessible to the entire team (such as in a Google Doc), or by recording notes on a hard copy of the template to be photocopied and distributed to teammates after the meeting.

Learning target: With prompting and support, students ask questions about key details in a text.

Here's what.
Based on the student data and work samples for this assessment, identify specific trends, observations, or outcomes. (Five minutes)

What strengths do students demonstrate that reflect proficiency?

- Some students were able to craft questions correctly and base those questions on the key details in the story.
- Of those students, a few of them were able to develop inferential questions. They were thinking beyond the text.

What weaknesses do the data reflect?

- Some students are still having difficulty crafting questions correctly.
- Some students are asking questions unrelated to the key details in the text.
- A few students were able to write out (instead of needing to say their questions aloud); however, we noticed they had difficulty with concepts of print—particularly understanding that words move from left to right across the page, rather than right to left. Although this skill is not the focus of this assessment, we will keep the data in mind for upcoming team data discussions on students' writing skills.

So what?
Interpret results and determine what led to the results. (Fifteen minutes)

What instructional strategies help proficient students master the learning target?

- Teacher C helped her students remember how to craft a question by teaching them the five Ws and H of questioning.
- Teacher C also provided students with a story map to help them think about the key details in the beginning, middle, and end of the text before generating their questions.

Why might some students struggle with these concepts or skills?

- Students might need additional help remembering and focusing on the key details in the text.
- Students are still getting used to crafting their own questions rather than simply telling teachers what they think about a text.

Figure 5.4: Data-inquiry discussion template—Example.

continued →

Now what? Develop an intervention plan to address the trends or patterns in the data that you've collected. (Thirty minutes) (Buffum et al., 2018)			
Scoring Criteria	Not Mastering	Developing Mastery	Mastery or Extends
Criterion: Asks questions that begin with *who, what, when, where, why,* or *how*	**Students:** Kyle and Rohan **Instructional plan:** For students who need help distinguishing a question from a statement, reteach the lesson in which the teacher explains the difference between a question and statement, reads aloud a few sentences, and then asks students to hold up one finger to indicate *This is a question;* two fingers to indicate *This is a statement;* and a fist to indicate *I am not sure.* Provide feedback, correction, and reteaching until students can demonstrate mastery.	**Students:** Suzy, Anna, and Ritika **Instructional plan:** For students who can distinguish a question from a statement but need help crafting their own questions, engage students in a think-aloud of how to use the five Ws and H of asking questions while reading a story. Then give students an opportunity to practice the skill with the teacher and their peers before trying it on their own.	**Students:** Carlos, Latisha, John, and Ramon **Instructional plan:** N/A. This target does not extend.
Criterion: Asks questions about the key details in a text	**Students:** Suzy, Rohan, and Kyle **Instructional plan:** For students who have difficulty determining key ideas, read a short, simple story aloud to the group. After reading the text, ask students, "What is the most important thing that happened in the story? These important moments are the *key ideas.*" Listen to students share their key ideas and provide feedback as needed. For example, if students mention something from the text that is not a key idea, say, "The character's pretty dress is not one of the most important things in the story. Her dress has nothing to do with the events of the story, so it is not a key idea of the text."	**Students:** Latisha, John, Anna, and Ritika **Instructional plan:** For students who need help developing questions based on the key ideas in the text, provide them with a story map and show them how to use pictures, symbols, or words to record the key details from the beginning, middle, and end of the story. Students can reference the story map to generate questions.	**Students:** Carlos and Ramon **Instructional plan:** Teach students to think beyond the text by asking non-literal questions that require inferential thinking. For example, based on the events of a story, a student might ask, "How can the character's experience help me in my own life? Where might a similar situation take place in our community?"

Visit go.SolutionTree.com/literacy for a free reproducible version of this figure.

Figure 5.4 shows entries the kindergarten team recorded onto the data-inquiry discussion template for the assessment they issued on asking questions about a text. In the *Here's what.* section, although they kept the focus on questioning—which is this common formative assessment's learning target—they noted deficiencies in other skills that they will assess later in the unit. Specifically, they input that a few students who were able to write out (instead of saying aloud their questions) had difficulty with concepts of print, particularly the understanding that words move from left to right across the page—rather than right to left. In this regard, they took advantage of using this tool to record brief preassessment data for future reference. It may not always be the case to record such information, but if it occurs, embrace this opportunity.

The Data Are Action Oriented

Action-oriented data discussions ensure that teams make changes based on their decisions. All other steps of the data conversation process are in vain if this does not occur. *Action oriented* simply means that teachers proactively provide support to students based on the data because, to put it in frank terms, that is our job and common sense would even dictate that we respond based on the data we collect and analyze. Why collect it otherwise?

Teams embed dedicated time into their unit calendar for responsive teaching not only to address the needs of struggling learners but also to extend the learning of those students who are ready for more advanced coursework. This time is indicated on the team calendar by recording *Intervention: Corrective Instruction or Extension*. Instruction continues during this time; however, teachers must be cognizant of students who need either more scaffolding or challenge. The whole crux of the data-inquiry conversation is to ascertain next steps in instruction for each student knowing they are each at varying levels of proficiency. This can occur as a manner of responsive teaching in small-group instruction or in the RTI framework.

In order to make prudent instructional decisions and select appropriate support for students, teams should also consider alternate forms of data to augment the common assessment results. This means utilizing formal or informal data from a different assignment in literacy—and even across disciplines—to ascertain students' performance to assist with planning scaffolds and extensions. Since students experience a wide range and variety of texts across content areas and write for myriad purposes, teachers can analyze data from a social studies assessment, for example, to make a prediction about what support students might need to master a reading standard in ELA. As well, teachers may utilize previous writing data from an assignment other than the common assessment to inform their next moves. Taking these data into consideration gives a more complete picture.

Thus far in the chapter, we have provided the logistics and process of a data-inquiry meeting. Take time with your team to complete the following exercise.

EXERCISE

*Participate in a Collaborative Formative
Assessment Data-Inquiry Discussion*

After grading their common formative assessments and entering data into the collection tool, teams are ready to discuss student results, share instructional strategies and ideas, and develop a responsive teaching plan.

Use the following questions to guide this exercise.

★ What are the logistical plans for meeting together?
For example, have we set a date and location for our team data discussion?

★ Will team members be required to bring their students' assessment with them in case they need to reference them during the meeting?

★ Will the team utilize a data discussion protocol to help teachers focus on student results in a safe, nonthreatening environment?

★ Where will the team record their ideas for extending instruction for students who are ready to move ahead or providing scaffolds for students in need of additional support?

RTI

When we focus on learning, it is our obligation to address each student's unique learning needs. The reality in a heterogeneous classroom is that some students already possess the acquired skills to be taught, while others will require more time or practice to become proficient. RTI relies on student data to make decisions about what level of support individual learners need.

RTI is "timely, targeted, systematic interventions to all students who demonstrate the need" (Buffum, Mattos, & Weber, 2012, p. xiii). Figure 5.5 shows a visual of the tiers that comprise RTI.

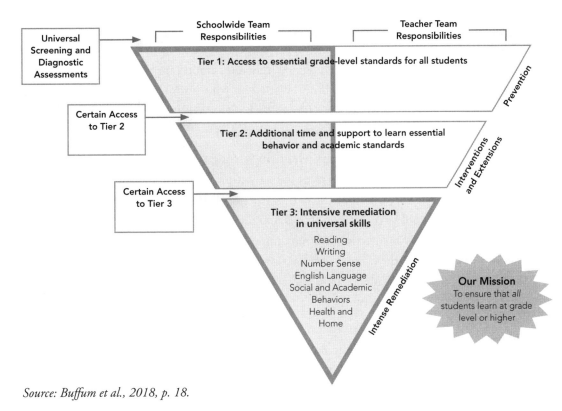

Source: Buffum et al., 2018, p. 18.

Figure 5.5: RTI at Work framework.

Tiers

What happens in each of the three tiers in the RTI framework? Tier 1 represents core classroom instruction for all students, Tier 2 is targeted small-group interventions for students who are struggling with standards proficiency, and Tier 3 is intensive individualized remediation targeted to students who are not experiencing improvement in Tier 2.

Among the many reliable and comprehensive books that provide details, resources, and guidance on RTI, we recommend *Taking Action: A Handbook for RTI at Work* (Buffum et al., 2018) to augment the discussion in this chapter.

Extension or Acceleration for Learners Who Are Proficient

Learners who demonstrate clear understanding on essential learning targets during current instruction need acceleration or extension. Teachers must strive to engage advanced learners in valuable, meaningful learning experiences rather than simply occupy their time with extra homework, busywork, or time fillers (Guskey, 2010). Unlike RTI, many states do not define opportunities for extension and acceleration. However, if your state or district has adopted legislation around these areas of instruction, refer to their interpretations. If not, work with your team to define criteria for those needing extension or acceleration and what that will look like, because all students deserve the opportunity to achieve at high levels.

Tier 2 *acceleration* is for students who demonstrate proficiency with nearly all the standards in a given grade level prior to instruction. The data that indicate these students are usually measured at the end of the previous school year or the onset of the current school year. An example is a kindergarten student moving to first grade just for literacy instruction but remaining in the kindergarten classroom for the rest of the school day. Tier 3 acceleration is for students who require intense acceleration in multiple subject areas and are advanced to the next grade level after meeting certain academic criteria.

Teachers can provide *extension* by moving students horizontally through the curriculum and encouraging them to dig deeper into current content, without moving them ahead vertically (Buffum et al., 2018). To accomplish this differentiated approach, teachers might challenge students to:

> Look at things from different perspectives, apply skills to new situations or contexts, look for many different ways to solve a problem (not just looking for the correct answer), or use skills learned to create a new outcome or product. (Buffum et al., 2018, p. 180)

For example, on the data-inquiry discussion template (figure 5.4, pages 129–130), students identified as needing extensions can tackle the more sophisticated skill of thinking beyond the text by comparing the characters or events from a reading to their own real-life experiences. To draw these comparisons, students must take the information they learned in the text and apply it to a novel situation. This allows students to think more deeply without moving them ahead to the next topic of instruction.

Students Who Need Additional Time and Support

For students who lack mastery, teams will spend additional time implementing an instructional *scaffold*, or temporary support structure, to help the students understand a concept or perform a task they could not typically achieve on their own (Northern Illinois University, 2015). When implementing scaffolds, teachers break down concepts into comprehensible chunks and implement strategies, perhaps providing a structure or a tool of some kind, to guide them in achieving the expected outcome.

Additionally, teachers use gradual release of responsibility, a sound instructional framework presented in chapter 6, to scaffold reading across the disciplines. Plus, they can implement the following research-based suggestions. Doing so can support students in becoming more proficient readers with a heightened sense of comprehension across different text genres they will experience across all subjects. Use any of the following scaffolding strategies alone or in combination based on students' characteristics and needs related to learning a specific skill.

Use Graphic Organizers

For kindergarten students identified as needing additional time and support on the scoring criteria, teachers might try using a graphic organizer. Students needing intervention in the standard of asking questions about key ideas in a text, for example, could benefit from a graphic organizer such as a story map, like that in figure 5.6. The story map helps them focus on and remember the key ideas in the beginning, middle, and end of the story. Students then use pictures, symbols, or words to record their ideas and reference them as they generate their questions.

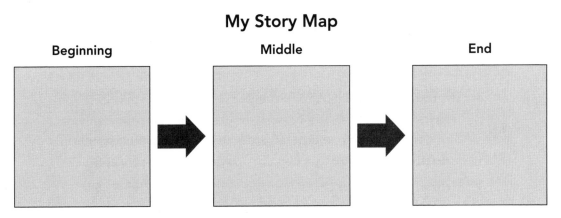

Figure 5.6: Kindergarten story map.

*Visit **go.SolutionTree.com/literacy** for a free reproducible version of this figure.*

Tell the Vocabulary

Prior to having students read the text, the teacher can carefully analyze it for any challenging and important vocabulary that cannot be determined by context. Teachers share the challenging vocabulary words with students and explain their meaning so that when the words appear in the text, students are able to make deeper meaning (Shanahan, 2019).

Build or Access Prior Knowledge

Struggling readers often have very little prior knowledge on the subject matter of a text; therefore, sharing background knowledge on the subject through a read-aloud, short video, or quick discussion can give students the information they need to make sense of a text (Neuman, Kaefer, & Pinkham, 2014). Students can also be guided to use their related experiences or prior knowledge to prepare them for the subject matter in the text.

Stair-Step Texts

To help increase students' ability to grasp the information in a challenging text, teachers can first have them read an easier *apprentice text*, or *stair-step text*, on the same topic (Shanahan, 2018c). Encountering important information in the easier text will help students notice and pay attention to it when they read about it in the challenging text.

Miscellaneous Scaffolds

Pair stair-step text with the following strategies to maximize effectiveness.

- **Encourage repeated readings:** Encouraging students to reread rigorous texts gives students the opportunity to revisit any challenging words, vocabulary, or concepts that may have interfered in their understanding. Multiple reading of texts brings down the rigor, making the texts more accessible.

- **Use realia:** Real-life objects or pictures of objects, *realia*, can help students make a connection between the objects and the word or phrase they represent. Giving students an opportunity to see and touch authentic materials helps increase their overall language-learning experience.

- **Help with coherence:** Coherence refers to the way words, ideas, and sentences are connected in a text. When authors use features such as pronouns and synonyms to connect ideas across a text, they can sometimes cause confusion for young readers, especially when ideas are far apart and referents are not repeated (Shanahan, Fisher, & Frey, 2012). Consider this simple passage: "Anne and her dog walked in the woods. They saw many different animals. They can't wait to do it again soon." Readers need to know that the word *they* in the second and third sentences refers to Anne and her dog from the first sentence. Readers also need to remember that the third sentence refers to walking in the woods, which is mentioned in the first sentence. Teachers can help by marking the text to show connections between words or replacing pronouns with their antecedents.

Figure 5.7 (page 138) features general interdisciplinary suggestions, many of which are successful scaffolding tools. Share these ideas with team members, and then sample and implement different strategies, making sure they match the right scaffold to a student's characteristics and needs related to learning a specific skill. Afterward, as a group, discuss how well a particular strategy worked or what teachers might recommend changing.

As students acquire a skill and learning continues, teachers remove the scaffolds to advance pupils to the next level in the learning progression. The key is to select the appropriate scaffold to facilitate productive struggle and then gradually release the scaffold so that students do not become too dependent. Over time, students should be able to employ the strategy or perform the skill without the need for additional support; however, for students with a severe disability, the scaffold can stay in place and serve as an *accommodation*.

If a scaffold allows students to accomplish a task too easily, the support is probably too enabling. In a classroom where teachers promote productive struggle, students feel empowered to persist despite a healthy struggle since the teacher encourages determination and curiosity. Students gain a sense of accomplishment as they try and try again to tease out something challenging. They feel the struggle is worthwhile because they can sense that by pushing through, success will come. Teachers offer cues and prompts to support students without giving them the answer outright. If this sounds like a learning environment that adopts the growth mindset philosophy—believing that intelligence is something that can be developed, rather than a fixed trait (Dweck, 2016)—it is.

The absence or mismatch of scaffolds or supports can lead to destructive struggle for students. Subsequently, no learning occurs due to missed learning opportunities. When confronted with this type of struggle, students feel overwhelmed and frustrated. As a result, they feel disengaged and ill-equipped to arrive at a solution. Sensing the learning target is out of their grasp and with failure in sight, they shut down. Overcoming these consequences requires immense teacher effort in terms of reteaching students and likely rebuilding their self-efficacy. To be clear, teachers are obligated to ensure productive struggle with students so they have the opportunity to grow academically and become more confident in general. To accomplish this, we position our students for success through teaching and assessing at rigorous levels, mindful that scaffolds might be necessary.

Given intense focus of instruction from the classroom teacher for multiple purposes, there might still be a time in which a student needs more. In that case, we suggest consulting dedicated RTI resources such as *Taking Action* (Buffum et al., 2018) as essential for implementing intervention practices.

Interdisciplinary Scaffolding Strategies

Use any of these alone or in combination based on students' characteristics and needs.

Let Them See It

- Show visuals, or point to something in the classroom environment, like a word wall or chart.
- Provide graphic organizers.
- Show a timeline to provide context.
- Use realia (objects or activities that relate what you are teaching to real life).
- Use gestures and animation.

Let Them Hear It

- Model how something works or how to do it; use the think-aloud strategy so they hear your brain at work.
- Rephrase it into simpler language or paraphrase.
- Read the text aloud.
- Use verbal cues, prompting, or questioning to elicit responses or elaboration, or to redirect.

Break It Down

- Divide the task or directions into manageable parts or steps.
- Create a calendar or timeline to plot milestones.
- Check students' progress after each part or step.
- Convert a text portion or a set of directions into a bulleted list.

Give a Clue

- Teach mnemonic devices for rote memorization (for example, acronyms like HOMES to remember the Great Lakes or chants like, "Thirty days hath September . . ." to remember the number of days in the months).
- Provide templates, sentence frames, or sentence starters.
- Offer hints to the solution.
- Partially complete a graphic organizer.
- Provide word labels.

Figure 5.7: Interdisciplinary scaffolding strategies.

*Visit **go.SolutionTree.com/literacy** for a free reproducible version of this figure.*

Common RTI Scenarios

The following sections present a few scenarios teachers might encounter.

Scenario One: Intervention Needs Outweigh Resources

Many of our students require targeted intervention. We can't keep up with the number of students who need reading intervention.

First, the team must re-examine core literacy instruction. When a team meets to analyze data and ultimately draws the conclusion that many students struggle with a particular target or skill, such as knowledge of letter names or letter sounds, the team must dig deep into the reasons for this struggle. They might determine that the assessment questions are unclear, the students don't speak English as their first language, or that students have an individualized education program (IEP). Although educators face these real concerns, they might unintentionally do a disservice to students. Teams need to move forward and reflect deeply about student needs, always seeking better ways to achieve goals. For example, very young readers often struggle to decode words as they are unable to break down phonemes in words.

A team might first need to determine if phonological awareness is the primary area of concern. A student must first hear sounds in words prior to being asked to read or write such words (Moats & Tolman, 2019). They must gather data in order to remove these types of barriers. This can be done using a quick assessment such as the Phonological Awareness Screening Test (PAST; Kilpatrick, 2016). Assessments such as this empower teachers to make immediate changes in their core instruction. These changes can be addressed in a whole- or small-group setting based on learner needs.

Once teams re-examine classroom instruction, they need to look closely at interventions for students who need further help, including, perhaps, small-group time or help in addition to classroom instruction. Teams can ask themselves the following questions.

- ▶ "Are these interventions aligned to grade-level standard deficits?"
- ▶ "What data did we use to determine which students require intervention?"
- ▶ "Did we implement a different strategy when students showed they did not master a skill?"
- ▶ "Do we need a wider range of skills to support students who struggle with reading?"

Timothy Shanahan (2008) says in relation to targeted interventions, quality and intensity are necessary to promote change. If students are not progressing, then teachers need to look at the wider range of skills to assist students in reading with comprehension.

Finally, teams should consider what intensive, targeted schoolwide intervention looks like by asking the following questions.

- "Who is still experiencing problems?"

- "What data did we use to determine what those problems are?"

- "Are we aligning core instruction with these interventions?"

- "What interventions are we using, and what others would be effective for these deficits?"

- "Have the problems decreased as a result of intervention?"

In all cases, students who need intense interventions have been working with professional educators who have provided core instruction, as well as additional help. If these students continue to struggle in their learning, the RTI team needs to reconvene and brainstorm potential solutions. The team might need to meet more often, implement more progress monitoring, and revise student intervention plans accordingly.

Scenario Two: First Graders Don't Know Letters and Their Sounds

We have first graders who still don't know the letter names and sounds. I can't teach them to read unless they know all of the letters and sounds.

As mentioned previously, research supports the two best predictors of success in early readers are knowledge of the alphabetic principle and phonemic awareness (Ehri & Roberts, 2006). As a reminder, *alphabetic principle*, explained simply, is the understanding that letters represent sounds that form words. *Phonemic awareness* is the ability to hear, identify, and manipulate individual sounds (phonemes) in spoken words (Adams, 1990). Without a deep knowledge of the English letters, as well as an understanding that words are made up of sounds, students cannot learn to read (Blevins, 2017). It would do our literacy learners a disservice, however, to remain in a holding pattern until letters and sounds are totally mastered. Jan Richardson and Michèle Dufresne (2019) suggest students who know fewer than ten letters by name work with an adult to trace only the letters they know, as well as the first letters in their name, on a daily basis.

Once students become more proficient with letters and sounds, they trace the entire alphabet. This is done by using his or her finger to trace upper and lowercase letters, as well as saying the name of the letter and picture (*B, b, ball*). In *A Fresh Look at Phonics*, Blevins (2017) notes that students best learn through active exploration and many experiences with print, including alphabet books such as *Alligators All Around: An Alphabet* by Maurice Sendak (1962) or *Eating the Alphabet: Fruits & Vegetables from A to Z* by Lois Ehlert (1996). These types of books are predictable, highlight each letter of the alphabet, and use illustrations to reinforce the topic of letter knowledge.

Many district reading programs dictate a scope and sequence of phonics skills. A strong scope and sequence constructed from less difficult to more demanding skills is paramount for student achievement. Blevins (2017)notes, "While there is no one 'right' scope and sequence, programs that strive to connect concepts and move through a series of skills in a small stair-step way offer the best chance at student success" (p. 138). Marie M. Clay (2005) teaches us:

> Early in the lesson, the teacher helps the child gain footholds in print. The child learns some letters and begins to work with some simple words. The teacher asks herself, "What detail in print is the child already attending to?" (p. 8)

For this reason, it is important for teachers to help students become proficient with a handful of letters to begin, such as *s, m, a, t,* and *d*. Once students have mastered these letters and sounds, they can begin manipulating letters to create and read words like *at, am, sad,* and *mad*.

Students become motivated and see themselves as readers when they work with words and apply them in the context of reading rather than overly practicing flash cards in order to memorize letters and letter sounds. In addition to working with simple words, it is important to engage students in activities surrounding both phonological and phonemic awareness. Nursery rhymes, songs, and poetry help students find patterns and parts in words as they develop a strong phonological awareness. Explicit experiences with phonemes in order to fully understand phonics are critical (Blachman, 1991; National Reading Panel, 2000; Wood & McLemore, 2001).

Hearing beginning, middle, and ending sounds in words; manipulating words by omitting or substituting sounds; and blending and segmenting sounds in words are the key to early reading success. Chapter 7 (page 163) explains these concepts in detail and provides concrete examples.

Scenario Three: Small-Group Decisions

I have a first-grade student with a fluency deficit in regard to rate and expression late in the school year. Do I need to add intervention for additional support?

As mentioned previously, a high-quality core literacy small-group setting should be implemented to address the needs of this reader before recommending him for additional intervention.

A first grader might already have well-developed skills in phonics and alphabetic principles yet lack skills in fluency in regard to reading at an appropriate pace, proper phrasing, intonation, expression, and emphasis on the correct words. Timothy V. Rasinski (2012) teaches that readers need to read not only accurately but also automatically. When students read in a word-by-word, robotic fashion, they may struggle to remember what they've read. This decoding struggle ultimately leads to a breakdown in making meaning and comprehending text, which is the ultimate goal (Rasinski, 2012). In this situation, a teacher needs to determine how to best meet the needs of this reader.

Many teachers use a guided-reading structure at the small-group table; however, a student with a specific deficit in fluency will strongly benefit from a skill-focused small-group experience focusing solely on reading fluency. You can differentiate small-group core instruction, in the classroom setting, by two things: (1) the instruction intensity and (2) the group structure.

Beyond using a screener such as a curriculum-based measurement, a teacher will have observed this student by listening to him or her read. The teacher has noticed the reader not only struggles to read at an appropriate rate, but also lacks expression and intonation. Literacy author Jennifer Serravallo (2015) explains for small-group strategy lessons to function well, with the teacher able to provide individualized support to each learner, it is critical that the learners have a clear, explicit strategy to support their practice. The teacher states the strategy up front for the group at the beginning of the lesson, and "strategies are deliberate, effortful, intentional and purposeful actions a reader takes to accomplish a specific task or skill. Strategies make the often-invisible work of reading actionable and visible" (Serravallo, 2015, p. 8).

However, just as we offer strategies to students, we want them to outgrow those strategies. Looking at the first grader in this particular scenario, we want to determine which strategy will best address this skill deficit. In *The Reading Strategies Book*, Serravallo (2015) shares a multitude of strategies such as Make the Bumpy Smooth, Read It Like You've Always Known It, and Say Good-Bye to Robot

Reading. The first strategies ask readers to return to words and phrases they may struggle with, and either smooth them out or reread with confidence. The latter, inspired by Sharon Taberski, teaches readers to "scoop up" a few words at a time instead of reading word by word; read all the words in one scoop together, in one breath, before pausing; and then scoop the next few words.

Scenario Four: Writing Struggles

Many of our primary students can't write. We need the reading specialist to work with them.

Writing presents numerous challenges. Many students struggle in writing due to the sheer challenge of forming letters through handwriting, while others wrestle with issues when spelling words. Students may also grapple with planning, organizing, and expressing ideas in writing. Teachers must gather data to determine the primary barrier for their students.

When handwriting is determined to be the primary deterrent, teachers offer tracing and letter-writing practice during playful learning experiences. Writing opportunities during playful learning allow students to build confidence with controlling a pencil, tracing lines, and forming letters and shapes. Building hand strength is also important. Allowing opportunities to play with and mold clay into letters or using tongs to pick up small objects in a sensory table may accomplish this goal (Kid Sense, n.d.).

Parents often look for ways to help or ask what they can do at home, and handwriting practice is a great way to get families involved. Written directions or video demonstrations showing how to properly form letters can be sent home with students. Scaffolded practice that follows your particular scope and sequence with a few letters at a time, rather than a packet with all upper- and lowercase letters, will likely yield a more positive result. Much like decoding in reading allows for deeper comprehension, building strong handwriting skills allows for fuller idea development in writing (Spear-Swerling, 2006).

Elementary students can also find spelling to be a roadblock when writing. Wiley Blevins (2017) suggests dictation be a regular part of phonics instruction for students. Dictation practices allow teachers to guide their students' thinking about not only spelling and phonics, but also writing conventions, reinforcing concepts such as punctuation, capitalization, and finger spacing. This practice allows teachers to connect skills taught in reading to their student's writing. *The Next Step Forward in Reading Intervention: The RISE Framework* (Richardson & Lewis,

2018) highlights the importance of guided writing in the primary classroom and recommends following a four-step process such as the following.

1. Teachers dictate a sentence connected to the guided reading text. This sentence includes important sight words, as well as words that reinforce explored phonics concepts, such as words with the short *a* or *o* sound.

2. Students are encouraged to say the words slowly. Serravallo (2017) tells students to "talk like a turtle" and write the sounds they hear (p. 299).

3. Once students have all the sounds on the page, they say it again *like a turtle* and run their fingers under the letters they wrote. After students have completed and reread their sentence, they are encouraged to write more about the book they are reading.

4. If any sounds are missing, teachers guide students to make corrections. An alternative strategy is to encourage students to spell as well as they can on the first go-round, allowing writers to spell it as best they can and keep going, circling words they're unsure of to revisit later (Serravallo, 2017).

Not all students struggle with handwriting and spelling. Some are unsure of what they want to say, while others need to determine how to organize their ideas. Young writers often are not sure how to begin their writing. When planning, organizing, and expressing ideas, teachers often help students navigate these hurdles by engaging in a task analysis. This first critical step ensures that students are clear about the purpose for their writing. In addition to providing clear understanding, teachers provide time and structures for creating a plan for writing. Sequence and T-charts support organization prior to writing. In addition to thinking ahead of the writing, teachers allow students time to discuss their ideas and share their stories with peers.

Compelling learning connections occur when students talk about what they are going to write before they write. Talking about stories and ideas is an informal introduction to each part of the writing process, and students need many experiences to discuss before they write.

Marie M. Clay (2004) notes oral language is the foundation to literacy instruction:

If we plan instruction that links oral language and literacy learning (writing and reading) from the start—so that writing and reading and oral language processing move forward together, linked and patterned from the start—that instruction will be more powerful. (p. 9)

All students, especially English learners, profit from opportunities to practice ideas and build their vocabulary. Students can participate in structures such as

Line-Ups, sharing stories with peers, or perhaps a Traveling Pair-Share where students utilize their graphic organizer and mix around the room taking turns *talking out* their story to multiple partners (Kagan & Kagan, 2009). Whichever method chosen, teachers should build time into the literacy block to ensure students have the opportunity to speak about their ideas before and after writing. Chapter 7 (page 163) will address whole-group and small-group writing in more detail.

Summary

In a PLC, collaborative teams are committed to finding ways to support all students in achieving at high levels. To uphold this promise, teams review and analyze data from a common assessment to find trends in students' performances. With this information, they capitalize on the findings and each other's expertise to devise ways to support struggling learners and challenge those who have achieved mastery. To help ensure that teachers speak candidly and feel comfortable to share and discuss data in a safe place, they establish norms. Additionally, teams must develop a robust, systematic data-analysis protocol—like Here's what. So what? Now what?—to secure a procedure for sifting through, analyzing, and acting on what the data reveal.

When a team meets to analyze data and ultimately draws the conclusion that some students struggle with a particular target or skill, team members must dig deep into the reasons for this struggle and develop a concrete action plan. They also must formulate learning opportunities for students ready to broaden and deepen their understanding of a skill. By working through an ongoing, continuous cycle of data inquiry, teams will deliver the quality core instruction and targeted interventions needed to ensure all students can read and write at grade level, fostering a love of literacy to carry them throughout their school-age years and beyond.

In chapter 6, readers will learn how to reach these goals by designing high-quality lessons using a research-based instructional model called *gradual release of responsibility*. When teachers devise lessons through this framework, they position students well to achieve desired goals.

Design Lessons Using the Gradual Release of Responsibility Instructional Framework

Instruction done well is no easy task. When teachers instruct, they employ appropriate strategies for the express purpose of meeting learning outcomes. To instruct, teachers have at their disposal an array of strategies. However, they must be judicious in selecting those that steer learning to the intended goals while taking into consideration their students' characteristics. During instruction, they collect evidence of student learning via formal and informal formative assessment (as discussed in chapter 2, page 39) and adjust their teaching based on how well students grasp the targeted skills.

Teachers' commitment to their students' reading and writing skills necessitates the planning and delivery of a literacy-focused, guaranteed, and viable curriculum (DuFour & Marzano, 2011). In the preceding chapters, collaborative teams engaged in the deep-dive PREP process to determine priority standards; developed a literacy-focused learning progression, complete with supporting assessments and rubrics; and established a process to gather and collaboratively assess data. This work is all vital to offering the curriculum preK through first-grade students deserve, but ensuring that all students learn requires more. It requires that teachers use the data they collect to inform and differentiate their classroom instruction each day. Figure 6.1 (page 148) illustrates how each step in this process has brought us to this point.

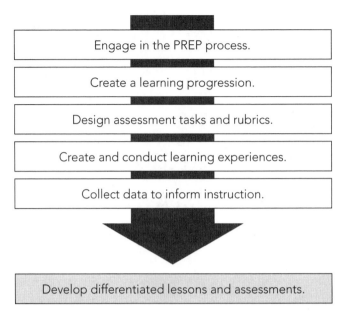

Figure 6.1: Overview of the instructional process.

Gradual Release of Responsibility

Research reveals that a direct instruction model can produce desired effects when teaching a new skill, strategy, or procedure (Fisher & Frey, 2014c). One such instructional framework, gradual release of responsibility, which originated with P. David Pearson and Margaret C. Gallagher (1983), involves an orchestrated, graduated cognitive shift from teachers modeling to students employing the new learning independently:

> When the teacher is taking all or most of the responsibility for task completion, he is "modeling" or demonstrating the desired application of some strategy. When the student is taking all or most of that responsibility, she is "practicing" or "applying" that strategy. What comes in between these two extremes is the gradual release of responsibility from teacher to student. The hope in the model is that every student gets to the point where she is able to accept total responsibility for the task, including the responsibility for determining whether or not she is applying the strategy appropriately (i.e., self-monitoring). But the model assumes that she will need some guidance in reaching that stage of independence and that it is precisely the teacher's role to provide such guidance. (p. 35)

Douglas Fisher and Nancy Frey (2014c) identify these phases of gradual release of responsibility inspired by Pearson and Gallagher's (1983) model. Taken together, the four parts contribute to an effective and fluid learning experience that can yield student achievement and contribute to high-quality Tier 1 instruction.

1. Focused instruction ("I do it.")

2. Guided instruction ("We do it.")

3. Collaborative learning ("You do it together.")

4. Independent learning ("You do it alone.")

All four components must be included in a lesson for maximum effect and to increase the likelihood of students mastering a new skill, strategy, or procedure. Teachers can rearrange or repeat parts of the model as dictated by the needs of students. For more simplistic skills, they can incorporate the four parts in abbreviated form in a typical class period or extend the model across several days to tackle more sophisticated skills. Only if teachers are reinforcing or reviewing a learning target should they judiciously omit parts.

Timothy Shanahan (2018c) humorously, albeit realistically, poses and responds to questions of how quickly teachers should relinquish their support by writing:

> Those decisions are hard because they need to be made on the spot. And, when they are wrong—that is, when it turns out that the kids can't take the reins successfully—the teacher has to take back the responsibility, for the time being that is.
>
> That's why I think of gradual release as: I do it, we do it, I do it again, we try to do it again but this time a little differently, we do it, we do it, oops, I have to do some of it with more explanation, you do it (no, not quite like that), you do it, we do it again, okay now you can do it. (I know it isn't catchy, but it is more descriptive of how the process really tends to work).

Teachers must use their professional expertise and knowledge of their students' characteristics to determine how to choreograph the steps of this model to best suit the needs of all students in their classrooms.

Focused Instruction—"I Do It"

During focused instruction, teachers take on most of the responsibility, accounting for the first person in *I do it*. Teachers establish the learning target, provide context, and show students what the skill, strategy, or process entails. While conducting focused instruction, teachers unobtrusively assess to determine how best to support students later during guided instruction. This portion of the lesson, which can include setting the purpose for learning and modeling or demonstrating and using think-alouds, might last around fifteen minutes.

Set the Purpose for Learning

Teachers can state the lesson's purpose at the outset by posing and posting the learning target (using an *I can* statement) and perhaps a guiding question in terms accessible to students. Or, teachers might wait to reveal the learning target and guiding question after engaging students in a brief activity. In fiction, for example, authors use key details in a story to reveal character traits. Before teachers share the learning target focused on characterization, they read aloud two passages—one with key details depicting a happy character and the other with key details depicting a sad character—and ask students to identify the character's feelings in each passage and justify their responses. After students articulate that the first character is happy and the second character is sad, teachers confirm their impressions. They then present the goal for the lesson: "Today we will focus on the guiding question, How do authors use key details to tell us more about a character? We also will address the learning target *I can use the key details of a story to learn more about a character*." To provide context for the work, teachers connect the learning to what students have done previously, what they already know, or how they will use the new learning.

Model or Demonstrate and Use Think-Alouds

After teachers establish the purpose, they model the new learning to present how one performs the task and what constitutes quality. For clarification, there's a technical difference between modeling and demonstrating. When teaching cognitive processes like reading, writing, or performing mathematical computations, teachers employ *modeling* to show students what high-proficiency work looks like and explain how they can replicate that work. When showing students how to perform physical tasks, such as swimming using the butterfly stroke or filling a measuring cup, teachers employ *demonstration* (Fisher & Frey, 2014c).

Concurrent with modeling or demonstrating, teachers employ the think-aloud strategy to reveal what goes on in their heads as they perform the task. This self-talk makes their thoughts transparent to students. For example, preK, kindergarten, and first-grade teachers often use the think-aloud strategy during a read-aloud by periodically pausing to verbalize their thoughts as they navigate a confusing moment. For instance, when reading Janell Cannon's (1993) *Stellaluna* to the class, teachers might choose to think aloud as they determine the meaning of a new word, such as *downy* in the following sentence: "Stellaluna landed headfirst in a soft downy nest, startling the three baby birds who live there."

To signal when they have stopped reading aloud and have begun thinking aloud, teachers can provide a clear gesture, such as a thinking pose, pointing to their temple, or tapping the side of their head. By making a gesture, students understand at that moment the teachers' words come from their heads—not from the text. After signaling, teachers begin sharing their thoughts aloud: "I wonder what the word *downy* means in this sentence. I will try to figure out the meaning of a confusing word by looking for clues in the text. According to this sentence, Stellaluna landed headfirst in the nest, but it seems that she didn't get hurt. Also, there are baby birds in that nest. If Stellaluna didn't get hurt from her fall and baby birds probably have soft nests, I think *downy* must mean soft." The think-aloud strategy in this example gives young readers the opportunity to listen to and learn more about the kinds of thinking they should use during their independent reading.

Teachers also talk about avoiding certain pitfalls, fending off misconceptions, revealing when the task might be difficult, and explaining how to deal with the challenging aspects of the task. For example, when prekindergarten students begin learning letter sounds, they often add an /uh/ sound to the end of consonant sounds—/buh/ rather than /b/, for example. Although this may not seem like a big deal, it becomes problematic as students advance in their phonics skills and begin blending sounds together to decode words. If students read the word *bat* as /buh/ /a/ /tuh/, they might not recognize it as the word *bat*. To avoid this confusion, teachers need to talk to students about *clipping* the /uh/ off the end of their consonant sounds. In other words, pronounce the sound for *b* as /b/ rather than /buh/.

Invite Minimal Participation

Teachers check for understanding at this early stage in the lesson. While modeling the task, they unobtrusively observe students. Additionally, they might gather students' responses to a question or prompt by quickly signaling with a thumbs-up (*yes* or *true*), a thumbs-down (*no* or *false*), or a fist (*not sure*). Or, teachers might model the task and ask students to turn and talk with a neighbor or elbow partner. All the while, teachers collect information to lead guided instruction.

During focused instruction, teachers present the learning target to students and connect what they will be doing so there's context. They explicitly show and narrate what proficiency looks like to prepare students for what they will eventually do on their own. Teachers attentively assess, albeit informally, in preparation for guided instruction.

Guided Instruction—"We Do It"

During guided instruction, teachers differentiate by arranging students purposefully in pairs, trios, or small groups of four based on similar needs. They work on a different task from the one previously modeled so that students can practice the new learning and apply it in a novel situation. While students practice how to transfer this skill, teachers supervise and provide guidance. They circulate around the classroom, constantly formatively assessing and offering actionable, immediate feedback by way of questioning, prompting, and discussing. They differentiate to redirect, remediate, or repeat information as needed. Additionally, they might scaffold instruction, which serves "to provide support, knowledge, strategies, modeling, questioning, instructing, restructuring, and other forms of feedback, with the intention that the student comes to 'own' the knowledge, understanding, and concepts" (Hattie, 2012, p. 144). For scaffolding suggestions, see chapter 5 (page 121).

Teachers might also need to extend or accelerate learning for those who would benefit from an additional challenge. If need be, teachers regroup students and allow them to work at different paces. For example, some students might have started an activity by working independently, but through unobtrusively assessing, teachers realize grouping certain students and working with them is prudent. Teachers can also direct students to monitor their own learning by providing them with a visual cue card of strategies to use when they get confused or a checklist of steps within a task if they forget a process. For instance, kindergarteners just learning to read might benefit from a visual cue card when they get stuck on a word. The cue card in figure 6.2 can remind students of the various strategies to use when decoding: *point* to each word, *look* carefully at each letter, *stretch* out the letter sounds, and *blend* the sounds together.

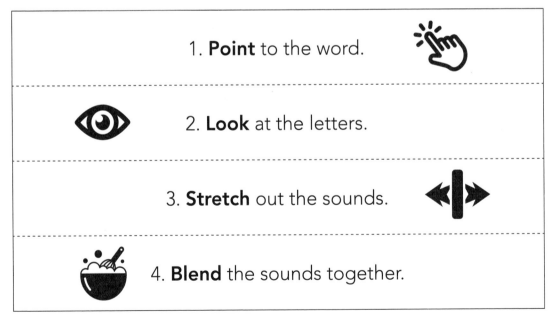

Figure 6.2: Visual cue card for beginning readers.

*Visit **go.SolutionTree.com/literacy** for a free reproducible version of this figure.*

Collaborative Learning—"You Do It Together"

By discussing and actively engaging in a task with peers, students derive deeper meaning and perhaps new insights based on the learning target. Together they seek validation and clarification, articulate their thoughts, and question each other (Fisher & Frey, 2014c). This collective involvement spurs students toward clarity and understanding; it represents an important component of gradual release that should not be overlooked.

As Douglas Fisher and Nancy Frey (2008) explain:

> When done right, collaborative learning is a way for students to consolidate their thinking and understanding. Negotiating with peers, discussing ideas and information, and engaging in inquiry with others gives students the opportunity to use what they have learned during focused and guided instruction. (p. 7)

Collaborative learning is an opportunity for students to work with partners or in small groups around targeted skills. As they put collaborative learning into practice, students' output becomes stronger than what they would have produced on their own.

After students participate in a collaborative exercise, teachers determine the next instructional moves, such as leading a debriefing session, conducting another formative assessment, returning to guided practice for particular students as needed, or moving to independent learning.

Independent Learning—"You Do It Alone"

As a final step in the lesson model, students fully assume responsibility for the cognitive load to independently demonstrate understanding of their new learning. To accomplish this, each student applies the skill, strategy, or procedure in a novel situation to show that he or she can transfer learning and provide evidence of mastery. For example, if students practice capitalizing the first word in a sentence and the pronoun *I*, they apply this skill of proper conventions of capitalization in their own narratives. If some students still exhibit difficulty applying the new learning, repeat certain phases of the instructional model accordingly.

Gradual Release of Responsibility Strategies

This section provides a specific example of a gradual release lesson that teachers can conduct with students in kindergarten to first grade to increase students' ability to blend—a critical strategy for helping students sound out, or decode, words.

As Blevins (2017) explains, teachers who spend time frequently modeling and applying blending strategies to phonics instruction achieve greater student results.

During a word-building lesson, students practice blending by using a set of letter cards or tiles to form words in a particular sequence that varies by about one or two letters. The teacher directs students to form a word, read it, and then add, delete, or substitute a letter to transform the word into a new word (Beck & Beck, 2013). For example, students could use the word-building set *a, h, b, t, m,* and *s* to build this sequence of short-*a* words: *at, bat, mat, sat, Sam, ham.* Engaging in activities such as word building not only gives students time to play with and explore letter sounds but also provides them an opportunity to "consolidate and solidify their learning of how words work" (Blevins, 2017, p. 112).

As you will read in chapter 7 (page 163), instruction on the foundations of reading is never an isolated event. In fact, it permeates every component of the literacy block—from whole-group reading instruction to small-group writing lessons and even independent work time. When students have opportunities to systematically apply newly learned skills to authentic reading and writing experiences, such as those offered throughout the literacy block, students will make greater gains (Armbruster, Lehr, & Osborn, 2006).

During word building, as you will see in the sample lesson, after students have learned and practiced blending, they are ready to take on the challenge of applying this strategy to a variety of literacy activities, such as using the same words to craft a story or reading similar words in decodable books. According to Blevins (2017), "Because the focus of these connected texts is not solely on words with the target skill, students must use all they know about letters and sounds to read the words and make sense of the text" (p. 78). Such a task is much more cognitively demanding than simply reading isolated words lists. Just imagine a student's excitement when he uses his new skill to independently read a book or write his own story. Filling out worksheets or participating in other skill-and-drill activities are not engaging or motivating.

Example Word-Building Lesson

For students new to blending, teachers should, at first, focus instruction on simple CVC (consonant-vowel-consonant) words that begin with continuous sounds, such as /s/, /m/, /r/, /l/, /n/, and /f/. These sounds are easier for students to blend because they can be stretched and held without distortion unlike stop sounds, such as /b/, /c/, /d/, /g/, /p/, /t/, /k/, or /j/, which can only be pronounced for an instant and are easily distorted.

As students become more adept at blending, teachers can gradually introduce more complex phonics patterns, such as CVC words with a silent *e* (CVC*e*) or with two consonants for the initial sound (CCVC) or final sounds (CVCC). For example, students could make the word *mate* after *mat*, *flat* after *fat*, and *card* after *car* (Foorman et al., 2016). Subsequent phonics lesson suggestions appear at the end of this section. Collectively, these learning experiences help lay a solid foundation to support students in becoming independent readers and writers of text.

The following word-building lesson is adapted from literacy authors Isabel L. Beck and Mark E. Beck (2013).

1. **Focused instruction ("I do it."):** I can blend the sounds of letters together to build words.

2. **Guided instruction ("We do it."):** We use letter cards to build new words, working with the teacher step by step.

3. **Collaborative learning ("You do it together."):** Our small group builds words using a new set of word cards.

4. **Independent learning ("You do it alone."):** I can read texts that incorporate words with the same letter-sound patterns from the previous word-building lesson.

Prepare for the lesson by doing the following.

▸ **Gather a set of large letter cards for teacher demonstration:** As you add, substitute, and delete letters to build words at a pocket chart in the front of the room, students will manipulate their own letter cards at their seats.

▸ **Make student letter cards:** You can deal with student letter cards in different ways.

- Photocopy and laminate a letter card set for every student to store them in envelopes or plastic baggies.

- Give each student a photocopied sheet of the letters for the upcoming lesson only. Before the lesson begins, students cut out their letter cards like the ones in figure 6.3 (page 156). Finding the method that works best for you and your students might take a little bit of trial and error.

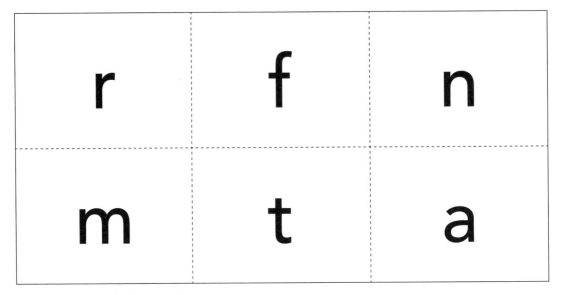

Figure 6.3: Sample letter cards.

Focused Instruction—"I Do It"

Take these eight steps for focused word-building instruction.

1. In the front of the room, display the large letter cards for *r, f, n, m, t,* and *a* in a pocket chart.

2. Review the name of each letter and the sound it makes. Point to a letter and ask students, "What letter is this?" and "What sound does it make?"

3. Say the answers chorally with students, modeling the correct response while paying close attention to any incorrect responses.

4. After reviewing the letters in the word-building set, say, "Today we will use these letters to build some words together. The lesson will focus on the question, How do letter sounds blend together to make words? and address the learning target *I can blend the sounds of letters together to make words.*" To help build relevance for students, explain the importance of learning these skills by telling students, "Blending sounds together will help you sound out words more easily so you can read and write texts on your own."

5. Model what students will do: *use the letter cards to make words.* Concurrently, think out loud to explain how you blend the sounds of the letters together to decode the word. Using the large demonstration letters, make the word

ran in the pocket chart. Tell the students, "I can read this word by blending together the sounds of each letter."

6. Use successive blending to stretch out the sounds of the word. You can do this by slowly running your finger underneath each letter as you melt one sound into the next without pausing: /rrraaannn/ (Blevins, 2017).

7. Repeat this process a few times, slowly condensing the stretched sounds until you get to a normal pace: /rrraaannn/, /rraann/, /ran/.

8. Tell the students, "This is the word *ran*. I am going to change one letter in *ran* to make a new word. I am going to change the *r* to *f*. Sound out the new word with me: /fffaaannn/, /ffaann/, /fan/. The new word is *fan*."

Guided Instruction—"We Do It"

The next steps have you and students building words together. For the first word in the series, you tell students the specific order of the letters.

1. Distribute letter cards to each student and say, "Now let's make some new words together. Take out your letter cards and line them up in front of you. I will tell you which letters to use to build your words. Take your *m* and place it at the beginning of the word. Then, take your *a* and place it in the middle of the word. Finally, take your *n* and put it at the end. Let's stretch out the sounds to read this word together: /mmmaaannn/, /mmaann/, /man/."

2. Ask students, "What word is this?" Ask them this each time students make a word.

3. When they respond, write down each word on the board. That way, by the end of the lesson, the entire sequence of words is listed.

4. Continue leading students through the series of words by telling them which letter (or letters) to change: "Next, let's take away the *n* from the end of the word *man* and replace it with *t*. Let's stretch out the sounds to read this word together. What is the new word?"

5. With each new word, direct students to stretch the sounds and read the word chorally with you: "Replace the *m* in *mat* with *f*. What's the new word?" "Change the *f* in *fat* to *r*. What's the new word?" "Substitute the *r* in *rat* with *s*. What's the new word?"

Once students have gained a better understanding of both the skill and procedure for making words, they are ready for collaborative learning.

Collaborative Learning—"You Do It Together"

The potential benefit of working collaboratively raises students' awareness, clarifies their thinking, and develops their critical-thinking and communication skills (Frey, Fisher, & Everlove, 2009).

For this learning target on blending letter sounds, students will work in groups of three or four to build a series of short /i/ words. We find that students are more engaged in the lesson when each student can manipulate his or her own set of cards rather than sharing one set with group members.

1. Ask students to add the letter *i* to their word card set, so that they have *r*, *f*, *n*, *m*, *t*, *a*, and *i* displayed on their desks.

2. Announce the next word in the sequence with, "Change the *a* in *sat* to *i*." Students collaborate with each other to locate the correct letters, build the word, and then chorally blend the sounds together to read the word aloud (*sit*).

3. Keep adding new words to the list on the front board.

4. While students work through the word-building sequence, move between groups offering scaffolding or extensions, as needed. For example, some groups may need more teacher support to identify the correct letter cards from their set. In this case, teachers can provide students with an alphabet chart to reference during the word-building sequence. For students having difficulty blending the letter sounds, focus the word-building sequence on VC (vowel-consonant) words, such as *it*, *at*, *am*, and *at*.

Once students gain more proficiency with the skill, the teacher can increase the rigor of the task by moving on to CVC words (*sit*, *cat*, *ram*, *bat*). Likewise, for students who need extended learning, teachers can ask students to make the next word in a sequence without telling them which specific letters to change. For instance, if students are directed to change *hat* to *sat*, they must determine on their own which letters in *hat* need to be changed to form *sat*. As Blevins (2017) explains, this skill is more cognitively demanding than blending-focused word building.

Independent Learning—"You Do It Alone"

Individually, students read texts comprised largely of words with the same letter-sound relationship from the word-building lesson as well as several high-frequency words that students have been working on in other phonics-based lessons throughout the unit of study.

1. Launch this task by saying, "Let's read through the list of words on the front board to review all the words we have built so far:

   ran

   fan

   man

   mat

   fat

   rat

   sat

   sit

   fit

   fin

   tin

   "Notice how making a small change to each of the words helped us build brand new words with a similar sound pattern. Knowing the pattern of words can help you when you read a text and come to a word you don't know.

   "In the next lesson, you will get to use what you have learned about blending sounds together, along with high-frequency words, to read a book. You will see lots of the words from the word-building activity, but you will also have to sound out some words that are new to you."

2. To ensure that students are prepared for the upcoming lesson, write on the front board a simple sentence incorporating words from the short *a* and short *i* word families: *The **fat rat** can **sit** on the **mat**.*

3. Listen in on students as they pronounce the words to formatively assess their ability to decode. Offer further assistance if needed.

Phonics

Before or after the lesson just described, you might develop one or more of the following ideas into a gradual release lesson for decoding words and increasing overall word awareness. Or, use another idea for an extension for students who have mastered these skills.

Word Sort

Teachers give students a set of words with similar spelling, sound, or semantic categories and ask students to cut out and sort the words according to their common feature. A word sort like the one in figure 6.4 allows students to "organize what they know about words to form generalizations that they can then apply to new words they encounter in their reading" (Bear, Invernizzi, Templeton, & Johnston, 2012, p. 55).

rat	pig	big
wig	hat	pat
sat	fig	cat

Figure 6.4: Sample word sort set for early readers.

For beginning readers, the focus is typically on sorting short-vowel words into rhyming categories. There are two types of word sorts.

1. In *closed word sorts*, teachers provide the categories, and students then match the words with the features to create the word collections. For example, students could sort words into two columns, each representing a different rhyming category.

2. In *open word sorts*, teachers provide only the word list; students must determine the common features and label the categories for each word group.

Word Ladders

Source: Rasinski, 2005.

Students build a sequence of words from beginning to end, changing one word into another by altering a single letter at each step. Word ladders differ from building words because they require students to analyze both the structure and meaning of words. For example, teachers can ask students to change one letter in the word *mat* to name something you use when you need directions: *map*. Students can then be asked to change one letter in the word *map* to name something you do when you are tired: *nap*.

Elkonin Boxes

Source: Blevins, 2017.

Teachers pronounce a target word as students listen carefully, repeat the word slowly, and mark the individual sounds by placing counters in the cells of an Elkonin box, or sound box (Elkonin, 1963). For the counters, teachers can use any small objects, such as poker chips, blocks, animal figures, or even Matchbox cars. For example, when using poker chips as counters to segment the word *hop*, students' sound boxes would have three chips, one for each sound. Teachers would then help students determine how to replace each chip with a letter: "What is the first sound you hear in the word *hop*? What letter makes the /h/ sound? Remove your first chip and write the letter *h*." As teachers continue working through each target word by breaking it apart into sounds and "rebuilding it letter by letter," students have "a huge *aha*," and "if done consistently, teaches them to carefully think about the component sounds in a word when writing" (Blevins, 2017, p. 96). Figure 6.5 is an Elkonin box example.

Figure 6.5: Elkonin sound boxes.

EXERCISE

Design a Lesson Using Gradual Release of Responsibility

This chapter provides a research-based model for building well-orchestrated lessons—gradual release of responsibility. Chapters 7 (page 163) and 8 (page 217) will dig deeper into instructional planning, addressing aspects of high-quality literacy instruction and myriad instructional strategies, and chapter 8 ends with an activity that asks teams to design lessons implementing gradual release of responsibility. For now, discuss this model with your team, and record ideas your team can revisit after reading the upcoming chapters.

Use the following questions to guide this exercise.

★ How can we think aloud while modeling word-sorting activities to make our thoughts more transparent for students?

★ How can we design collaborative learning opportunities that engage all learners in the task of segmenting and spelling words using Elkonin boxes and counters?

★ How can we differentiate word ladder activities to account for the array of learners in our classrooms, from those who already know how to read to those who are just learning letter sounds?

Summary

When acquiring a new skill, strategy, or procedure, any learner benefits from a direct instruction model such as gradual release of responsibility. This instructional framework is predicated on four parts that teachers use to plan lessons in an orchestrated way: focused instruction, guided instruction, collaborative learning, and independent learning. Although teachers can change the order of these components, if what is taught is new, educators must capitalize on each of them to cement learning. After reading about this approach, as well as the subsequent chapters around lesson design, work with your team to design solid, cohesive lessons that address learning targets.

CHAPTER 7

Plan High-Quality Literacy Instruction

Delivering high-quality and comprehensive literacy instruction in preK through first-grade classrooms requires ample and dedicated time. That time is the *literacy block*—a specific and sacred segment built into every day's schedule. This particular period is dedicated specifically to the teaching, refining, and practicing of literacy skills and standards. *Sacred* makes it clear that it is a priority and it is safeguarded as a fundamental part of a student's day. The literacy block is conducted whether there is an abbreviated school day, a fire drill, or a school assembly.

Due to scheduling demands at each grade level, a block of literacy time may occur in one sustained time frame or as separate segments throughout the day, and constitutes a significant portion of the classroom teacher's contact time with students—often upward of 30 to 50 percent of the teaching minutes in a classroom (often ninety to one hundred twenty total minutes). During this time, embedded classroom structures, routines, and engagement opportunities establish a comfortable, familiar learning environment focused on accountability and student growth—a "predictable, bedrock schedule, one that students could count on and plan for" (Atwell, 2007, p. 120).

A well-organized and structured literacy block, the components of which are detailed in this chapter, is one where students know precisely what, when, why, and how learning takes place. There, students engage in explicit, systematic literacy instruction, articulate the purpose for their learning, and work as a classroom community toward the common goal of becoming independent comprehenders, communicators, and writers.

Literacy Block Components

Delivering a guaranteed and viable curriculum (Marzano, 2003) that meets the needs of all students requires a well-thought-out, collaborative blueprint. To ensure high-quality instruction across all classrooms, teams in a PLC work closely together to construct and uphold an all-encompassing literacy block—a daily time for deep and intentional teaching, thinking, and practice. They do the following.

▸ Complete and use the PREP template (figure 1.1, pages 14–16) and established learning progressions (chapter 3, page 61) as the team examines and develops curriculum to ensure students meet the demands of the learning standards and overall objectives.

▸ Familiarize themselves with the stories, poems, and fiction and nonfiction pieces chosen purposefully for whole- and small-group purposes.

▸ Identify elements of the texts that will lead to authentic teachable moments in developing reading, writing, vocabulary, and foundational skills (such as concepts of print, phonological awareness, phonics and word recognition, and fluency).

▸ Meet regularly—weekly if schedules permit—to discuss plans for explicit teaching, modeling, differentiating, and assessing, as well as possible scaffolds and opportunities for student engagement.

Though teachers will undoubtedly apply their own unique teaching styles in their individual classrooms and adapt instruction to meet the diverse needs of their students, working as a team allows teachers to capitalize on their expertise and collective thinking to plan high-quality instruction. As teachers meet to collaborate over upcoming literacy instruction, they can use the questions in figure 7.1 to guide their thinking and discussions.

Though the structures, timing, and procedures for each literacy block component may vary by classroom, school, and district, the following daily learning experiences are suggested in building a comprehensive literacy program that meets the needs of a diverse group of students in preK through first grade.

▸ Phonological awareness training

▸ Letter-sound skills

▸ Interactive read-alouds

▸ Shared reading

What learning targets do we need students to meet for upcoming lessons?

Where are our students at on the learning progression of knowledge and skills leading up to the overall learning standards? What learning still needs to take place?

What curricular materials will we use for whole- and small-group instruction? What explicit instruction will we provide as we utilize these texts?

How will we deliver whole- and small-group instruction to meet the needs of our learners?

How will we collect evidence of student learning?

Which students are already proficient, and how will we extend their learning?

Where might our students struggle the most? What differentiated approaches, supports, and scaffolds do we need to implement to help all learners succeed?

How will we gradually remove scaffolds to move students toward independence?

Figure 7.1: Questions to guide collaborative literacy planning.

*Visit **go.SolutionTree.com/literacy** for a free reproducible version of this figure.*

- ▸ Whole-group writing
- ▸ Small-group reading
- ▸ Small-group writing
- ▸ Literacy skill application

A literacy block has many moving parts—often quite literally! Step inside any classroom and you're sure to find an impressive array of authentic and active learning experiences taking place. Whether as a whole class, in small groups, or through play-based learning, each component of a literacy block plays a distinct role in developing skilled readers and writers.

Though specified times will be set aside for the explicit instruction of reading, writing, foundational skills, and vocabulary in both whole- and small-group settings, skillful teachers continuously embed all domains of literacy in their instruction throughout the day. They guide students in making natural connections between these skills, and work to develop well-rounded, independent readers and writers.

Phonological Awareness Training

We have an innate ability for figuring out the rules of language used in our environment without the need for any explicit instruction (Brynie, 2009; Genishi, 1998). However, unlike oral language development, reading involves a much more complicated process. As literacy experts Louisa Moats and Carol Tolman (n.d.) explain, our brains work unconsciously to:

> extract the meaning of what is said, not to notice the speech sounds in the words. It is designed to do its job *automatically* in the service of efficient communication. But reading and spelling require a level of metalinguistic speech that is not natural or easily acquired.

Simply put, our brains are not wired for reading. Nevertheless, many educators intuitively believe that we learn to read in much the same way that we learn to speak, and if we simply expose students to words enough times, they will learn them. For some students, this belief holds true. In fact, about 60 to 70 percent of students will naturally develop the foundational skills necessary to become proficient readers (Kilpatrick, 2016). However, other students will require direct and explicit instruction to prime their brains for reading.

An important foundational skill in learning to read is *phonological awareness*— an individual's awareness of the sound properties of spoken words. Phonological awareness typically develops in a predictable progression from recognizing larger units of sound (including words, rhymes, and syllables) to smaller units of sound (including onset-rime and the individual sounds in words called *phonemes*; Kilpatrick, 2016). *Phonemic awareness*, the most advanced level of phonological awareness, helps students recognize that the word *map* has three distinct sounds (/m/, /ă/, /p/) and that by changing the /m/ in *map* to /c/, they get a new word—*cap*.

Phonemic awareness is crucial to reading. However, for many students, the ability to distinguish the discrete sounds in spoken language does not come naturally. In fact, as Wiley Blevins (2013) explains, most students start school thinking of words as whole units (*dog, cat, run*) rather than a series of individual sounds (/d//o//g/, /c//a//t/, /r//u//n/). Without explicit and systematic phonological awareness training, these students will eventually struggle to make sense of phonics instruction and decoding. Although students with weak phonemic awareness might make it through a couple of years of reading instruction by memorizing words, this strategy will fail them by third grade, when they encounter more and more unique words in a text (Blevins, 2013). Without help, these students will develop a serious reading deficit.

According to psychologist and educator David A. Kilpatrick (2016) and his extensive research in early reading acquisition, phonemic awareness is essential for helping young readers build a foundation for immediate, effortless word retrieval. If students can recognize that the *letter sequences* in printed words match the individual *sounds* in spoken words, they have an easier time storing printed words in their long-term memory and thus increasing their overall sight vocabulary. Kilpatrick (2016) argues that:

> Limited sight vocabulary is a threat to reading fluency. If a student is poor at word recognition and fluency, reading comprehension typically suffers. When reading comprehension suffers, all of a student's school experience is negatively affected. This whole chain of events is preventable in most cases. (p. 43)

Before explicit and systematic phonological awareness training can begin, teachers must assess students' current phonological awareness. To guide teachers in this process, Moats and Tolman (2019) separate phonological awareness into three levels.

1. **Early phonological awareness:** These skills typically develop in the preK years. At this level, students learn to segment syllables (kan-ga-roo), rhyme words (Do *mat* and *bat* rhyme?), and play with alliteration (*curious*

cats can climb). The goal of these tasks is to help students move toward an awareness of words at the phoneme level.

2. **Basic phoneme awareness:** In kindergarten and first grade, students begin developing their basic phonemic awareness skills. At this level, students learn to orally segment and blend the phonemes in simple, one-syllable words—a critical skill for eventually decoding and accurately spelling.

3. **Advanced phonemic awareness:** In a typically progressing student, these skills will continue developing through fourth grade. They involve manipulating phonemes through sound deletion ("Say *sit* without /s/") and sound substitutions ("Change the /s/ in *sling* to /f/. What's the new word?").

To determine where students fall within these levels, teachers can collect data from several tasks related to rhyming, alliteration, syllable counting, blending, segmentation, isolation, and manipulation (Kilpatrick, 2016). Table 7.1 contains sample tasks and activities that can be used to both assess and promote phonemic awareness at each level. Please note that these activities are designed to help students develop *oral* language skills that will eventually help students learn to read and write. Students must first focus on speech *sounds* before focusing on letters. Learning how to match speech sounds to print is the next crucial step in instruction (Moats & Tolman, 2019).

Table 7.1: Phonemic Awareness Activities

Phonemic Skill	Activity
Early Phonological Awareness (PreK to Beginning Kindergarten)	
Rhyme	• **Read-aloud:** Use read-aloud texts with rhyme patterns and alliteration. Give students plenty of opportunities to engage in the text by supplying the rhyme or adding to the alliteration. • **Rhyme matching:** "Which one of the following words rhymes with *did*—*hid, nod,* or *bad*?" • **Odd word out:** "Which two words rhyme—*ham, jam, hope*?"
Alliteration	• **Matching words:** "Do the words *near* and *nest* start with the same sound? Yes or no?" • **Tongue twisters:** "Let's make a silly sentence with /p/ words. Purple petunia petals …"

Syllable Counting	• **Tapping syllables:** "Tap the table for every syllable you hear." Examples include *bread* (one tap); *cookie* (two taps); *chocolate* (three taps); and *hamburger* (three taps).
Onset-Rime Manipulation	• **Onset-rime division with squares:** Students divide words into their onset and rime using two different colored squares, tiles, or markers. As students say each part of the word, they touch a colored square to indicate the sound. One example is, "Let's divide some words into parts. I'll say a whole word. Then you repeat the whole word and divide it into two parts. Touch a colored square for each part of the word." Another example is, "If these two squares say *m--an*, change one square to make *p--an*. Which square needs to change? If these two squares say *p--an*, change one square to make *p--it*. Which square needs to change?"
Basic Phoneme Awareness (Kindergarten to First Grade)	
Onset-Rime Blending	• **What's the word?:** The teacher says an onset and rime aloud, and students orally blend the word parts together to make a word. Examples include the teacher asking, "What word is tr--ack?" (Student: "Track.") Teacher: "What word is p--ath?" (Student: "Path.")
Phoneme Segmentation	• **Simple syllables with two or three phonemes (using words with no blends):** Students say the separate phonemes in a word while they tap the sounds or move a chip for each sound. /h/-/a/-/m/ (ham) /p/-/e/-/g/ (peg) /h/-/e/ (he) • **Three or four phonemes, including blends:** Students say the separate phonemes in a word while they tap the sounds or move a chip for each sound. /r/-/a//-/ck/ (rack) /ch/-/o/-/m/-/p/ (chomp) /cr/-/a/-/t/ (crate)
Syllable Manipulation	• **Deleting part of a compound:** The teacher directs students to delete a word from a compound word. For example, the teacher says, "Say *airplane*." (Students: "Airplane.") The teacher says, "Say *airplane* again, but this time don't say *air*." (Students: "Plane.") • **Deleting a syllable:** The teacher directs students to delete a syllable from a word. The teacher says, "Say *enter*." (Students: "Enter.") The teacher, then, says, "Say *enter* again but this time don't say *en*." (Students: "ter.")
Phoneme Substitution	• **Building new words:** "If I change the /f/ in *fit* to /m/, what new word do I have?" (mit) "If I change the /l/ in *lap* to /t/, what new word do I have?" (tap)

Source: Adapted from Moats & Tolman, 2019.

In addition to these informal check-ins, teachers can evaluate phonological awareness through formal assessments, such as Kilpatrick's (2016) Phonological Awareness Screening Test (PAST). The PAST not only provides a point of instruction for students but can also help monitor student progress. The PAST (www .thepasttest.com) is available to educators online as a free, public domain test.

Teachers need to have a firm understanding of students' phonological awareness in order to plan for and provide the appropriate level of instruction. Although many students will develop a solid foundation of phonological awareness throughout the preK to first-grade years, other students will require more intensive, targeted instruction in small groups or individual settings. Once teachers understand where students fall on the progression of phonological awareness, they can work on advancing students to the next level by routinely engaging them in a few brief phonological awareness lessons throughout the course of the literacy block. About five or ten minutes of training is really all students need for skill development. This training can take place in whole group, small group, or individually depending on student need.

In addition, Kilpatrick (2016) suggests punctuating the school day with multiple exposures to phonological awareness training in order to solidify students' learning into long-term memory. For example, phonological awareness activities can be done during transition times, such as on the way to the gym, before bus dismissal, or after snack time. Teachers can even sneak activities in during interactive read-alouds and writing instruction, which we will discuss later in the chapter. Through a series of brief lessons and repeated exposures, teachers can help young readers develop the automatic and effortless phonemic skills necessary for efficient sight word development (Kilpatrick, 2016).

Although phonological awareness lessons are brief, teachers should apply the gradual release of responsibility model of instruction to help guide students toward mastery of skills. (See chapter 6, page 147, for more about the gradual release of responsibility.) During focused instruction (*I do it*), teachers will need to model new skills for students while providing plenty of multisensory supports. At first, students will not be able to complete tasks mentally (in their heads) and will benefit from the following visual or verbal supports.

▸ Using objects (tokens, buttons, or chips) to represent sounds

▸ Tapping or clapping out the sounds

▸ Stretching out the sounds (/faaaaaaaan/)

For example, a student might not be able to change the /a/ in *mat* to an /i/ (to make *mit*), but when he taps the sounds aloud using colored buttons, he can. In this instance, the student cannot mentally manipulate the sounds but can do it with the support of the buttons (Kilpatrick, 2016).

As students advance in their learning, they will need opportunities to practice new skills with teacher guidance and support (*we do it*). Throughout the guided support phase of the lesson, Moats and Tolman (2019) recommend giving immediate corrective feedback. For example, if students provide a letter name rather than the sound, be sure to explain the difference and then ask for the correct response. Along with teacher support, students will benefit from actively engaging with peers as they consolidate learning and practice applying the targeted phonological skills (*you do it together*). Once students grasp the new skills, they are ready to independently demonstrate their understanding and transfer their learning to novel tasks.

It's important to note that phonemic awareness training should not be taught as an isolated skill. In order to develop efficient sight word storage and retrieval, students must be able to apply their phonemic awareness skills to the process of mapping sounds to letters (Kilpatrick, 2016). Therefore, in combination with phonemic awareness training, students should work on mastering letter sounds.

E X E R C I S E
Plan for a Literacy Block in a PLC

Facilitate a collaborative discussion about the current structures and learning experiences in your literacy block. Use the questions in figure 7.1 (page 165) to guide initial collaborative discussions.

Use the following questions to guide this exercise.

★ What literacy structures and experiences are built into our current literacy block?

★ How much time is allotted to whole-group, small-group, and independent learning?

★ What refinements might we need to make to our current literacy block?

★ When will our team meet regularly to collaboratively plan and discuss upcoming lessons for the literacy block?

Letter-Sound Skills

To become an efficient and skilled reader, students will need automatic and effortless recognition of letter sounds (Foorman et al., 2016). However, as any preK through first-grade teacher can tell you, learning letter-sound correspondences can be quite confusing for new readers. Without explicit instruction, practice, and review, many students will acquire letter-sound skills too slowly, or possibly not at all.

To help students with this critical foundational skill, we recommend the following strategies and sequencing considerations.

▸ Use a developmentally appropriate scope and sequence for access to a "wealth of words" (Blevins, 2017, p. 28).

▸ Use multisensory learning methods.

▸ Practice writing letters.

▸ Teach to mastery.

▸ Provide opportunities to apply skills.

Use a Developmentally Appropriate Scope and Sequence for Access to a Wealth of Words

For most students, certain letter sounds are more difficult to learn than others. Typically, students have an easier time remembering the sounds of letters whose names hold clues to their sounds (Piasta & Wagner, 2010). For example, students can make clear connections between the names of letters that begin with the sounds they make (*b*[bee], *d*[dee], *k*[kay], *p*[pee], *t*[tee]). By contrast, students have a harder time remembering letter sounds that appear second in their letter name, such as *f* (ef), *l* (el), *m* (em), *n* (en), *r* (ar), and *s* (es). Overall, students struggle the most when a letter sound is not present at all in the letter's name, as in *h*, *w*, and *y* (Block & Duke, 2015).

When developing a scope and sequence for teaching letter-sound correspondences, it's important to keep in mind that learning should build from simple to complex, from the known to the unknown. Therefore, teachers should begin instruction with simple letter sounds before moving on to sounds that present more difficulty.

In addition, teachers need to consider the frequency of occurrence of letter sounds. In the English language, certain letters, such as *e*, *t*, *a*, *i*, *n*, *o*, *s*, *h*, *r*, *d*, *l*, and *c*, occur more often than others (*z*, *y*, *w*, and *v*). By teaching high-utility letters early in the scope and sequence, teachers can give students access "to a wealth of words for reading and writing" (Blevins, 2017, p. 28). It's important to note that these high-utility letters include vowels. Although vowels can be challenging to master, students cannot study words without them. Teaching vowels in combination with consonants will generate more opportunities for blending, segmenting, and decoding.

Use Multisensory Learning Methods

Students will benefit from using hands-on activities and manipulatives to experience letters in a variety of ways, such as building letters with blocks or modeling clay, tracing letters in shaving cream or sand, or assembling letter puzzles. As students engage in these activities, teachers should point out the physical details of letters, drawing attention to letters that share similar features, such as *b* and *d* or *p* and *q*, while helping students learn ways to distinguish them (Kilpatrick, 2016). For example, a good trick to help distinguish *b* from *d* is to tell students that *b* always faces *d*. Displaying a visual of the two letters smiling at each other, as shown in figure 7.2, helps reinforce the idea.

Figure 7.2: Letter *b* facing letter *d*.

Teachers should also expose students to the similarities and differences in the upper- and lowercase forms of letters. To reinforce this learning, an alphabet arc like the one in figure 7.3 can help students match uppercase to lowercase letters, and locate letters by name (Moats & Tolman, 2019).

a b c d e f g h i j k l m n o p q r s t u v w x y z

Figure 7.3: Alphabet arc.

*Visit **go.SolutionTree.com/literacy** for a free reproducible version of this figure.*

In her book *Letter Lessons and First Words: Phonics Foundations That Work*, reading instruction scholar Heidi Anne Mesmer (2019) also recommends using alphabet arc lessons to help students practice quickly saying the letter sounds of both known letters and those being taught. Students can use the following routine to match a set of letters (foam or plastic) to the corresponding letter on an alphabet arc (Mesmer, 2019).

1. **Name it:** The student chooses a letter and says its name.

2. **Sound it:** The student says the letter's sound.

3. **Place it:** The student places the letter on the corresponding letter of the alphabet arc.

4. **Check it:** Once all letters have been placed, the student checks the work by touching and saying each letter.

Practice Writing Letters

Teaching students how to write letters will improve their overall letter recognition skills. To learn how to properly write each letter, students need explicit instruction on letter features, spatial relationships, and sequences of strokes (Moats & Tolman, 2019). When introducing a new letter, Moats and Tolman (2019) recommend the following routine: "First, the teacher explicitly describes and models the sequence of strokes in the letter. Then, he or she provides guided practice with immediate feedback before having students practice independently" (p. 192). To help model the correct sequence of strokes, teachers can name the lines on students' writing paper. For example, the top line is the hair line, the middle line is the belly line, and the bottom line is the shoe line. The instruction might follow these steps.

1. While forming the letter *t* at the whiteboard, the teacher says, "I start at the hair line and draw a straight line down to the shoe line. Then, I make another, shorter line right across the belly line. Now, let's try to write the letter *t* together."

2. The students follow along on their own paper as the teacher explains the strokes and models the formation again.

3. Finally, the students practice writing the letter *t* several times on their own while the teacher observes and offers feedback: "Be careful. The first line needs to go all the way from the hair line to the shoe line."

Learning to write letters will help students make connections between the names, sounds, and forms of letters, anchoring them into memory for quick, automatic retrieval.

Teach to Mastery

As Blevins (2017) explains, students need purposeful, systematic review and repetition of basic phonics skills in order to achieve mastery. Unfortunately, with many reading programs, teachers must teach "so much, so fast" that instruction becomes "'exposure' focused rather than 'mastery' focused" (Blevins, 2017, p. 51).

To become proficient with letter-sound skills, students require plenty of practice, review, and repetition over a period of several weeks, until the letter sounds become automatic. After first introducing a set of letter sounds, teachers can reinforce them throughout the day with several brief reviews. For instance, before lining students up for recess, teachers can engage students in a quick flash card activity by holding up a letter and asking students to make its sound. After a lesson, the teacher could randomly point to known letters on the alphabet strip and ask students to provide the sound. In general, "the more reinforcements, the stronger the letter-sound skills" (Kilpatrick, 2016, p. 104).

Provide Opportunities to Apply Skills

As students build their knowledge of letter-sounds and phonemic awareness, they will need plenty of opportunities to apply their skills to actual reading and writing activities. It is through the application of skills that learning is solidified and consolidated (Blevins, 2017). However, as Moats and Tolman (2019) lament, "designing text-reading experiences for students who can barely read anything is a challenge!" (p. 216).

To accommodate new readers who have yet to learn the alphabetic code or have sufficient word-recognition skills, teachers can begin decoding instruction using texts containing words with sound-symbol correspondences that have already been taught (Moats & Tolman, 2019). These decodable texts allow for explicit teaching of phonics patterns while providing ample practice for students. For example, if students know the letters *a*, *s*, *f*, *r*, *m*, *c*, *n*, *t*, and *d* and the high-frequency words *is*, *the*, and *on*, then they can read the following decodable passage:

Sam is a fat cat.

Sam sat on the mat.

A rat can tap the mat.

The cat is mad at the rat.

Reading decodable texts allows students to tap into their understanding of letter-sound correspondence rather than relying on other less effective methods, such as guesswork based on picture clues or rote memorization. In fact, teaching new or struggling readers guessing strategies actually interferes with the development of sight vocabulary and word-reading skills (Ehri, 2013).

After reading a decodable text, Blevins (2017) recommends having students write about it. This task provides an ideal opportunity for students to practice and apply targeted phonics skills since their writing will undoubtedly need to include words from the text. (See the Whole-Group Writing section, page 188, and the Small-Group Writing section, page 198, for more information.) Students could write an additional line of text, a continuation of the story, or a separate event based on a character or situation. The writing task could even be as simple as asking students to list five or ten words from the story. As students attempt to spell words, encourage them to say the word, segment each sound in the word, and write the words as they say each sound (Moats & Tolman, 2019). This will help students make the connection between their phoneme awareness and letter-sound skills.

Along with letter and sound training, students will need explicit teaching in other critical aspects of literacy, such as reading comprehension, vocabulary development, and general background knowledge. In the next section, we will discuss the benefits of using interactive read-alouds in helping students work toward these goals.

EXERCISE

Train for Phonological Awareness and Letter-Sound Skills

Use the information provided about phonemic awareness training and letter-sound skills to guide a collaborative discussion about the current foundational skills experiences in your classroom. Discuss any refinements you might make to your method of phonemic awareness training and letter-sound lessons to make a greater impact on student achievement.

Use the following questions to guide this exercise.

★ How can we assure that the scope and sequence of skills build from simple to complex and provide students with access to a wealth of words for reading and writing?

★ How will we incorporate the gradual release of responsibility during these lessons?

★ How can we provide opportunities throughout the day for practice and review?

★ How can we design learning opportunities for students to apply new skills to actual reading and writing experiences?

Interactive Read-Alouds

In the preK through first-grade literacy block, interactive read-alouds play an essential role in developing students into proficient and independent readers of complex text (Liben & Liben, 2017). An interactive read-aloud is a systematic and explicit method of reading aloud that allows students to listen to, speak about, and engage in complex text they would not be able to access on their own. Throughout a read-aloud, teachers use a combination of guided conversation and thoughtful reflection to actively involve students in processing the language, ideas, and meaning of a text while building their overall knowledge of the world around them. As education scholars David Liben and Meredith Liben (2017) argue, there "is likely no better way to draw students to the treasures stored in the written word than through reading aloud to them as much as possible" (p. 4).

Prior to the lesson, the teacher previews the text for key events or challenging content. At the start of the lesson, the teacher briefly shares background knowledge on the text to generate student interest, activate prior knowledge, or preteach potentially difficult concepts and vocabulary. Here are some of the key characteristics of an interactive read-aloud lesson.

▶ Students listen to fluent, modeled reading.

▶ The teacher embeds authentic opportunities for knowledge building and vocabulary instruction. This might include a lesson on pushing and pulling objects for a science unit or aligning texts with a concept that students are learning about in a separate class, such as music or physical education.

▸ Students engage in authentic discussions and share thoughts, ideas, and experiences related to the text.

▸ The teacher facilitates a close reading (when applicable) to guide students through the language, ideas, and meaning of a text. Teachers would provide a close reading if that is the focus of the lesson. Otherwise, teachers might choose an active read-aloud for a variety of purposes—sharing a lesson in friendship, taking turns, whole-body listening. Or, they might just need to build background knowledge on a topic.

▸ The teacher provides explicit strategy instruction aligned to learning targets, such as asking and answering questions about a text, determining the key details of a text, or comparing two events from the text.

Text Selection

Productive read-alouds require intentional text selection, interactive read-aloud implementation, and close reading. Read-aloud texts should be content-rich, complex, and loaded with sophisticated academic vocabulary (Coleman & Pimentel, 2012b). In other words, students need exposure to texts that are worthy of reading and rereading. Since read-alouds have the potential "to bring the world into the elementary classroom," they should provide students with a "wide array of knowledge about the artistic, historical, literary and scientific spheres while engaging [students] in rich academic discussions" (Liben & Liben, 2017, p. 4–5).

When choosing texts, CCSS recommend building a coherent curriculum focused on topics or themes that "systematically develop the knowledge base of students" (NGA & CCSSO, 2010, p. 33). By using several titles based on a single topic, students have the opportunity to build a deeper understanding of the ideas, concepts, and vocabulary related to that particular topic. As students advance through the grade levels, teachers can develop and expand on this knowledge to ensure increasingly deeper levels of learning (NGA & CCSSO, 2010). While students in the upper elementary grades are expected to independently read and reflect on these texts, students in prekindergarten to first grade need opportunities to participate in teacher-led interactive read-alouds, allowing students to orally compare and contrast as well as analyze and synthesize "in the manner called for by the *Standards*" (NGA & CCSSO, 2010, p. 33).

In figure 7.4, increasingly complex nonfiction texts build foundational knowledge of the federal government. In prekindergarten, students learn about important members of a community, and then, in kindergarten, students learn why communities need rules, and, finally, in first grade, students learn about the people, organizations, and concepts that make up the government.

Interactive Read-Aloud Implementation

Typically, teachers begin each read-aloud by generating student interest in the upcoming text. During this introduction, teachers might provide information on the topic, ask a few questions about students' prior knowledge, or share a brief background video. Since read-alouds help students acquire academic language not typically used in everyday speech, teachers should preselect about five or ten vocabulary words to highlight and define during the reading (Himmele & Himmele, 2012). This selection should include words that are critical to students' understanding of the story in addition to words that students are likely to encounter in other books or in real life (Beck, McKeown, & Kucan, 2013).

Grade	Focus Area	Books
Prekindergarten	Community helpers	*National Geographic Readers: Helpers in Your Neighborhood* by Shira Evans (2018)
		Mail Carriers by Cari Meister (2014a)
		Police Officers by Cari Meister (2014b)
		I Want to Be a Firefighter by Dan Liebman (2018)
Kindergarten	Rules and laws	*Signs in Our World* by John Searcy (2006)
		Why Do We Need Rules and Laws? by Jessica Pegis (2017)
		The Purpose of Rules and Laws by Joshua Turner (2018)
		Safety in My Neighborhood by Shelly Lyons (2013)
First grade	Introduction to the Federal Government	*U.S. Symbols* by Ann-Marie Kishel (2007)
		The Next President: The Unexpected Beginnings and Unwritten Future of America's Presidents by Kate Messner and Adam Rex (2020)
		Shh! We're Writing the Constitution by Jean Fritz (1987)
		The US Congress for Kids by Ronald A. Reis (2014)

Figure 7.4: Increasingly complex texts about community.

Throughout the read-aloud, the teacher does the following.

▸ Embeds authentic opportunities for knowledge building, such as a lesson on pushing and pulling objects for a science unit or aligning texts with a current concept from a separate class, such as music or physical education.

▸ Provides explicit strategy instruction aligned to learning targets, such as asking and answering questions about a text, determining a text's key details, or comparing two events from the text.

▸ Facilitates a close reading—if that is the focus of the lesson—to guide students through a text's language, ideas, and meaning. Otherwise, the teacher might choose an active read-aloud for a variety of purposes— sharing a lesson in friendship, taking turns, whole-body listening. Or, they might just need to build background knowledge on a topic.

Close Reading

Through careful instruction and support, teachers then can choose to engage students in a "close and thorough exploration" of the text so that they can "discover how to learn from reading" and, over time, "grow their knowledge, vocabulary, and understanding of syntax" (Liben & Pimentel, 2018, p. 7). Fisher and Frey (2012) refer to this type of instructional routine in which students "critically examine a text, especially through repeated readings" as *close reading* (p. 179).

To integrate close reading into an interactive read-aloud lesson, teachers first preview the text for challenging or pivotal points when understanding is crucial or for moments when comprehension might break down. For example, the picture book *Chrysanthemum* by Kevin Henkes (1991) provides an opportunity for young readers to analyze the changes characters undergo throughout the course of a text. In the story, a little mouse named Chrysanthemum feels depressed and sad on the first day of school after her schoolmates laugh at her for having such an unusual name. After previewing the text, the teacher might decide that a pivotal yet confusing moment comes at the end of the story when several characters undergo a change of heart after the music teacher, an expectant mother, tells the class that she loves Chrysanthemum's name and is even considering naming her own baby Chrysanthemum. With this announcement, Chrysanthemum becomes the envy of the class. She realizes that she loves her name, and the students who once bullied her yearn to be her friend.

With this key moment of the text in mind, teachers then develop a series of questions that will lead students to notice these moments and analyze their deeper meanings. Rather than simply asking generic questions that might rely heavily on students' background knowledge and personal experience (Have you ever felt sad about the way a friend treated you? Why do friends sometimes treat each other badly?), teachers should craft text-dependent questions that require students to draw on insights and knowledge they gleaned from engaging with the text (Liben & Pimentel, 2018). Students need opportunities to focus on the text itself and learn how to gather information and support from their reading.

Fisher and Frey (2012) have several broad categories of text-dependent questions that invite students to think about and engage in thoughtful reflections and rich discussion regarding the events, details, and knowledge in text. Figure 7.5 has a description and examples of each category of text-dependent questions.

Throughout the close reading, as students dive into the text, they will need space to turn and talk to each other or to form small discussion groups. Encouraging cooperative learning and allowing students to share their thoughts, ideas, and experiences with others helps build a community of readers with a shared literacy experience (Fountas & Pinnell, 2006).

Question Category	Example from *Chrysanthemum* (Henkes, 1991)
"**General understanding** questions draw on the overall view of the piece, especially the main ideas or arguments."	What happened at the beginning, middle, and end of the story?
"**Key detail** questions are the who, what, when, where, why, and how questions that are essential to understanding the meaning of the passage."	Why did the children make fun of Chrysanthemum? What about her words and actions helped you understand how Chrysanthemum was feeling?
"**Vocabulary and text structure** questions bridge explicit with implicit meanings, especially in focusing on words and phrases, as well as the way the author has organized the information. Text structure questions may include text features and discourse structures (problem/solution, cause/effect, compare/contrast, and so on)."	How did the author help us understand the meaning of the word *wilted*? What event caused the children to change their minds about Chrysanthemum's name? Compare how they treated her at the beginning of the book to how they treated her at the end.

"**Author's purpose** questions draw the reader's attention to genre, point of view, multiple perspectives, and critical literacies, such as speculating on alternative accounts of the same event."	How is the music teacher's reaction to Chrysanthemum's name different from the students' reactions?
"**Inferential** questions challenge students to examine the implicitly stated ideas, arguments, or key details in the text."	What changed the students' opinion of Chrysanthemum's name? Why? How do you think the music teacher feels about the way the children are treating Chrysanthemum? How do you know?
"**Opinion and intertextual questions** allow students to use their foundational knowledge of one text to assert their opinions or to make connections to other texts, using the target text to support their claims."	In your opinion, do you think Chrysanthemum should forgive the other students for making her sad? What lesson about friendship and acceptance does this story teach us?

Source: Adapted from Fisher & Frey, 2012, p. 185.

Figure 7.5: Categories and examples of text-dependent questions.

For read-aloud text suggestions, see the following resources.

▸ Achieve the Core's Read Aloud Project (https://achievethecore.org /page/944/read-aloud-project)

▸ Common Core State Standard's "Appendix B: Text Exemplars and Sample Performance Tasks" (www.corestandards.org/assets /Appendix_B.pdf)

Shared Reading

Though many frameworks for shared reading exist, the purpose of shared reading is unwavering. It is during this portion of the daily literacy block when we share not only the experience of reading with students, but our knowledge of *how* to read and comprehend as well. In preK through first-grade classrooms, the instructional support and guidance provided by the teacher through a shared group reading experience "provides the bridge that enables a student to gain new insights that later allow him or her to successfully engage in the reading process independently" (Stahl, 2012, p. 48). Whereas an interactive read-aloud has only the teacher reading the text, a whole-group, or shared, reading lesson involves students reading the text as well. Teachers become the models from which students mimic and develop their own reading habits and skills. Students tune in to our fluent and expressive voices, watch closely as we deliver explicit instruction on specific reading standards, and listen intently as we orally make our thinking concrete. Then, students try it out for themselves, echo reading, choral reading, and actively engaging in thoughtful discourse with their peers to make meaning.

A whole-group reading lesson is a daily staple in preK through first-grade classrooms. Usually fifteen minutes in length, its purpose is twofold, providing (1) focused instruction on itemized learning standards and skills and (2) continuous exposure to myriad effective reading strategies and foundational skills critical to the development of proficient independent readers. A shared reading experience does many things (Fountas & Pinnell Literacy Team, 2019):

- Provides enjoyable, successful experiences with print for all students
- Promotes the development of all aspects of the reading process
- Builds language skills and enhances vocabulary
- Provides opportunities to engage in expressive, meaningful, fluent reading
- Builds understanding of various types of texts, formats, and language structures

Students benefit when teachers do the following for a whole-group reading lesson.

- ▶ Explicitly state learning objectives.
- ▶ Help build background knowledge.
- ▶ Engage all students in grade-level texts.
- ▶ Provide explicit instruction-aligned learning targets.
- ▶ Share text in a way that is physically visible to all students.
- ▶ Embed instruction on vocabulary, word work, and foundational skills.
- ▶ Enable opportunities for engagement and student discourse.

To help students with this critical foundational skill, we recommend the following strategies and sequencing considerations.

- ▶ Consider text selection carefully.
- ▶ Ensure student engagement.

- ▸ Embed early literacy skills.

- ▸ Use gradual release of responsibility in shared reading.

Consider Text Selection Carefully

Katherine A. Dougherty Stahl (2012) explains that "in shared reading, all children have their eyes on the text and are held accountable for participating in text reading and activities at some stage of the shared reading process" (p. 48). To prepare for this essential learning opportunity, teachers work in their collaborative teams to carefully select the reading material.

In late kindergarten to first grade, whole-group shared texts are rich, grade-level texts (or beyond grade level if most students are ready) from a variety of genres. During the lesson, all students engage in the challenging text with the careful guidance of their teacher, allowing for the explicit teaching of the knowledge, foundational skills, comprehension strategies, and vocabulary necessary for continued reading growth.

Though some students in the class may not yet read grade-level material independently, "novice readers with instructional levels that tend to be limited by their decoding abilities are able to stretch into texts containing more words, richer vocabulary, and more sophisticated themes" during this teacher-guided lesson (Stahl, 2012, p. 48). This whole-group experience allows all students to engage in rigorous texts, deepen their thinking, and exercise their reading brains in new and powerful ways.

Team collaboration for lesson preparation is vital. Teachers must know the nuances of the text and have an intentional plan for instruction delivery that is purposeful, robust, and engaging. If your district uses a purchased reading program, it is equally important to carefully review the details of the text prior to a shared reading lesson. To maximize time and amplify the learning experience, teams collectively devise a distinct plan for the delivery of the lesson, embed engagement opportunities for students, and ensure that the plans and instructions outlined in a teacher's manual directly correlate to the standards and lesson objectives.

Ensure Student Engagement

Critical to the success of a shared reading lesson is students' ability to actively engage in the text. Whether displayed electronically on a large screen or interactive board, shared by way of a big book with large font, or distributed as individual copies to all students, it is imperative that every student can access and view the text effortlessly.

This means that students are looking at the text before, during, and after the lesson. Their eyes are on the precise words, sentences, and illustrations that artfully make up the page, and their minds are focused on making meaning. We cannot expect students to memorize the subtle details of every text after a first or even second read, just as a ballplayer can't develop a home-run-hitting swing after one single attempt. Therefore, to strengthen reading skills, a shared text is typically reread and revisited throughout the lesson and over the course of a few successive days. As students dig into the text to answer questions or participate in collaborative discussions, teachers should see them flipping pages, pointing at words, and explaining their thinking as they reference explicit details from the text.

Embed Early Literacy Skills

For students just learning to read, shared reading provides an ideal opportunity to foster early literacy skills. For instance, teachers could model for new readers concepts of print, such as how to handle a book by turning the pages, pointing to the words, and reading from left to right across the page. If students have a copy of the text in front of them, they can practice along with the teacher, setting the stage to one day read on their own. In addition, teachers can build students' phonological awareness by focusing their attention on the language of the text. As teachers read selected sections aloud, they can direct students to listen for any repeated words, rhyming patterns, or alliteration.

By rereading and revisiting these texts, teachers can slowly shift the lesson's focus from early phonological awareness skills to more advanced phonics skills. For instance, after several repeated readings of a Dr. Seuss book, teachers can eventually point to the rhyming words in the text while students chorally read them together with the teacher. In addition, after rereading a text heavy in alliteration, such as Shel Silverstein's (1974) poem "Sarah Cynthia Sylvia Stout Would Not Take the Garbage Out," students can point to or circle the similar letters in their own copies of the poem to practice their letter identification. As students' decoding abilities advance, they can engage in "fill-in-the-gap reading" in which the teacher reads the majority of the words but pauses to allow students to read the simple decodable text. When students dive back into the text each day, they build on previous learning while also digging deeper to take thinking and learning about the text, and about the art of reading, to the next level.

To maximize the impact of each lesson, students engage as *active* participants throughout the whole-group lesson. A common misconception is that the teacher's role throughout the entirety of whole-group reading is to read aloud to the students. Reading aloud is a piece of the lesson, as we know that listening to proficient readers model fluent reading provides students with a sense of what fluent reading should sound like, and therefore leads to increased comprehension (Rasinski, 2014).

Remember that the goal is to produce independent readers, and when all reading is reserved solely for the teacher, the students' learning becomes a task based merely on auditory comprehension, limiting the independent practice necessary for students to become masterful readers. Even the youngest readers need opportunities to apply early reading skills to authentic reading tasks. We can draw these young readers into the lesson in a variety of simple ways—from practicing a rhyme pattern, to clapping the syllables, or even decoding simple words in a shared text. As their skills and confidence grow, they will eventually take on more complex and demanding reading tasks.

Use Gradual Release of Responsibility in Shared Reading

The gradual release of responsibility is especially effective during the shared reading experience as the lesson moves from teacher directed to student centered.

Though the following example moves primarily from teacher-directed instruction to independent practice, the order in which the structures occur will differ from day to day. On particular days, teachers may choose to begin with a cooperative component, allowing pairs of students to engage in upfront discoveries or synthesize previous learning. On other days, teachers may want students to begin by approaching a task independently to observe how they grapple with a concept on their own. Ample opportunities for teacher modeling, guided support, and independent practice are embedded into the whole-group lesson, but do not necessarily happen in this particular order on any given day (Fisher, 2008).

Setting a Purpose

The teacher begins by setting the lesson's purpose and building background knowledge. Objectives are communicated clearly so that students can make connections to previous and current learning, and background knowledge is established by way of visuals, meaningful discussions, and other scaffolds that establish context for the new learning taking place. For example, in a kindergarten whole-group lesson on decoding, the teacher could set the lesson's purpose by providing a quick summary of the upcoming content and how it relates to their previous learning of letter sounds. The teacher might say, "In today's lesson, we are going to learn how to use what we know about letter sounds to help us decode, or sound out, words. We have been working hard on our letter sounds, and now it's time to put them to good use—to read on our own."

Practicing Explicit Modeling

The teacher transitions into the explicit modeling of a skill, or strategy, usually by way of a think-aloud. Students listen to fluent and expressive reading as they follow along in the text, and the teacher makes her thinking visible by explaining precisely *how* she makes meaning of the text. For example, a kindergarten teacher would explain the process used to decode a word by blending its letter sounds together, and then engage in a demonstration, or modeling, of blending while reading aloud from the text. For students in this grade band, shared reading provides ample opportunities to embed the teaching of phonics, phonemic awareness, fluency, vocabulary, comprehension, and fix-up strategies as authentic opportunities arise in the text. Although this initial part of the whole-group lesson is primarily teacher-led, brief moments for engagement (pair-share with a peer, for example) allow students to process and synthesize their learning. With daily exposure to the intricacies of skilled reading and intermittent opportunities for engagement, students develop comprehension skills at new levels.

Guiding Student Practice

After reading aloud and modeling the target skills, it is now time for the students to take a more active role in the shared reading experience. Here, students dive into the text with intent to begin practicing the modeled skills and strategies with the support of their peers and teacher. For example, they may circle or locate words belonging to the same word family, work with a partner to describe an important event from the text, or complete a graphic organizer to sequence story events in chronological order. During this time, students work cooperatively to practice their learning, sharpen their skills, and gain a deeper understanding of the explicit and implicit meanings in the text.

Allowing Independent Practice

By the end of a whole-group reading lesson, students take on more responsibility as they bridge their learning to independent practice and application. As they transition to independent practice, students transfer their knowledge and skills by applying their learning in new ways. Whether continuing with the same shared text or using an alternative independent text, students read closely, integrate strategies, and are held accountable for their learning by engaging in meaningful tasks that demonstrate their precise levels of mastery. Often, this time for independent practice occurs as the students transition to the part of the literacy block that is set aside for small-group reading or writing instruction.

Whole-Group Writing

Throughout the literacy block, it is essential to set aside time for the teaching and modeling of writing skills. During the whole-group writing experience, explicit writing instruction typically rotates among the study of three distinct writing genres—(1) informative, (2) opinion, and (3) narrative—but may also include letters, poems, or how-to books. Depending on the lesson's objective, teachers deliver instruction on a variety of writing techniques, and lessons may shift focus.

▸ In preK and early kindergarten, lessons most likely focus on stringing together ideas at the word and sentence level.

▸ In late kindergarten to first grade, lessons shift to helping students craft larger compositions, such as an opinion piece with relevant reasons and supporting details.

Additionally, teachers naturally embed instruction on vocabulary and foundational skills as authentic teachable moments arise during instruction. In the early stages of writing development, the goal is to help students see themselves as real writers and to view their work as legitimate text (Rowe & Flushman, 2013). By placing the "pen in the child's hand," creating a supportive writing environment, and encouraging them to write, teachers can help students understand the purposes, processes, and joys of writing (Rowe & Flushman, 2013, p. 239).

Writing instruction for preK through first grade presents an ideal opportunity to build off students' curiosity about language by encouraging them to share their thoughts and record their ideas in any way they can. According to early education researcher Shannon Riley-Ayers (2013), "Writing development begins long before children's writing resembles true print" (p. 67). As emergent writers mark up the pages with pictures, mock handwriting, and letter strings, they are, in fact, producing writing. If teachers can help students expand on their ideas, attach meaning to what they have written, and tell the story behind what their words actually "say," then they are in essence "demonstrating an understanding that print communicates a message" (Riley-Ayers, 2013, p. 67). Over time, with appropriate modeling and support, the markings students record on a page will make more sense in conveying their ideas to others. As literacy education expert Timothy Shanahan (2018b) aptly explains in his blog *Shanahan on Literacy*, "Once you have kids writing—not just scribbling on a page or drawing pictures, but really trying to write messages using letters (albeit with invented spellings), then things get really interesting."

Students benefit when teachers do what's listed in figure 7.6 for a whole-group writing lesson. It is impossible to include each of these in every lesson.

☐ Explicitly state learning objectives.

☐ Explicitly teach narrative, informative, and opinion writing.

☐ Use teacher write-alouds.

☐ Introduce interactive writing experiences.

☐ Explicitly teach and model standards-aligned skills.

☐ Instruct on vocabulary, word work, and foundational skills.

☐ Ask students to apply skills to authentic writing experiences.

☐ Use the gradual release of responsibility model.

☐ Embed opportunities for engagement and student discourse.

Figure 7.6: Whole-group writing checklist.

*Visit **go.SolutionTree.com/literacy** for a free reproducible version of this figure.*

To help students, we recommend the following strategies and sequencing considerations.

▶ Apply early literacy skills.

▶ Create a supportive writing environment.

▶ Use writing to improve reading.

▶ Use gradual release of responsibility in whole-group writing.

Apply Early Literacy Skills

Writing practice provides authentic and engaging opportunities to develop students' phonemic awareness and letter-sound skills. According to early education scholars Renée M. Casbergue and Dorothy S. Strickland (2016):

It does a child little good to recite letters of the alphabet if he or she doesn't know what letters actually are or how they are used to understand and convey messages. And while children certainly need to recognize and form the letters of the alphabet, it is equally important for them to learn how to use those letters to share their thoughts. (pp. 8–9)

If students only practice foundational skills through isolated, repetitive activities "devoid of any meaningful context," then they are unlikely to "retain or apply their understanding of the alphabet over time" (Casbergue & Strickland, 2016, p. 3). It is through authentic writing experiences that students can show what they know about the letters and sounds and see firsthand the benefits of using new skills.

Throughout these writing tasks, students should be encouraged to use their letter-sound and phoneme awareness skills to spell out words, even if they have yet to learn correct spellings. Inventive spelling provides teachers with teachable moments to show "1) how the oral phonemes relate to what the student wrote and 2) how these phonemes related to the actual spelling of the word" (Kilpatrick, 2016, p. 63). In addition, inventive spelling opportunities can be used informally to assess students' level of phonemic awareness and knowledge of letter sounds. Data from these student samples can help teachers plan differentiated instruction, especially when forming small groups for writing instruction.

Create a Supportive Writing Environment

To create an environment that fosters and supports writing, teachers should distribute an abundance of writing materials throughout the classroom and provide plenty of opportunities to use them. Students will need access to pens, markers, crayons, finger paints, colored paper, index cards, sticky notes, small chalkboards, whiteboards, and magnetic writing boards as they practice and experiment with new writing skills.

Teachers can provide opportunities for writing beyond the literacy block by embedding writing into daily routines and everyday tasks. For example, preK and kindergarten students can practice writing their names by signing a classroom attendance board or by signing up for an activity during choice time.

These frequent writing tasks will also help to develop the fine motor skills and finger dexterity necessary for writing. Throughout the classroom, teachers can add labels to various objects and items, helping students connect words with the things they represent. In addition, displaying signs, schedules, charts, and calendars will allow students to see the use of words in their everyday activities. As students become more adept at writing, teachers can create word walls to display high-frequency words that students commonly need to use in writing, encouraging students to practice spelling and using words correctly in their writing.

Use Writing to Improve Reading

Even with our youngest writers, research supports the claim that writing serves as an impactful tool to improve reading: "In particular, having students write about a text they are reading enhances how well they comprehend it. The same result occurs when students write about a text from different content areas, such as science and social studies" (Graham & Hebert, 2010, p. 6).

Based on their findings of the correlative influence of writing on reading, literacy authors Steve Graham and Michael Hebert (2010) recommend using writing to bolster students' reading skills and comprehension as well as learning about subject matter content. Graham and Hebert (2010) sort their findings into three core categories.

1. **Teachers ask students to write about what they read.** When students write a response based on a text-based task—for example, a personal reaction, interpretation, or summary—reading comprehension improves.

   - In preK and early kindergarten classrooms, students rely heavily on drawings, dictations, and symbols to craft these responses.
   - At the end of kindergarten and into first grade, responses include words, sentences, and even well-developed paragraphs.

   Students' understanding of a text deepens and their content knowledge increases when they write responses to both teacher-crafted text-dependent questions, which are typically interjected throughout the reading or at the end of the text, and student-designed questions, which students generate on their own. To help preK through first-grade students craft their own text-dependent questions, teachers will need to provide explicit instruction on questioning skills. Students will need to know what makes for a good question and have ample time to practice developing quality questions with the support of teachers and peers prior to implementing the skill on their own. Although students engage in question and answer discussions, they derive more benefit from writing their responses (Graham & Hebert, 2010).

2. **Teachers conduct lessons around writing skills and processes to create text.** Since both areas of literacy share common processes and knowledge, teaching students to write improves reading skills. Therefore, teachers conduct lessons on the following processes.

   - Writing (planning, editing, revision, and so forth)
   - Text structures (compare-contrast, problem-solution, cause-effect, sequence, description)
   - Sentence construction
   - Spelling

3. **Teachers increase the amount of writing that students do.** Providing students with more time to write their own texts—self- or peer-selected topics, letters to pen pals, journal entries—correlates to an uptick in reading comprehension.

The recommendations are woven into various learning experiences throughout the school day, but initial explicit teaching typically begins in the whole-group setting, where teachers employ a number of instructional strategies to facilitate the learning of new writing concepts. As one approach, Fisher and Frey (2008) suggest making the composing process concrete by utilizing write-alouds during explicit writing instruction—a teacher's detailed verbal explanation of thinking as he artfully works through a key component of the writing process. In preK through first grade, the writing process typically includes the following steps (Gibson, n.d.).

1. **Prewriting:** This is the planning stage when students brainstorm ideas, often using graphic organizers, such as a chart or story web, to help capture their thoughts. Prekindergarten through first-grade students will rely heavily on a combination of pictures and invented spelling throughout the writing process.

2. **Drafting:** Using the ideas generated during prewriting, students work independently to write their story, poem, or nonfiction piece. As students write, teachers can confer with students to offer suggestions and guidance while gathering data on skills that are difficult for students and that they might need to address through additional whole-class instruction or focused small-group or individual minilessons.

3. **Revising and editing:** Students share their rough drafts with their classmates and make suggestions to each other. Teachers provide explicit instruction and modeling of giving effective peer feedback. For instance, if students have written fictional text, teachers can demonstrate how to ask *who, what, when, where, why,* and *how* questions to better understand an event, character, or setting in a story. For all types of writing, teachers can also show students how to suggest better words or pictures to express ideas.

4. **Rewriting:** Students rewrite their draft based on the feedback from their peers.

5. **Publishing:** After completing their final draft, students celebrate their accomplishments by publishing—sharing—their writing. Students can display their writing on a class bulletin board, add it to a class book, or post it to the classroom blog.

Teachers of preK through first-grade students typically focus a write-aloud lesson on a key writing concept or skill students find particularly challenging within the writing process. For instance, teachers might choose to write aloud as they brainstorm a topic during the prewriting stage, develop a concluding sentence during the drafting stage, or add punctuation to sentences during the rewriting stage.

Composing writing is an intricate exercise due to the thought processes necessary to formulate coherent ideas and sentences, as well as the physical demand of writing a composition. Therefore, modeling writing for the entirety of the write-aloud would be counterproductive. Marzano (2017) affirms that "when information is new to students, they best process it in small, understandable increments. This is because learners can hold only small amounts of information in their working memories" (p. 30). For this reason, the gradual release of responsibility is especially effective during a write-aloud, since the lesson moves from teacher directed to student centered. In addition, because oracy is the first step in producing language and articulating thinking—and is the foundation for producing writing—teachers should embed time for processing, collaborative discourse, and verbalizing thinking in the lesson (Kirkland & Patterson, 2005). Just a few minutes devoted to students articulating ideas with others can lead to more in-depth, focused writing. Immediate opportunities for trial and practice are also essential to helping students actualize learning.

Use Gradual Release of Responsibility in Whole-Group Writing

Teachers can use the gradual release of responsibility with a write-aloud. The following four steps (Gibson, n.d.) help make this a success. Please note that prior to the lesson, teachers should prepare for their write-aloud by writing out the text they plan to construct in front of students. This preparation develops the teacher's awareness of his or her decision making and helps anticipate any confusion students might have.

1. **Set a purpose:** Let students know what you plan to share with them during the write-aloud and why it is important for them to learn. For example, if you are showing how to determine spelling by orally segmenting it into its individual sounds, you might say the following.

   I am going to show you how to use what you know about letter sounds to help you write out words in your story. This is an important skill for helping you learn how to add writing to your stories.

   Begin the lesson by telling students that they will have the opportunity to listen in on your thoughts as you write in front of them. Let students know that as you write and share your thoughts, they are expected to listen carefully and pay attention to the decisions you make because they will need to do the same in their own writing.

2. **Use explicit modeling:** Using a whiteboard, chart paper, or projector, display your text as you write in front of students. As you write, make verbal statements that describe the steps you take or the decisions you make to help you generate the text. When modeling the spelling strategy, the teacher might verbalize the following thoughts.

> *I want to write a story about a fish. What are the sounds I hear in the word* fish? *I'm going to say* fish *aloud and listen to the sounds: /f/ /i/ /sh/. First I hear /f/, so I will write an* f *on paper. Next, I hear /i/, so I will write an* i. *The last sound I hear is /sh/. I know that the letters* s *and* h *together make /sh/, so I will write down* s *and* h. *The word* fish *must be spelled f-i-s-h.*

3. **Guide student practice:** After the write-aloud, ask students to reflect on and discuss with their peers what they noticed about your thinking during the activity. For the spelling example, the teacher might ask the following questions.

> *What steps did I follow to figure out the spelling of the word? How can you use this technique in your own writing?*

Then, give students the opportunity to practice the writing skill or concept with their peers. For the spelling example, the teacher could give students a few words to practice segmenting and spelling with a small group before trying it out on their own.

4. **Allow independent practice:** When students seem comfortable and confident with the concept or skill, they are ready to apply it to their own writing. As students practice, teachers provide individual guidance and support as needed.

Similarly, teachers might also implement interactive writing into their whole-group lessons. Writing authors Kate Roth and Joan Dabrowski (2014) define *interactive writing* as a "dynamic instructional method during which the teacher and students work together to construct meaningful text while discussing the details of the writing process." This shared writing experience allows group collaboration and discussion as the teacher guides students through the steps of the writing process, and promotes active participation because students are invited to "share the pen" with the teacher at particular points in the lesson (Roth & Dabrowski, 2014). Norine Blanch, Lenora C. Forsythe, Jennifer H. Van Allen, and Sherron Killingsworth Roberts (2017) assert, "Teachers should take courage in their ability to model authorship, providing ample opportunities to emulate writers and learn from mentor texts through explicit teaching and use of the writing process" (p. 50).

EXERCISE

Guide a Discussion About Whole-Group Lessons

Use the information provided about whole-group reading and writing instruction to guide a collaborative discussion about the current whole-group experiences in your classroom. Discuss any refinements you might make to whole-group reading or writing lessons to make a greater impact on student achievement.

Use the following questions to guide this exercise.

★ How can we assure that the texts we are using in the whole-group experiences are appropriately challenging for our students?

★ How will we ensure that the texts utilized during whole-group lessons are accessible and visible to all students?

★ How will we incorporate the gradual release of responsibility during whole-group reading and writing lessons?

★ What texts will we use as mentors or models during writing instruction?

Small-Group Reading

Throughout the literacy block, teachers gather flexible groups of students to provide differentiated instruction and support in a more personalized setting. Flexible grouping allows students to work together in a variety of ways based on such factors as student interest, prior knowledge, and skill level. During small-group reading, teachers often group students who have similar needs, and, with the teacher's guidance, students work intently to develop identified skill gaps, practice strategies aligned to grade-level reading standards, and even extend their learning when they are ready for more. On any given day, students may meet with the teacher to work on fluency, word work, foundational skills such as phonics or decoding, comprehension strategies, and standards-aligned skills.

As you explore the topic of small-group reading, you'll notice a repeated emphasis on the notion of flexibility. To be successful, small groups must be flexible in a number of ways, such as the following.

▸ *Who* is in a small group

▸ *How long* a small-group session takes

▸ *What* differentiated support to provide

As education scholars Carol Ann Tomlinson and Marcia B. Imbeau (2010) put it, "A flexible approach to teaching 'makes room' for student variance" (p. 14). The flexible approach is in the teaching.

During small-group reading instruction, teachers pull students together—typically no more than six—for a narrowed focus informed by assessment data and tailored to the current needs of the group's students.

To help students, we recommend the following strategies and sequencing considerations.

▸ Determining who

▸ Determining what

Both address the variable *How long?*

Determining Who

To implement an effective differentiated classroom that meets every student's needs, Tomlinson and Imbeau (2010) remind teachers to continually ask themselves, "What does *this* student need at *this* moment in order to be able to progress with *this* key content, and what do I need to do to make that happen?" (p. 14; emphasis in original). Like a catchy new pop song that won't leave your head, this question resonates in a teacher's mind. Teachers are eager to find the answers so they can support students in a small-group setting.

To help students make strides in their reading abilities, teachers form groups by identifying particular students who need extra practice and support with a specific *skill*. They can determine these students based on informal and formal assessment data gathered throughout a learning progression. Perhaps the teacher has identified four students who are struggling to retell the key events in a story, while six students are still developing their basic knowledge of one-to-one letter-sound correspondences, and three others are working on decoding multisyllabic words. Clearly, the needs vary greatly. When the teacher gathers each different group during small-group instruction, she will orchestrate support using differentiated strategies, teaching tactics, and scaffolds. Teachers need to be strategic when dividing their time among groups. While some groups might require more time and attention, other groups might grasp the learning more quickly, allowing additional time for independent practice and application.

Additionally, since students in kindergarten and first grade will eventually need to demonstrate mastery of a skill using texts at their own grade level, the teacher will provide guided practice opportunities using grade-level texts. Here, during the small group, the teacher becomes the scaffold as he or she assists students in navigating challenging texts that are currently beyond their instructional level, while teaching explicit strategies that will aid comprehension. At each small-group reading session, student groups might need to be reconfigured for different purposes, with the goal of continuous improvement and growth. Systematic, ongoing assessment data ensure the accuracy and flexibility of group membership. Although formal assessments can provide a wealth of information, teachers typically rely more on their informal observations of students during small-group instruction to inform their grouping. For instance, as students apply their reading skills and strategies in authentic situations, teachers can jot down anecdotal records. (See chapter 2, page 39, for more information about anecdotal records). Teachers often keep a stack of sticky notes or a clipboard close by during small-group reading sessions to quickly record these observations. Based on the data, teachers can determine whether students have reached proficiency and shift group membership to accommodate progress.

Determining What

A primary focus at the small-group reading table is on the explicit teaching of strategies used to construct meaning. Author on reading instruction Jennifer Serravallo (2010) defines *strategies* as the "step-by-step how-tos for internalizing skills such as determining importance, questioning, inferring, monitoring for meaning, activating prior knowledge, visualizing, and retelling/synthesizing" (p. 12). In other words, strategies are a type of scaffold, explicitly taught to students, that aid in conquering the skills needed for proficient reading. Shanahan and his colleagues (2010) offer another definition of strategies as "intentional mental actions" and "deliberate efforts by a reader" to better comprehend what is being read, and that, moreover, a strategy is *not* a worksheet or exercise, as those are merely activities (p. 11). Unless coupled with direct and explicit instruction on the thinking one must employ to make meaning, worksheets and exercises rarely help students become better at reading (Allington & Gabriel, 2012). These kinds of activities allow students to show what they know at their current level of proficiency, but don't offer any *new* strategic instruction to actuate growth.

Additional literacy skills are developed and refined at the small-group table as well, reiterating the need for classroom flexibility as students are called together for various reasons. Since students come to school with a range of literacy experiences and abilities, students receive differentiated support in homogenous groups to strengthen foundational skills such as phonics and fluency. Kindergarten and first-grade teachers can gain valuable insights on individual students as readers by conducting running records and using the data to identify skill gaps, such as the ability to decode. To broaden their knowledge and understanding of how language works, teachers facilitate differentiated word work lessons as well, which equip readers with strategies for word attack skills, leading to greater reading independence (Morrow & Gambrell, 2011).

If your district uses a purchased vocabulary or spelling program, explicit word work instruction will begin at the small-group table. From there, students resume word study tasks and sharpen newly learned word concepts during literacy skill-application time, since repeated exposure is critical to student growth. With focused and guided support during small-group instruction and a variety of strategies in their reading toolboxes, students make great strides in reading abilities.

Small-Group Writing

Much like small-group reading, small-group writing is a time for focused differentiated instruction tailored to students' specific writing needs. Karen R. Harris, Steve Graham, Barbara Friedlander, and Leslie Laud (2013) define *skilled writing* as a complex process "requiring extensive self-regulation of a flexible, goal-directed, problem-solving activity. In addition to basic skills, students must also develop knowledge about the writing process, genre knowledge, and strategies for writing and self-regulating the writing process" (p. 539).

Students benefit when teachers do the following for a small-group writing lesson.

- ▸ Flexibly group students
- ▸ Use specific strategies for instruction
- ▸ Differentiate writing supports and scaffolds
- ▸ Guide instruction at various steps in the writing process
- ▸ Guide practice on identified skill gaps
- ▸ Periodically hold one-on-one writing conferences with students
- ▸ Give specific, individualized feedback
- ▸ Provide individualized writing goals

During small-group writing, teachers bridge the learning from the whole-group experience and assist students as they craft their ideas into written compositions. Data-informed decisions are made when flexibly choosing who to meet with and what skills and concepts to address. Students with emerging alphabet awareness and concepts of print will rely heavily on pictures, symbols, and letter strings to capture their ideas on paper. In the small-group setting, these young writers will need help developing the fine motor skills necessary to properly grip a pencil and move it across the paper. In addition, they will need support conveying the meaning of their writing. Often, at this early stage of writing development, students express ideas orally by dictating words, phrases, or sentences while the teacher records them on paper. As students gain more proficiency with their writing skills, the teacher can move onto more rigorous writing tasks.

Throughout the writing process, preK through first-grade students will likely need additional small-group support in the following areas.

- ▸ Generating ideas
- ▸ Sounding out and spelling words
- ▸ Crafting topic sentences
- ▸ Gathering evidence from a text
- ▸ Adding descriptive words
- ▸ Composing complete sentences
- ▸ Organizing ideas to develop coherence
- ▸ Using capitalization and end punctuation
- ▸ Editing and revising a rough draft

Observational data collected during small-group writing instruction helps teachers determine which students can independently apply the new learning to their own writing and which students require further instruction. When students continue to struggle with writing, a one-to-one conference is an ideal opportunity to deliver individualized instruction targeting their specific needs.

To impel continuous growth, the teacher provides differentiated instruction on explicit writing strategies at the small-group table as students strengthen, fine-tune, and practice composition skills. Additionally, scaffolds such as sentence frames, graphic organizers, word banks, templates, mentor texts, visuals, and checklists provide the proper amount of support. Graham et al. (2012) emphasize the following about strategy instruction:

Teachers can help students become effective writers by teaching a variety of strategies for carrying out each component of the writing process and by supporting students in applying the strategies until they are able to do so independently. Over time, students will develop a repertoire of strategies for writing. Teachers should explain and model the fluid nature in which the components of the writing process work together, so that students can learn to apply strategies flexibly—separately or in combination—when they write. (p. 12)

With guidance, support, and feedback from the teacher, the small-group writing table becomes a safe, comfortable environment where students find themselves writing with originality and taking risks to express their ideas in thoughtful and creative ways. Teacher feedback plays a key role in helping students take risks and challenge themselves as writers. According to Carol S. Dweck (2007), professor of psychology at Stanford University with over thirty-five years of research on student motivation, the type of praise teachers give "is intricately connected to how students view their intelligence" (p. 34). For example, when teachers praise students for their intelligence ("You must be a gifted reader"), students tend to develop a fixed mindset, believing their ability level is a trait they simply possess. Although teachers deliver this type of *person praise* in the hope of building students' self-confidence and overall enjoyment of learning, instead, the students often become preoccupied with their intelligence, looking for tasks that substantiate their beliefs about their intelligence and steering clear of those that challenge them (Dweck, 2007). Sadly, students who fear making mistakes lose the motivation to learn. On the other hand, when teachers praise students' effort ("You must have worked hard to learn all the letter sounds"), students tend to develop a growth mindset, believing their ability can increase through their hard work and effort. Students exposed to *process praise*—"praise for engagement, perseverance, strategies, improvement, and the like"—step up to a challenge, taking on rigorous tasks without the fear of making mistakes or worrying how they will look (Dweck, 2007, p. 35).

While working with preK through first-grade students in small-group writing instruction, the desirable process praise often sounds like the following.

- ▶ "I like how you tried several strategies to help spell that tricky word."
- ▶ "You are working hard to add details to your story. I can picture this character because you took the time to add vivid words."
- ▶ "You really took on the challenge to create this how-to book by making pictures, labeling the steps, and writing some important details. You learned so much, and you will help others learn, too."

In this safe environment where students see that their hard work and efforts are paying off, their desire to learn truly thrives. With their teacher there to guide and support, words flow more easily onto the paper, and students begin to see themselves as authors.

Students may meet as a small group during any step of the writing process, from brainstorming and planning to editing and revising. Just as with small-group reading, small writing groups are flexibly formed based on identified student needs. With a narrowed focus, select students may work with a teacher to refine a number of writing skills such as those listed in the Whole-Group Writing section (page 188).

However, at times, this specialized writing instruction might also take the form of an individual student conference. During conferences, teachers meet with individual students to discuss current writing projects and provide feedback so students know what precise changes or additions need to occur next to improve. Especially for younger writers, feedback must be as concrete and explicit as possible. Avoid vague directives such as "add more description" or "include evidence from the text," which give little direction to students on the precise next steps to take for notable improvement.

For feedback to be effective, education author Grant Wiggins (2012) suggests seven key elements. Table 7.2 delineates each with examples.

Table 7.2: Effective Feedback for Writing Conferences

Key Element	Element Description	Writing Example
Goal referenced	Students need to know the goal of the feedback, how it will accomplish a task, and what criteria can be used for self-assessment and for critiquing peers' work.	You can mention a standard directly and refer students to their rubric for further guidance: "Adding details to your characters is one of the goals of this assignment and is listed on the rubric. These particular words and phrases help readers imagine what your character looks like and sounds like. Reread your paper and decide where you need to add more details."
Tangible and transparent	The feedback must be clear and obvious so students can understand what it means and can actually use it as a learning tool.	Writing comments such as "What?" or simply adding "sp" in the margin to indicate a misspelled word can confuse students, who may skip over the input because they do not know what it means. Instead, clearly tell students, "This word is misspelled. To help spell it correctly, you can say the word aloud, listen for the sounds within the word, and jot down the letter or letters that make those sounds."

Actionable	The feedback must provide specific details or facts that students can use to improve. Avoid adding praise, value judgment, or blame.	Rather than commenting, "Good job!" and "You did that wrong," provide students with specific, actionable feedback on how to improve. Actionable feedback includes reinforcing what works (so students can continue implementing a skill) and pointing out what didn't (so they can revise). A teacher might say, "In your story, you used lots of vivid action words to show what the character is doing. Add some more descriptive words to help the reader imagine what the character looks like."
User friendly	Feedback should use language that students can understand. Do not overwhelm students by offering too much detail at once.	Rather than offering, "Your topic sentence should draw the reader into the text and prepare him for your thesis statement," to help a first grader develop a topic sentence, offer this less technical comment instead: "Your topic sentence should hook the readers and get them ready for your main point."
Timely	Throughout the writing process, provide feedback in a timely manner so students can apply the input as soon as possible to their drafts.	Research shows that students are most likely to benefit from immediate feedback as opposed to delayed feedback (Irons, 2008; Opitz, Ferdinand, & Mecklinger, 2011). For example, if students get feedback after turning in a published piece, they cannot learn from salient comments that may contribute to improvement. Timely feedback can come from myriad individuals—peers, those outside the classroom, and the teacher.
Ongoing	Integrate continuous opportunities for students not only to receive feedback but to use the feedback to reshape their performance and to better achieve the learning goal.	The ongoing nature of feedback is built into the writing process not just during revision—where it is most typical—but also in other stages, as appropriate. For example, if students struggle to stay on topic throughout their opinion writing, provide them with feedback by suggesting a strategy on how to maintain their focus throughout an essay, give them an opportunity to revise their work, and check on their progress again to make sure they successfully implemented the strategy.
Consistent	Feedback must be consistent among teacher teams so students receive stable, accurate, and trustworthy information. Therefore, teams need to get clear on what high-quality work is.	Collaboratively created rubrics and collected anchor papers consistently show what students need to do to show proficiency. Teacher teams' calibrated grading efforts also create consistency. (See chapter 4, page 93.)

Source: Adapted from Wiggins, 2012.

During one-on-one conferences, students who might be intimidated to share in front of peers might feel more comfortable talking with the teacher alone. Plus, even though the dialogue between them centers on instruction, it concurrently builds a relationship between the student and teacher. On the culmination of individual (or small group) conference sessions, teachers set individual and specific goals for each student, and send them off to apply newly learned skills and concepts during independent work time. To help students self-monitor as they work independently, teachers can provide a list of tasks, such as an editing checklist, or a visual aid detailing a specific writing skill, such as generating ideas for a story. Figure 7.7 is for generating story ideas.

Story Ideas	
1. Think	
2. Draw	
3. Write	

Figure 7.7: Story idea tool.

*Visit **go.SolutionTree.com/literacy** for a free reproducible version of this figure.*

EXERCISE

Guide a Discussion About Small-Group Instruction

Use the information provided about small-group reading and writing instruction to guide a collaborative discussion about the current small-group experiences in your classroom. Discuss any refinements you might make to small-group reading or writing sessions to make a greater impact on student achievement.

Use the following questions to guide this exercise.

★ How will we use data to decide which students to pull together for small-group differentiated instruction?

★ What differentiated supports or extensions do students need at this time?

★ What reading and writing skills do students need to master learning standards, and what strategies can we explicitly teach to help them reach proficiency?

Literacy Skill Application

During the facilitation of small-group reading and writing instruction, students who are not gathered into a small group typically engage in literacy skill-application time. Though this time in the literacy block is often referred to by a host of names—centers, workstations, rounds, rotations, or independent learning time—we use *literacy skill application* to denote its precise purpose in the larger literacy block.

As the teacher conducts small-group lessons with select individuals, the rest of the students in class are given ample time to practice and apply, either independently or collaboratively, the newly learned strategies and skills explicitly taught during whole- and small-group reading and writing lessons. Students try the strategies for themselves, engage in tasks that let them practice and refine those skills, and strengthen the bridge toward independence.

Literacy skill application requires the following considerations.

▶ Structure with teacher outside the rotation

▶ Student engagement and accountability

▶ Reading time

▶ Play

▶ Vocabulary

Structure With Teacher Outside the Rotation

With the teacher's attention focused on a select few students, careful consideration must be made in how to structure and design the learning opportunities for every student in the room. To maintain levels of continuous engagement during small-group time, teachers often follow one of two rotation models. In the first, the small-group session with the teacher is included *inside* the rotation of independent workstations; in the second, more flexible, and recommended approach, group time with the teacher is positioned *outside* the rotation. Figure 7.8 depicts these two approaches to independent learning stations, with the *T* representing the teacher's position during small-group instruction.

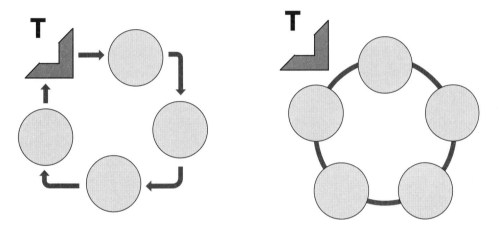

Structure A: Teacher inside the rotation   **Structure B: Teacher outside the rotation**

Source: Adapted from Bates, 2013.

Figure 7.8: Structures for small-group and independent learning.

When included inside timed rotations, groups of students make their way around the room to a set of predetermined workstations. Rather than flexible, this framework is quite rigid. When the timer goes off after approximately fifteen minutes, students stop what they are doing and move to the next station, one of which is the small-group session with the teacher. While this rotational structure allows for the regimented movement of students in and out of small-group reading and writing sessions, there are pitfalls associated with this approach.

First, dynamic, higher-order-thinking tasks and activities cannot always be accomplished in the limitations of timed stations, and as we know, learning is not a one-size-fits-all experience. Not all students move at the same pace, and what one student accomplishes in ten minutes could easily take another student twenty. Additionally, when teachers position themselves in the cyclical movement of the rotation as one of the learning stations, time spent on guided support in each small group is restricted to a set duration, *and* the teacher is limited to working only with those students who show up to the table as a group in the rotation. This leaves little to no flexible room for pulling individual students based on timely data-driven decisions.

Instead of fastening themselves inside a rigid rotation structure, teachers are encouraged to take themselves *outside* the rotation. This allows for both flexible groupings of students, as well as flexible timing. Some small groups may only need five minutes to quickly receive the differentiated support they need, while other groups may require more intense guided support over the course of fifteen or twenty minutes. Celeste C. Bates (2013), assistant professor at Clemson University, affirms that "flexible grouping allows teachers to call children from centers based on the children's interests and needs, recognizing that as these needs change, so do the grouping arrangements" (p. 30).

With the freedom to move in and out of small groups flexibly based on student data, teachers can make a greater impact on reading achievement and maximize small-group time to benefit each student in the room. Table 7.3 summarizes the benefits of positioning the teacher outside independent station rotations, rather than inside.

Table 7.3: Positioning the Teacher Inside the Rotation Versus Outside the Rotation

Don't: Teacher Inside Station Rotations	Do: Teacher Outside Station Rotations
• Duration of small-group instruction is equivalent and fixed for all groups.	• Duration of small-group instruction is flexible and tailored to the group's needs.
• Small groups are restricted to those students placed together during rotations.	• Teachers pull students from any center on an as-needed basis.
• Homogenous groups of students travel together to all work rotation stations.	• Heterogeneous groups of students can travel or work together at various workstations.
• Duration of each workstation is restricted and dictated by a timer.	• Duration of workstations is flexible and can be adjusted to the task.
• Rotation centers typically involve identical tasks for all students.	• Workstation and independent activities can be differentiated for each student.

Alternatives to timed rotation stations can also enhance the skill-application practice taking place during small-group instruction. For example, teachers can implement and display a "must do, may do" learning menu of skill-application tasks related to vocabulary, word work, fluency, foundational skills, writing, or reading skills.

▶ **Must-do tasks:** Required learning tasks are listed for the students to accomplish during skill-application time. These tasks are a priority, as they are meaningful to the development of current priority standards and aligned to recent whole-group reading and writing lessons. A student accountability piece—distinct evidence of student thinking and learning—is also linked to each task so that teachers (and students) can monitor and measure individual progress. The accountability piece could take many forms, depending on the learning task. For instance, students writing a comparison of penguin and otter habitats could complete a Venn diagram; students independently reading a challenging text could write a journal entry to reflect on new learning; or students using magnetic tiles to build words could jot down a list of the words they generated during the activity. All students must accomplish these tasks first, but can typically choose the order in which to complete them.

▶ **May-do tasks:** These are optional activities to engage in after meeting requirements. Though not a priority, they are meaningful and practical in strengthening and advancing literacy skills, and available to those students who finish the must-do items with time to spare.

Teachers structure skill-application time in a number of ways, but the primary goal of any independent learning framework is to engage students in a variety of relevant and growth-producing learning experiences with embedded accountability measures in place to monitor growth and determine next steps for each student.

Student Engagement and Accountability

Despite our valiant efforts to establish routines and hold high expectations for all, preK through first-grade students don't always have the stamina, attention, or motivation to follow through when working individually at their own pace. For this reason, it is critical that time spent working individually is highly structured, and that directions and expectations for all tasks and activities are crystal clear to every student.

To optimize literacy skill-application time, some students may require differentiated supports beyond what is provided to the whole class. For example, in addition to a must-do/may-do menu, students may benefit from a detailed checklist with step-by-step procedures on which to track individual progress. Figure 7.9 (page 208) is a customizable checklist for student-friendly language and picture cues.

Step	Brief Description of Procedure	Picture of the Procedure
1.		
2.		
3.		
4.		

Figure 7.9: Tracking progress.

*Visit **go.SolutionTree.com/literacy** for a free reproducible version of this figure.*

Others may require extra scaffolds or materials such as graphic organizers, high-lighters for locating text support, sequencing strips, or sticky notes for annotating or tracking one's thinking. Before we send students off to work on their own, we must equip them with the various tools they'll need to be independently successful.

Perhaps most critical to the success of independent skill-application time is continuous cognitive engagement. Fisher and Frey (2018) admit what many teachers know to be true: some students pretend to be engaged when their minds are not actually focused on the task at hand; still others are struggling to keep their minds on task because of developmental or physiological issue. To facilitate effective independent work time, teachers must ensure that students are consistently engaged, self-monitoring to understand their current level of understanding, and accountable for their learning. If students are not cognitively engaged and actively thinking throughout their independent practice time, valuable minutes in the literacy block are lost, resulting in missed opportunities for student growth. Therefore, teachers must ensure that every moment is maximized in promoting high levels of thinking.

Marzano (2017) illustrates four components of engagement, which often dictate students' mental readiness throughout the teaching-learning process: (1) paying attention, (2) being energized, (3) being intrigued, and (4) being inspired. Just as teachers stop often and ask themselves *which* students need support, it is equally imperative that they pause to consider just *what* their students are currently doing and precisely *how* it is helping them to become skilled independent readers, writers, and thinkers. For instance, while students engage in individual literacy skills application, teachers can pause their small-group instruction to quickly scan the room and identify specific students who appear disengaged.

To help refocus students, teachers might need to refine structures and procedures as needed. Jennifer Serravallo (2010) suggests explicitly teaching students how to identify when they lose focus and start to drift away from the task at hand. For example, to help students refocus on their book, teachers can share the following strategies (Serravallo, 2010).

▸ Use a bookmark or sticky note ahead in your book to mark your reading goal. When you get to the desired page, pause your reading, take a break, and silently retell yourself what you just read.

▸ If you catch your mind wandering, stop reading and look back in the text to find the spot you last remember reading. Reread this section and try again.

▸ Use a timer to set a reading goal. When the timer goes off, take a break and reflect on the text. Try adding a bit more each time you read.

Educator Jennifer Gonzalez (2018) of the Cult of Pedagogy blog explains this quite adeptly:

If we want our students to actually learn the facts and concepts and ideas we're trying to teach them, they have to experience those things in some way that rises above abstract words on paper. They have to process them. Manipulate them. To really learn in a way that will stick, they have to DO something.

Student engagement demands *doing*. Literacy skill-application time requires students to engage in cognitive, purposeful tasks such as the following.

▸ Sorting words

▸ Sequencing story events

▸ Monitoring progress by way of a checklist

▸ Responding to the events in a story

> ▸ Drawing a visual representation

> ▸ Using sentence stems to compose explanatory text

> ▸ Editing or revising in different colored ink

Reading Time

During the literacy skill-application segment of the literacy block, time is set aside for reading with a partner, listening to reading, or reading independently. On most days, reading in some capacity is listed as a requirement for students, given that the volume of reading students do is linked to increased comprehension and overall reading achievement (Allington, 2014). During this time, students will need access to a wide variety of both fictional texts (stories, plays, and poems) and informational texts (trade books, magazines, online resources, biographies, and how-to books). Students get the freedom to pick a book that interests them, allowing for an element of autonomy. As teacher and author Nancie Atwell (2007) affirms, "This is a time and a place for students to behave as skilled, passionate, habitual, critical readers" (p. 120).

In prekindergarten and kindergarten classrooms, students can independently "read" the pictures of their books or revisit the texts from the interactive read-aloud or shared reading lesson. In addition, students can engage in paired reading of these same texts by looking over a book with a partner, silently discussing what they see, and making up stories or developing inferences based on the pictures and any words they recognize.

Developing the appropriate behaviors and building the stamina necessary for these students to engage in independent reading will take plenty of practice. Students from prekindergarten, kindergarten, and first grade can't focus on reading for a sustained period of time—even just five minutes!—simply because we give them a book and tell them to have at it. Instead, education authors Gail Boushey and Joan Moser (2014) recommend building reading stamina in intervals of minutes (or even seconds) over a period of several days or weeks. Using the gradual release of responsibility model, teachers first share with students the expectations for independent reading time and model the expected behaviors. These behaviors could include the following.

> ▸ Quickly choose your text, find a comfortable workspace, and begin reading.

> ▸ Keep your eyes on your text.

> ▸ Use a whisper when needed.

Teachers model these behaviors by demonstrating both desired and undesired behaviors. For instance, to model *keep your eyes on the text*, the teacher could show students how she holds the book close, looks down at the page, and directs her eyes to the page; then she could show students what *keep your eyes on the text* does *not* look like by glancing around the room, staring off into space, or holding the book far away from her. She clearly explains to students that these are the behaviors they should *not* do. To help students reference and understand the expectations, teachers record the desired behaviors on a visual chart.

Students are now ready to practice and build their stamina by working independently to follow the behaviors on the chart. Boushey and Moser (2014) recommend observing students as they work to determine when they can no longer maintain their stamina with the task. When this happens, students might begin wandering around the room, talking to each other, or zoning out. When these students first start practicing independent reading, they do not last long—maybe two minutes. Once their stamina begins to wane, teachers should signal the students to gather together for a whole-class reflection and debriefing. During this discussion, teachers encourage students to think about their performance and compare their behaviors with the expectations listed on the chart. Teachers will ask students, "How did it go? Which of the behaviors were you able to do? Which behaviors were hard for you?" After reflecting on their personal challenges and success, students set a goal for the next practice session.

With each session, students' stamina will slowly increase. Teachers can track student progress by marking their time spent on task on a large bar graph like the one in figure 7.10 (page 212). After each practice session, teachers can mark the total time and then reflect with students on what they can do next time to reach the overall class goal. The bar graph in this figure shows kindergartners' progress as they work toward a class goal of independently reading for ten minutes.

Though simply reading for pleasure and practice is certainly beneficial and should be offered as an option, time for reading is often utilized for the application of newly acquired skills and strategies. As they read or listen to reading, students practice the concepts taught during whole- and small-group instruction. Whether students read for pleasure or dig into a text to practice standard-aligned skills, teachers establish expectations and accountability measures (if necessary) to ensure that students remain focused and on the path toward continuous growth. For instance, a first-grade student reading a science text on the topic of weather might be expected to jot down key ideas in a notebook, draw a detailed picture of a

Figure 7.10: Bar graph of independent reading goal.

new concept (such as the water cycle), or keep a list of new vocabulary words (*evaporation, condensation*) gathered throughout the text. The student could share this new learning with a partner or with the teacher during a one-to-one conference.

E X E R C I S E
Guide a Discussion About Independent Learning

Use the information provided about literacy skill-application time to guide a collaborative discussion about the current independent learning experiences in your classroom. Discuss any refinements you might make to independent practice time to make a greater impact on student achievement.

Use the following questions to guide this exercise.

★ How will we structure independent skill-application time to allow for the flexible grouping of students?

> ★ What engagement structures and activities will we embed into the independent segment of the literacy block to ensure students are actively and cognitively engaged in their learning?
>
> ★ What opportunities can we provide for students to practice skills collaboratively?
>
> ★ What accountability measures will students complete to demonstrate progress?

Play

In the preK, kindergarten, and first-grade classrooms, play is critical to a student's learning and development (Gronlund, 2013). Through this highly social interaction, students learn about the world around them, naturally developing their literacy skills, along with their imaginations, as they construct tiny cities out of blocks, perform a puppet show for their friends, or simply read a book aloud to a stuffed animal.

By providing students with props, such as costumes, blocks, and stuffed animals, and giving them paper and pens for writing, we create opportunities for students to involve text in their make-believe worlds. For example, students might use paper to jot down a shopping list at the grocery store, create traffic signs for a roadway, or plan out dialogue for an upcoming play. Students often stretch their literacy skills during these moments, experimenting with concepts and skills that are better suited for playful learning rather than the traditional instructional setting. However, when students see the benefits of reading and writing in their everyday lives:

> They are more likely to find a purpose that matters to them. In short, by exposing children to many texts and giving them the opportunity to create their own, they are more likely to include text in their lives, not just in their play. (Bennett-Armistead, n.d.)

When students have the time and opportunity to write their own stories, act out scenes from a favorite book, or design a blueprint for a building, they are, in fact, strengthening their literacy learning and developing the skills needed to become independent readers and writers.

Vocabulary

To address the question of where vocabulary instruction best fits in the block, we're inclined to begin with a rather simple answer: *everywhere*. Vocabulary plays a prominent role in the development of adeptly literate students across the domains of reading, writing, speaking, and listening. In fact, increased vocabulary equates to deeper meaning from text: "There is much evidence—strong correlations, several causal studies, as well as rich theoretical orientations—that shows that vocabulary is tightly related to reading comprehension across the age span" (Beck et al., 2013, p. 1).

For instance, to comprehend complex read-aloud texts brimming with rich themes, scientific explanations, or detailed historical accounts, students need word knowledge. Guiding students as they explore the nuances of language, such as figures of speech, "shades of meaning among verbs describing the same general action (e.g. walk, march, strut, prance)" (NGA & CCSSO, 2010, p. 27), and words with multiple meanings (the noun *duck* is a bird and the verb *duck* means to bend down), will help them eventually comprehend a range of texts on various topics, as well as artfully tell a story or strongly support an opinion. To communicate clearly and accurately with others, students must be equipped with vocabularies that allow for effortlessly exchanging original thoughts and ideas. For this reason, vocabulary skills are continuously strengthened and refined throughout the literacy block.

Vocabulary instruction must extend beyond a surface level of haphazard introductions to new words as they appear in various texts. Rather, teachers need to place an emphasis on vocabulary instruction that works and make it a daily part of a student's learning experience. The texts teachers choose for read-alouds are one way to address this. To import words into their personal working vocabularies, students require repeated exposures to new words and multiple opportunities to observe, write, and use the words in meaningful contexts. Therefore, direct instruction proves more effective when teaching new words to students:

> The case for direct instruction is strong. From a number of perspectives, the research indicates that wide reading probably is not sufficient in itself to ensure that students will develop the necessary vocabulary and consequently the necessary academic background knowledge to do well in school. In contrast, direct instruction has an impressive track record of improving students' background knowledge and the comprehension of academic content. (Marzano, 2004, p. 69)

Not all unknown words necessitate direct instruction. To determine how to best choose words for instructional purposes, teachers should be familiar with the three-tier system of categorizing words that Beck and her colleagues (2013) devised.

> ▸ **Tier one:** These are basic words used more in conversation. Children acquire these words in everyday life; therefore, explicit instruction is

usually unnecessary for native English speakers. Examples comprise sight words and other common words like *boy, chair, pretty, red,* and *hand.*

▶ **Tier two:** These words are "likely to appear frequently in a wide variety of texts and in the written and oral language of mature language users" (for example, *investigate, determine, claim,* and *infer;* Beck et al., 2013, p. 25). The denotation of these words change based on their contexts. For example, a music teacher might *direct* the school chorus; in science, the teacher may *direct* students to view a demonstration; and in literacy, students may study *direct* characterization.

▶ **Tier three:** Often referred to as *domain-specific words,* these appear in a content area and are limited to a particular topic such as *nucleus, genes, treaty,* or *electoral.*

To structure strategic vocabulary instruction, Marzano (2004) suggests implementing a six-step process during literacy instruction.

1. The teacher provides a thorough description, explanation, or example of a prechosen vocabulary word to students so they develop a keen understanding of its explicit and implicit meanings.

2. Students restate the meaning in their own words.

3. Students draw a picture, symbol, or graphic to create a visual representation of the word.

4. Students engage in activities.

5. Students discuss words with each other.

6. Students participate in vocabulary games.

Summary

Although reading and writing should transpire throughout a student's day, the specific literacy block is time teams must safeguard specifically for literacy instruction and learning. During this time, those students with gaps in reading readiness and language development receive differentiated instruction and guidance to develop essential foundational skills, putting them on the path toward grade-level learning. During the preK through first-grade years, all students learn to decode simple words, receive ample time to improve fluency, and become word wizards as they broaden their vocabulary knowledge. In addition, they learn and apply a variety of strategies to aid with comprehension, and they engage in an abundance of shared reading and writing experiences, including playful learning. They write frequently and passionately, read abundantly, and radiate with the motivation to become better each and every day.

To develop truly literate students with the capacity to engage in higher-order independent thinking requires a strategically planned and implemented literacy block that honors and celebrates the interconnectedness of reading and writing. Dividing and confining the teaching of skills and concepts into their own separate chambers of instruction leaves students short of developing all facets of the multi-dimensional complexities of literacy. Though teachers will set aside specific times for explicit instruction of reading, writing, and vocabulary in both whole- and small-group settings, skillful teachers continuously embed all domains of literacy within their instruction, in every subject area, throughout the day. They guide students in making natural connections between these skills.

In chapter 8, we'll continue our focus on providing quality literacy instruction by exploring three instructional strategies that teachers can use to facilitate learning throughout each component of the literacy block. When implemented thoughtfully, these strategies and teaching tools support students in grasping literacy concepts and mastering a variety of grade-level targets and standards.

CHAPTER 8

Select Appropriate Instructional Strategies

The previous chapter provides suggestions for planning and conducting a literacy block. In this part of the school day, teachers conduct direct instruction to assist students in acquiring a new skill, strategy, or procedure using sound models like gradual release of responsibility. The learning progression provides a path for instruction and compels teacher teams to ask, "If the assessment expects students to produce X to show evidence of learning, what does the instruction actually look like?" Therefore, this chapter provides guidance in using the learning progression to select and implement appropriate instructional strategies that yield an assessment. While reading, consider how to integrate any strategy with learning activities that implement the gradual release of responsibility.

Sometimes a strategy overlaps with the actual assessment. When delivering lessons, teachers pair instructional strategies (and methods) with learning activities since the two go hand in hand. *Instructional strategies* (or *teaching strategies*) are the techniques teachers use throughout instruction—whether it be a structure, procedure, or process—to make learning attainable for all students. *Learning activities* are the tasks students engage in to practice and demonstrate their learning. Sometimes the tools teachers use for a strategy during instruction also serve as the activity or assessment. For example, students completing a graphic organizer is an effective strategy *and* learning activity useful for multiple purposes, such as organizing information, preplanning a writing piece, or demonstrating knowledge of a concept. This is a tool that students use to facilitate their learning and which teachers can collect and use for formative assessment (Glass, 2012).

This chapter features three specific teaching strategies that we find particularly useful for preK through first-grade literacy instruction.

▶ Cooperative learning

▶ Graphic organizers

▶ Concept attainment

Each strategy is thoroughly explained, including its key principles, and has detailed steps for preparing, conducting, and adapting an activity that relies on the strategy. When perusing the presented strategies and capitalizing on your own inventory, consider ways to tailor any strategy for other learning targets. As you do so, heed researcher John Hattie's (2012) advice: evaluate the methods you choose. Hattie (2012) explains further, "When students do not learn via one method, it is more likely that it then needs to be re-taught using a different method; it will not be enough merely to repeat the same method again and again" (p. 96).

Cooperative Learning

Teachers strive to keep their students actively engaged in their learning throughout the entire school day. This is particularly important in the primary classroom as young learners endeavor to build stamina in focus and attention.

Cooperative learning is a powerful instructional strategy in which small groups work together to complete tasks. Cooperation among students enhances active listening as well as student confidence and motivation as they collaborate with peers to verbalize ideas, resolve conflict, and come to consensus. In step 1 of the kindergarten team's learning progression, students distinguish between a question and statement (figure 8.1). This paves the way for readers to ask questions to understand the author's message.

	Learning Progression Steps	Learning Progression Components	Assessments
↑	Step 1	**Knowledge Item:** Know the difference between a question and statement.	**Unobtrusive Formative Informal Preassessment: Teacher observation** From a list, identify examples of statements and questions.

Figure 8.1: Excerpt of learning progression—Step 1.

To cultivate an understanding of the distinction between statements and questions, teachers might implement a cooperative learning strategy called Numbered Heads Together, which allows students to work cooperatively and reach consensus on an answer (Kagan & Kagan, 2009). Individual and group accountability, as well as group behaviors such as active listening, taking turns, and cooperation, are strengthened through this process. The following five steps are a synopsis of the structure. We discuss it in more detail when explaining how to conduct the lesson.

1. Teachers begin by presenting students with a problem—in this case, distinguishing between sentences that are questions and sentences that are statements.

2. Teachers give students time to think about their responses and then participate in a team discussion.

3. Students privately record their answers using a whiteboard or choose an answer from prepared cards.

4. Students then stand up and discuss with teammates. During the discussion, students coach or praise each other, and sit back down to signify readiness.

5. Each group has one representative who shares with the whole class. The teacher calls a number, and students with that number answer simultaneously.

Cooperative learning as an instructional strategy shifts focus from teacher to student. Students actively participate in their learning as they share and discuss their ideas with peers.

Ensuring Key Principles

Professors David W. Johnson and Roger T. Johnson (n.d.) have identified five key principles of cooperative learning (and they are the steps of the Numbered Heads Together activity).

1. Positive interdependence

2. Face-to-face interaction

3. Individual and group accountability

4. Group behaviors

5. Group processing

Embedded within these principles is the idea that all students can be engaged at high levels. In addition, cooperative learning fosters positive socialization in early learners by addressing rudimentary academic and social skills such as taking turns, active listening, sharing ideas, and following directions (Price-Mitchell, 2015).

Positive Interdependence

Positive interdependence allows students to feel responsible for their own efforts as well as the group they are part of, whether the group consists of one, two, or three other members. When all members of a group contribute, the success of one student is connected to that of the others. This not only creates cooperation, but also boosts achievement as students seek to support each other's learning. Once positive interdependence is in place, a caring, cooperative community exists, which ultimately leads to an increase in student achievement in the process (Kagan, 2013).

Face-to-Face Interaction

Face-to-face interaction enables students to encourage and support one another and prevents a sit-and-get learning environment. In cooperative learning classrooms, teachers build time into the instructional day for face-to-face interactions, allowing students to share ideas, information, and materials with each other, as well as offer necessary support and feedback, and promote high-quality decision making and problem solving. This builds students' self-esteem and deepens social relations. Face-to-face interaction is particularly important for preK through first grade, because oral language surpasses reading and writing abilities. However, these skills must be explicitly taught, with teachers devoting time to helping these young learners master the art of active listening.

Individual and Group Accountability

Individual and group accountability confirm that each student is responsible for doing his or her part; each student is accountable for meeting her or his goal, just as each group is accountable for meeting its goal. Well-developed cooperative lessons build group members' capacity throughout the learning process, resulting in immense achievement gains. When individual accountability is in place, all team members master the learning target set before them (Slavin, 2014).

Because powerful literacy discussions don't happen naturally with primary learners, educators Laura Beth Kelly, Meridith K. Ogden, and Lindsey Moses (2019) suggest the LET'S Talk protocol:

- **L**isten and look at the speaker
- **E**qual participation

> ▸ **T**ake turns

> ▸ **S**it up and show respect

Using a structure such as Timed Pair-Share, primary learners individually share ideas with each other. Each partner takes a turn as both the speaker, as well as listener (Kagan & Kagan, 2009). Utilizing protocols like LET'S Talk ensures individual accountability as one hundred percent of students are sharing ideas, rather than the traditional *call on one student* at a time atmosphere present in many classrooms.

Group Behaviors

To successfully collaborate and work with others, students must possess interpersonal and small-group skills (Guido, 2017). Embedded within the cooperative learning environment lies a plethora of skills, such as active listening, taking turns, taking responsibility, apologizing, leadership skills, and teamwork skills. These nonacademic skills are imperative for students in all facets of life, in and beyond the classroom environment. Teachers need to be extremely intentional when planning for cooperative learning in selecting specific skills that match the learner's needs. As mentioned, when using the LET'S Talk protocol, teachers must reinforce expected behaviors such as listening to one another and taking turns (Kelly et al., 2019). In the very youngest learners, these skills take time to develop and need to be explicitly taught. These social skills aren't simply acquired. Just as we teach students how to read and write, so must we teach them how to get along with and listen to others.

Group Processing

Group processing offers members the opportunity to reflect on, analyze, and refine the work at hand, developing higher-level-thinking skills through feedback and building strong relationships. When group processing occurs, members analyze their own as well as the group's ability to work together. Certainly primary students are capable of reflecting and processing their collaborative efforts. Figure 8.2 (page 222) illustrates a reflective activity in which group members self-evaluate and evaluate peers following a literature discussion.

Table 8.1 (page 223) lists some kinds of cooperative learning structures that kindergarten teachers might use throughout a fiction unit. Although cooperative learning helps students engage in various aspects of a text, teachers employ others as well. This ensures students benefit from a wide array of learning experiences to fully delve into the richness and rigor of a text.

	Yes, I have it!	I am working on this.	My partner agrees.
I talked the whole time.			
I looked at my partner with my eyes.			
I listened to my partner with my ears.			
I took turns.			
I kept the events in order.			
I gave my partner praise.			

Figure 8.2: Group-processing reflection.

*Visit **go.SolutionTree.com/literacy** for a free reproducible version of this figure.*

Table 8.1: Cooperative Learning Activities in a Kindergarten Fiction Unit

Target or Skill	Structure	Student	Teacher
Answer questions about key details in a text.	Timed Pair-Share	In pairs, students share answers to questions with a partner for a predetermined amount of time while the partner listens.	Teacher asks questions and observes students as they share answers with a partner, gathering anecdotal notes for informal assessment.
Identify characters' traits using details from the story to describe what the character looks like, thinks, or feels, and what the character does.	Round-Robin	Working in small groups, students take turns responding orally to questions. Team member A begins, and, going clockwise, students each share their ideas.	The teacher asks questions and provides sentence stems to help students construct their answers (such as *I think Chrysanthemum is ____ because ____.*) Once teams are up and running, the teacher gathers unobtrusive data from students.
Recognize all upper- and lowercase letters of the alphabet.	Mix and Match	Students receive one card labeled with one upper- or lowercase letter. They move around the room to find their match. For example, a student with *A* finds the student with *a*.	The teacher observes students who may need support identifying their letter or their corresponding letter. Once all matches are found, the teacher scrambles cards and students repeat.
Segment syllables in spoken words.	Rally Coach	Using pictures or words, partners take turns. One answers the question, "How many syllables does ____ have?" while the other coaches. Partners then switch roles.	The teacher gathers informal data on students to determine proficiency seeing a picture or reading a word and breaking the word into parts as well as providing feedback to students who still need support.
Demonstrate basic knowledge of one-to-one letter-sound correspondences by producing the primary or many of the most frequent sounds for each consonant.	Quiz-Quiz Trade	Students receive one card labeled with a letter and move around the room quizzing one person at a time, posing the question, "What sound does this letter make?" Person A quizzes person B; then B quizzes A. Before they move onto another person, A and B trade cards. If either person A or B is incorrect, the other person coaches and gives hints for support.	The teacher gathers informal data on students to determine levels of proficiency on the ability to identify and name letters and letter sounds.

Source for standards: NGA & CCSSO, 2010.

Source: Kagan & Kagan, 2009.

Preparing

The following suggestions can help teachers prepare for an activity using cooperative learning and ensure that it runs smoothly.

▸ **Choose the appropriate structure to match the task at hand:** Learning and assessment objectives must be at the forefront when choosing a structure. The main objectives in cooperative learning are allowing students opportunities to demonstrate knowledge and interact with peers, while also providing teachers the ability to gather data unobtrusively.

▸ **Determine logistics:** Based on the learning target, teacher teams prepare questions and statements from a selected text. A visual representation is displayed on a SMART Board or poster. Students benefit from visuals as well; therefore, it is recommended to utilize pictures in addition to text to reinforce concepts. Student cards are created in advance. In this particular example, the teacher would distribute two cards to each student: a card with a *Q* for *question* and *S* for *statement*. An alternative method is to distribute whiteboards to the class and ask students to record *Q* or *S*.

▸ **Determine a recordkeeping tool:** Students record responses on a whiteboard or hold response cards in hand. During individual student work time, the teacher monitors student responses and records them in the form of anecdotal notes. As mentioned in chapter 2 (page 39), notes can be quickly jotted down or recorded on a premade template like that in figure 2.2 (page 45).

Conducting

To introduce how to correctly distinguish questions from statements, teachers ask students to participate in a read-aloud of a story, such as *Hooway for Wodney Wat* by Helen Lester and Lynn Munsinger (1999), which aligns nicely within the friendship and acceptance theme. Consider the following steps.

1. Students number off *one, two, three, four* in their own groups.

2. On a SMART Board or the like, teachers pose a problem for students to consider. For example, figure 8.3 offers a question or statement selected from the text *Hooway for Wodney Wat* (Lester & Munsinger, 1999). Students have individual think time before they privately write their answers on a whiteboard. As mentioned, each student might instead have a response card.

Question	"What's your name, Wodney?" (p. 6)
Statement	"His real name was Rodney Rat, but he couldn't pronounce his r's." (p. 5)
Statement	"To make matters worse, he was a rodent. A wodent." (p. 5)
Question	"What's another name for bunny?" (p. 6)
Question	"And how does a train travel?" (p. 7)
Statement	"A twain twavels on twain twacks." (p. 7)

Source: Adapted from Lester & Munsinger, 1999.

Figure 8.3: Questions and statements—Example.

3. Once all students have recorded their responses, they stand up and "put their heads together," showing their answers and discussing, thus engaging in face-to-face interaction and teaching each other. After everyone has shared and teammates have reached consensus, all members sit down to indicate their readiness. Because this structure is for recalling information, all team members erase their boards.

4. When all teams are seated, the teacher calls a number between one and four.

5. The students with the corresponding number simultaneously reproduce the team response and stand up to display their board as team representative. Teachers gather data and provide correction when needed.

6. Classmates celebrate their teamwork, and the process begins again.

Adapting

Teachers can utilize the Numbered Heads Together structure for determining if something is fiction or nonfiction, fact or opinion, a synonym or antonym. In addition, or in lieu of distinguishing information, this structure can be a tool like the one in figure 8.4 (page 226) for determining meaning in vocabulary words, identifying appropriate verb tense, counting syllables in a word, or creating compound words.

To differentiate, teachers can create smaller groups of three rather than four members. To scaffold, consider using picture support to provide context. Teachers can also conduct the activity ahead of time with a small group of students who may struggle. Or, rather than have students initially respond to the problem with individual think time, teachers can pair students at the beginning of the activity as a way of launching students' thinking together. Teachers continue recording unobtrusive data in this situation as they observe students working in pairs.

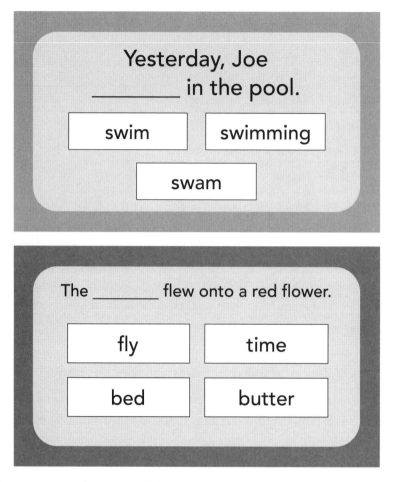

Figure 8.4: Appropriate verb tense and determining meaning.

Graphic Organizers

Graphic organizers are a staple in teachers' repertoire of instructional strategies across content areas. Teachers often collect a completed organizer to use as a formative assessment in determining levels of competency. In literacy, a graphic organizer serves as an effective reading and writing tool in myriad ways. It can do the following.

▶ Identify and explain the structure of a text.

▶ Brainstorm and collect ideas for a writing task.

▶ Organize information in a reading selection to deepen understanding.

▶ Demonstrate comprehension and communicate ideas.

▶ Record and categorize research notes.

▸ Learn new words and terms.

▸ Plot the sequence of a text.

In the friendship and acceptance unit example, the team created its own graphic organizer for students to use to determine different types of questions one could ask about details within stories.

In step 3 of the sample learning progression (an excerpt of which is in figure 8.5), students focus on ways they can frame questions.

	Learning Progression Steps	Learning Progression Components	Assessment
	Step 3	**Knowledge** Questions can ask *who, what, when, where, why,* and *how*.	**Unobtrusive, Informal Formative: Teacher observation** Students will engage in a small-group round-robin sharing of questions they generated about a text while the teacher observes.

Figure 8.5: Excerpt of learning progression—Step 3.

In this activity, teachers ask students to listen to a story and generate their own questions pertaining to details from the text. At this juncture, students revisit the text to deepen their understanding. This collaborative learning activity compels students not only to make inferences individually, but also rely on the input of group members to crystallize and extend their thinking together.

Ensuring Key Principles

Since all texts that students read (or listen to) and write maintain a structure, graphic organizers should mirror one of these common structures.

▸ Compare-contrast

▸ Problem-solution

▸ Cause-effect

▸ Sequence

▸ Description

To optimize its value, teachers select a specific type and format of organizer that focuses on a learning target. To do so, they can access these online resources or design their own organizer.

- edHelper.com at www.edhelper.com/teachers/graphic_organizers.htm
- Education Oasis at https://bit.ly/386nw5Y
- Freeology at http://freeology.com/graphicorgs
- Houghton Mifflin Harcourt Education Place at www.eduplace.com /graphicorganizer
- Teacher Files at www.teacherfiles.com/resources_organizers.htm
- TeacherVision at www.teachervision.com/lesson-planning /graphic-organizer

Several available organizers align to a particular text structure; therefore, teachers can differentiate by assigning or offering choices to students within an overarching structure. For example, a story map typically requires students to sequence ideas from a story from beginning, to middle, to end. That might be sufficiently challenging for some students, whereas others would benefit from an extended story map with five or more rungs to examine a more comprehensive sequence of events. Furthermore, some students prefer a story map organizer in a story mountain form, which leads to discussion around how stories change throughout.

Preparing

To prepare, teachers select a text, create a graphic organizer, and arrange students into pairs. Figure 8.6 has examples of questions from *Corduroy* by Don Freeman (1968), which complements the theme of friendship and acceptance.

Conducting

In the very early stages of the learning progression, students must know that questions can be asked and answered in a variety of ways. Participating in small-group discussions, sharing questions generated about text, helps make this clear. Organizers like the one in figure 8.6 ensures young learners are prepared for and able to fully participate in these conversations.

The five steps for the Read-n-Review activity follow.

1. The teacher reads the story aloud and leads the class in a brainstorming session to revisit key events, people, and places in the story.

2. The teacher then distributes a graphic organizer to each student pair. Early in the school year, young learners may not have the skills necessary to record ideas in writing. The teacher should encourage students to take

Who?		Who bought Corduroy?
What?		What did Corduroy lose on his shoulder strap?
When?		When did Corduroy look for his button?
Where?		Where did the night watchman put Corduroy?
Why?		Why was Corduroy happy at the end of the story?

Figure 8.6: Five Ws graphic organizer—Example.

*Visit **go.SolutionTree.com/literacy** for a free reproducible version of this figure.*

risks and record ideas in writing, as well as offer the option of drawing ideas in picture form.

3. Student pairs work together to recall details from the text. Partners take turns asking questions that begin with "Who." Rallying back and forth, partner A creates a question and asks partner B if he or she agrees with this question (Kagan & Kagan, 2009). An example follows.

Partner A: "I think a good who *question about this story is, Who bought Corduroy? Do you agree?"*

Partner B: "Yes, I agree!"

Partner B: "I think a good who *question about this story is, Who found Corduroy under the covers? Do you agree?"*

Partner A: "I agree!"

4. Repeat this process with questions beginning with *what, when, where,* and *why.* The partners alternate starting each time.

5. The teacher records anecdotal notes, which he or she will use to determine next steps for students.

Adapting

Teachers can utilize this graphic organizer strategy for fiction or nonfiction, to support identification of important details from the text. In addition to or in lieu of determining important details, this strategy can be a tool for students retelling a story or planning their own story when writing a narrative piece.

A structure such as Read-n-Review will enable students with opportunities to ask questions about details within a text (Kagan, Kagan, & Kagan, 2016). Within this structure, partners alternate; partner A reads or listens to a read-aloud while partner B has the opportunity to ask a question in regard to what has just been read. Partner A then answers. The process continues as partner A asks a question about what partner B has read.

To differentiate, teachers can arrange groups based on appropriately challenging text that appeals to the varying reading levels of students. To scaffold, consider working with students on one or more examples such as *why* or *when* questions, which might be more difficult for students to generate on their own. Teachers can partially complete the graphic organizer for groups that struggle. Or, they can participate at the beginning of the activity to launch students' thinking or prod them with hints, clues, or questions at any point students get stuck.

Concept Attainment

Concept attainment, a collaborative strategy that fosters critical thinking and decision making, produces a situation in which students productively struggle to process and understand concepts. To accomplish this, teachers orchestrate a well-planned series of directives aligned to a learning target across content areas. Specifically, teachers ask students to perform several tasks in the lesson to discern examples that do not have certain attributes, or *nonexamples.* Concept attainment challenges learners to identify categories and attributes, create definitions, and apply the new learning. In literacy, for example, teachers can implement this strategy to distinguish between characters, settings, and events; distinguish between questions and statements; determine methods of syllabication; identify patterns in words and word families; identify types of feelings; or identify types of writing.

Concept attainment can prove useful in disciplines other than literacy, such as when students identify plants or animals or investigate seasons. Concept attainment is particularly powerful for English learners, because it pairs a large variety of pictures and images, and it offers the chance to share ideas orally.

The following list articulates the concept-attainment steps at a high level (Glass, 2018). The next section applies those directions for a specific exercise to see this strategy in action.

1. **Examine and group a set of items according to their commonalities:** For this first step, teachers prepare a set of items for students to sort based on a learning target, such as pictures, words, or sentences. They can design this step in one of two ways—either students sort the items into categories (for example, characters, settings, and events), or students group in a yes-or-no construct in which some items represent examples (they belong together) while a random collection of other items are nonexamples. The following provides instruction to students for each approach.

    • *Option A*—"Study the _____ (pictures, words, or sentences). Group together items that share common elements. Be ready to share your reasoning."

    • *Option B*—"Study the _____ (pictures, words, or sentences). Group together those items that share common elements on one side. Put random items that don't share these elements on the other. Be ready to share your reasoning."

2. **Identify the specific attributes of this grouped set and name the set:** Instruct students to list the common attributes or distinguishing characteristics of the items of the grouped set and verify them with the class. Students state the name or concept for their groups (for example, *narrative elements* or *characters and non-characters*). If they are unfamiliar with the name of the grouped set, provide it and tell them that the targeted group with similar attributes becomes the focus going forward. If they group all items into separate categories (as in the preceding option A), then identify which category will receive attention first. Later, you can focus on another group of like items.

3. **Provide a definition:** Ask students to define the term or idea that is the focus for this activity. Student groups share their definitions with the class to arrive at a consensus. Ask students to record the attributes and definition on paper.

4. **Find and critique examples:** Guide students to resources, such as a text-book, print or digital article, website, video, or picture, and have them find examples of this skill that published authors, artists, or professionals in the field use. Instruct students to discuss and analyze these examples with group members and then share their interpretations or observations with the class. In this example, our youngest learners would be very adept at finding pictures of characters, settings, or events in magazines and books to support this important step in the process.

5. **Create examples:** Students review the items in the grouped set and use their list of these items' attributes, the definition, and the published work from the previous steps to construct new examples. For instance, if the grouped set includes settings, students list settings from familiar stories such as the forest Little Red Riding Hood walks through, or the house where Chrysanthemum lives. Further, if the set includes pairs of rhyming words, students construct their own rhyming word pairs. (Teachers can switch this step and step 4, if they prefer.)

6. **Apply the skill:** Students independently practice the skill by applying it, for example, to a piece of writing, a speech, or a drawing.

To personalize this strategy, the example centers on narrative elements: characters, settings, and events. Teachers refer to the complex text students have been exposed to as a resource for teaching this skill, so students experience authentic instances of established authors incorporating any skill that they will learn.

Step 7 of the learning progression focuses on answering questions about a character, setting, or event in a story (figure 8.7). This skill can be tricky since it is multilayered. To address the learning target in its entirety, character, setting, and events need to be incorporated into instruction.

	Learning Progression Steps	Learning Progression Components	Assessments
	Step 7	**Learning Target (Skill):** Answer questions about a character, setting, or event in a story, drawing on specific details in the text.	**Common Formative Informal: Constructed response** Teachers ask students to use a combination of drawing, dictating, and writing to explain how a character changes in a text.

Figure 8.7: Excerpt of learning progression—Step 7.

In this activity, teachers use concept attainment to introduce how characters, settings, and events can change throughout a story, and then ask students to apply what they learn by finding examples in text and writing about changes in narrative elements. For instance, when focusing on changes in characters' feelings, students sort pictures representative of characters throughout the story from other nonexamples (perhaps of a setting from the story). Once students have separated the examples from nonexamples, they choose two pictures to explain their thinking about how the character changed in the story. This typically happens in either a one-to-one conversation or in a written response.

Ensuring Key Principles

High-quality concept attainment for learners in these grades includes using visuals, teacher modeling, and providing ample opportunities to discuss ideas and justify thinking.

Preparing

Concept attainment begins with students using picture-card manipulatives that they will categorize into groups with a partner. The following steps will aid you in preparing a concept attainment lesson.

1. Find examples of narrative elements from the complex text students have been reading.

2. Ensure copyright law is followed, copy the pictures on heavy bond paper, laminate them, and cut them out. Make enough copies and enough heading cards labeled *Characters*, *Settings*, and *Events* for each pair of students working together, or have enough sticky notes for students to create their own heading cards.

3. Place a set of picture cards with a combination of characters, settings, and events in an envelope.

Conducting

To introduce characters, settings, and events, and how they can change in stories, follow these steps.

1. The teacher explains the following.

   - Characters are *who* is in a story (including people, animals, and sometimes creatures like aliens or robots).

- Setting refers to not only *where* a story takes place (such as a school, forest, or outer space) but also *when* the events occur (such as summer, Monday morning, or during lunch).

- Events are the *what* and *why* in stories (for example, learning to ride a bike, losing a tooth, or buying a puppy).

2. The teacher asks students to revisit a story they read previously and to pay attention to the narrative elements in the story. That story should include distinctive characters, settings, and events.

3. Conduct a quick picture walk, reviewing just the pictures rather than rereading the entire text. Revisit characters from the story to begin.

4. The teacher repeats the process twice, first by discussing setting and then again to determine important events from the text. If the class used the five Ws graphic organizer for the same book they're discussing now, the teacher could refer to it (figure 8.6, page 229) to connect the learning targets and solidify the learning.

Now the teacher will focus on concept attainment with these following seven steps.

1. Examine and group a set of items according to their commonalities. Distribute a set of picture cards to each pair with these instructions. Try the following script.

   Partners will receive an envelope with pictures from the story we have been reading in class. Look carefully to notice what the illustrations show. Then, categorize the pictures into different groups based on the narrative elements shown. Use the heading cards as you sort the pictures. Afterward, you will share your thinking with others in the class.

2. Identify the specific attributes of this grouped set. Ask each group to share how they grouped the pictures by answering these questions:

   - "What is similar about the items in this group?"

   - "What heading did you use for each group?"

   While students specify each group's common attributes and provide a title (or use a provided heading), feature the picture cards on a document camera or other projection device. Invite volunteers to come to the front and point to an example from the picture that supports their explanations. For example, a student might say, "These two pictures belong together because they each represent a setting from the story. They show where the character is, so we placed them under the group Settings." [Point to the tag.]

3. Invite students to return to their pictures and ensure that they are properly grouped and have the right headings: characters, settings, events.

4. Ask students to return to their pictures and determine why pictures were sorted together. For example, characters include people and animals and refer to who is in the story. All these pieces represent someone who is in the story. Provide these directions:

   With your partner, you will now pair up with a new group. Pairs will meet together to make a group of four. Team A will choose one picture to share and explain why they placed the picture under a specific heading. For example, Team A might say: "This is a picture of Corduroy. We placed him under the Character tag because Corduroy is who the story is about." Teams should discuss their ideas and determine if it is appropriate to celebrate agreement or discuss differing interpretations. Once teams agree, Team B chooses a different picture, shares and explains their thinking, and the process continues until we discuss all the picture cards.

5. Find and critique examples. After the initial exercise of sorting preselected pictures or text examples is complete, instruct each student to participate in a scavenger hunt, going through books to find examples of each narrative element (one at a time). This allows students to apply their knowledge about narrative elements by noticing them in the stories they read. Students then check with others in their group to be sure that the examples they found are correct. Partners should share one at a time to ensure equal participation.

6. Students create their own drawing and include a character, setting, and event from the text they used on an exit ticket. The teacher gathers these as students leave class and check them for understanding.

7. Teachers assign the following practice activity for students to demonstrate understanding during independent literacy rounds or centers. Students create a picture including all three narrative elements discussed and illustrate how these elements change throughout a story, utilizing a familiar story from a book bin or whole-group session. Teachers distribute paper that is divided into two, the left side representing the beginning and the right side designated for how these elements have changed.

   During a literacy station devoted to writing, students might also go to their personal stories to guarantee they have included all narrative elements within their own writing, and have represented how characters, settings, and events change throughout a story.

Adapting

As stated in the introduction of this section, teachers can incorporate the concept attainment strategy not only for learning the mechanics of writing, but across disciplines to stretch students' learning and facilitate self-discovery of concepts or ideas in myriad ways.

To differentiate for the featured narrative elements lesson, teachers can ask some partners to sort and others to categorize the pictures based on ability levels.

- ▸ **Sorting:** The teacher supplies students with the headings for each group (for example, "Characters"). This gives students an advantage of knowing how many groups they will ultimately form, plus the name for each. Therefore, during preparation, the teacher inserts the heading labels into the envelopes with the picture cards.

- ▸ **Categorizing:** This more cognitively challenging exercise asks students to determine how many groups they will fashion and the name for each.

Because this activity is done with young learners, teachers may want to add an accountability component by adding the answer in small letters to the back of the card. Students who are confused or unable to come to consensus can use this as a check and remain focused on the task at hand.

Another option is asking students to distinguish between examples and nonexamples. In this case, the teacher uses picture cards but asks students to focus on one narrative element at a time. For example, if using the book *Corduroy* (Freeman, 1968), groups begin by concentrating on just characters. They would place Corduroy, Lisa, Lisa's mother, and the night watchman in a *Yes* or *Example* pile, and place other pictures in another pile labeled *No* or *Nonexample*.

E X E R C I S E

Design a Lesson Using Gradual
Release of Responsibility

Chapter 6 (page 147) provides a research-based model for building well-orchestrated lessons. With the strategies presented in this chapter, along with those you and your team have acquired, use the learning progression to develop gradual release of responsibility lessons or enhance existing ones.

Use the following questions to guide this exercise.

★ How can our team use line items on the learning progression to design effective lessons? Can we divide the line items, draft lessons, and share with each other to maximize our time?

★ What strategies presented in this chapter meet the needs of students and align to our team's learning progression?

★ What other strategies can we collectively share as a team to support student learning and embed in lessons?

★ How will we assess student learning in the lessons?

★ How will we account for learners who do and do not master skills or who show they are ready for more?

Summary

Within instruction, it is incumbent upon teachers to select an appropriate strategy that meets the needs of students in moving their learning forward and mastering standards based on a learning progression. As Robert J. Marzano (2017) purports in *The New Art and Science of Teaching*, the focus of instruction should rest on student outcomes as opposed to teacher outcomes.

Teachers should also aim to infuse lessons with strategies that pique students' interest and engage them in the task at hand. Therefore, teachers should deliberately select strategies designed for students to accomplish a skill and check for understanding to ensure the strategy is producing the desired results. If a selected strategy misses the mark and students are unfortunately still grappling with proficiency, teachers need an alternate one to ensure students learn the targeted skills. The next chapter will present why addressing culture with literacy education is a necessity.

CHAPTER 9

Consider Equity in Literacy

Consider daily literacy activities that require even the most basic reading and writing skills. What percentage of your day or week might you spend reading any kind of text? What literacy skills did you need to get yourself to work today? Did you read signs along the road while driving or consult maps when accessing public transportation? What else in your week required a form of literacy? Did you sign a contract or consent form? Read a list or determine a budget in order to grocery shop? Peruse a restaurant menu? Fill out a voting ballot? Can you think of a job that does not, in some way, involve written communication?

Now, consider every form of communication you rely on to connect with the people in your life, from the internet and email to social media and text messages. To fully participate in society in the Information Age, teachers must provide *all* students a literacy level that positions them to participate and effectively function in society. They cannot afford to allow even one student to leave their care without guaranteeing he or she can read and write at grade level, as well as engage in fruitful discussions. In preK–1, literacy skills pave the way to all future learning.

What does this have to do with equity in learning? Well, if society strives to truly honor the fundamental tenet that all humans are created equal, it must ensure equal access to the necessary skills for all members in that society to aim for success. Literacy is an essential prerequisite for this endeavor and for full engagement in the world. It equips students with the essential building blocks that form the gateway to all learning. Through reading, writing, speaking, and listening, teachers grant their students access to the skills and resources necessary to fully appreciate a richly diverse society.

Teachers are living and educating students during important times filled with defining movements. From racial- and gender-equality movements to simply understanding and accepting the formation of one's identity, committed people passionately work to generate a society where everyone recognizes and accepts one another for each of our unique qualities. Schools and, more specifically, classrooms provide a venue for students to learn about building toward a more equitable and welcoming society in all its diverse glory. Within the classroom's walls, teachers strive to create a cohesive and inclusive learning environment as a microcosm of a broader, accepting society. In this regard, educators model and teach how to be inclusive of others despite differences—or, rather, *because of* differences.

Learning about each individual, including his or her preferences and experiences, is important. Students who might, at a glance, have similar characteristics should not lead teachers to make assumptions. Remember, teachers are charged with creating experiences and environments that advance the belief that all humans are equal and appreciate differences.

This approach also helps to create environments in which all students are able and willing to take risks to learn. Teachers aim for this goal but often feel ill-equipped to establish it. Therefore, this chapter supports educators in this regard and addresses how teachers and administrators can answer the following compelling and difficult questions concerning equitable school practices. These queries require teachers and administrators to be vulnerable and face what could be brutal facts about the current state of equitable practices in their classrooms and schools. Since movements abound, and the richness of a diverse world has expanded, teams should also generate additional questions, such as the following, while reading to examine other issues that affect their students and school.

- "How can our team and school identify and eliminate invisible biases that might influence our instructional approach to students and affect their trust in us?"

- "How can our team and school avoid excluding any student from rigorous learning opportunities in curricula and promote high expectations for all students?"

- "How can our team ensure the resources we select or are asked to use authentically reflect the demographics of our students, diverse perspectives, and the experiences of others?"

Teachers can generate other questions to address issues that their teams or schools confront. Students will likely generate questions without being prompted to do so. These young learners are naturally curious, questioning issues that adults might be ill prepared to address.

The following sections address equity of access to three fundamental aspects of teaching that align to the previously posed questions: (1) instruction, (2) expectations, and (3) resources. These sections act as our final roadmap to ensuring all preK through first-grade students leave your team's care with a strong foundation in literacy skills that will serve them well in future grades and in life. Educators working together as part of a strong PLC culture have the potential to make a positive impact for students, schools, and society but only if they are willing to step up to do the hard, reflective work on an ongoing basis. It is an educator's obligation, as a person in a position to positively influence students, to ensure each student—regardless of gender, race, ethnicity, language, or abilities—feels included in his or her classroom's culture. Your team's approach to literacy instruction can be a critical part of making that happen. Focusing on the material in this chapter can facilitate open conversations and perhaps necessary change for the betterment of your students.

Access to Instruction

Before working toward equity in curriculum and resources, your teacher team might begin with the following steps.

1. Examine, privately or publicly, any personal biases that might be present in how everyone approaches students. This is not about blame or judgment. It's simply important and valuable to look critically at the intended and unintended messages we might send to students through words and actions. This critical introspection will prove challenging but rewarding because it fosters growth, perhaps uncovering instruction areas that require revision.

2. Invite team members to share and acknowledge examples of inclusivity from each classroom. Then, ask yourselves how your instructional approaches might foster or inhibit equitable practices in the classroom, particularly as they pertain to literacy.

3. Articulate what existing or new practices lead to more equitable outcomes. While engaging in this discussion, you might discover a sense of vulnerability or the need to confront some uncomfortable issues. Open, honest dialogue is healthy and might result in identifying one area as a team focus to promote the kind of change that benefits all your students.

To practice, this section offers an examination of factors teams should consider in how their approach to gender, as only one defining difference among people, might influence their instruction. After this reflection, we challenge educators to learn more about other defining differences and apply a similar analysis.

To begin, gender is not binary—but we encourage our students to identify either as either a boy or a girl. Researchers state that gender is multidimensional residing somewhere along a continuum or spectrum (Bockting, 2008; Connell, 2009; Harrison, Grant, & Herman, 2012). Some students may not explicitly identify solely with one gender, and gender does not always characterize one's inclinations and tastes. For example, women and girls can enjoy sports and play video games, which are often thought of as traditionally masculine preferences. Additionally, men and boys might choose to dress in pink or play with dolls, traits traditionally regarded as feminine. Transgender individuals might possess a sense that their gender identity misaligns to their physical anatomy around the time they enter second grade:

> Research indicates that there is a significant gap between a child's under-standing that their gender doesn't conform to expectations and when they communicate with others (namely parents) about it. In one study, the average age of self-realization for the child that they were transgender or non-binary was 7.9 years, but the average age when they disclosed their understanding of their gender was 15.5. (Gender Spectrum, n.d.b)

According to Gender Spectrum (n.d.a), "gender non-conforming behavior in preadolescents is particularly visible [and] . . . most of them are already aware that they do not fit expected gender norms," and while some youth communicate trans-gender or nonbinary identity with relative ease or confidence, others feel uncom-fortable, experience bullying, and become withdrawn (Gender Spectrum, n.d.b). A teacher's support and understanding can go a long way.

How do you group students? You or other team members may group them based on gender with the best of intentions, as this can be an efficient or familiar grouping strategy. However, this sends the message that students are defined based on their gender. Avoid singling out gender as a defining characteristic, which sig-nals to students that they ought to identify with all the associated aspects that a particular culture deems as the norm. In fact, grouping by gender, which implies a clear-cut identification of male or female, can be confusing to students grappling with their gender identity.

Grouping by gender can be harmful to students if their preferences are inad-vertently reinforced as being wrong. Instead, use themes, colors, or shapes to arrange students into groups; randomly assign them by drawing sticks; or leave it up to students to formulate their own groups. Research shows that "stereotyping in childhood has wide-ranging and significant negative consequences for both women and men, with more than half (51%) of people affected saying it constrained their career choices and 44% saying it harmed their personal relationships" (Fawcett Society, 2019). In the case of grouping, any students with a nonbinary identification who question their gender may feel forced to select one group or the other. When confronted with such a choice, no safe space exists for these students. Research also confirms the damage this causes.

Gender stereotyping "is harmful when it limits women's and men's capacity to develop their personal abilities, pursue their professional careers and make choices about their lives" (Office of the High Commissioner for Human Rights, n.d.).

Diversity education expert Dana Stachowiak (2018f) asserts that "literacy classrooms are spaces with unique opportunities to do the work of creating an environment that is gender inclusive" (pp. 29–30). Committing to the following six actions can increase gender inclusivity (Stachowiak, 2018f).

1. Learn and understand terms and definitions.
2. Work through your own biases and beliefs.
3. Be proactive, not reactive.
4. Plan to support gender-noncomforming students.
5. Integrate, don't separate, curricula.
6. Commit to growing.

To become more educated about this area so you can strive to create a gender-inclusive classroom environment, consider reading the full article, "The Power to Include" (Stachowiak, 2018f), as well as the following five-part blog series Stachowiak wrote to complement that work.

1. "Terms and Definitions for Gender-Inclusive Classrooms" (Stachowiak, 2018a)
2. "Interrogating Bias" (Stachowiak, 2018b)
3. "Classroom Inventory" (Stachowiak, 2018c)
4. "Supporting Gender Noncomforming Students" (Stachowiak, 2018d)
5. "Creating a Gender-Inclusive Curriculum" (Stachowiak, 2018e)

Gender is just one example of many that teams must consider when making instructional choices. Other dimensions that render us diverse are also important. For example, how does the various religions your students might practice impact the classroom? Celebrating the month of December with a high emphasis on typically Christian traditions surely confuses or potentially excludes your students who identify as Jewish or Jehovah's Witness, as two examples. Further, is the only time you celebrate rich African American history in the month of February when requested to do so? Students who identify as black deserve to see themselves represented in our curriculum all year long. We implore teams to consider reflecting on how literacy instruction might reflect invisible biases or suppositions that could send overt and covert, unintentional messages to students whose identities are still forming. Race, culture, and religion are all areas we implore teams to explore when reflecting on how instruction might reflect invisible biases or suppositions that could send overt and covert, unintentional messages to students whose identities are still forming. The following sections examine some of these through the lens of curriculum and resources.

Access to High Expectations

It may seem unnecessary to ask the question, "Should any student be excluded from rigorous learning opportunities?" Obviously, the answer is no. Sadly, some educators quickly jump to unfounded conclusions about student capabilities and determine that perhaps some students are not ready for or able to participate in rigorous learning experiences. Or, an educator may apply arbitrary reasoning to determine that certain students are not competent enough to learn all the standards that others typically address in their grade level. Both are fallacies. With the exception of those who have a significant cognitive impairment, all students are entitled to and obligated to master all standards.

Generally, we observe learning opportunities are withheld, to various degrees, from three different groups of students who are able to meet grade-level standards.

1. Students who are evaluated and qualify for an individualized education plan or who are entitled to specific learning goals as a result of having a disability and are therefore labeled as students in special education

2. Students who are culturally and linguistically diverse but not yet English proficient and are therefore labeled as English learners

3. Students who begin school disadvantaged in some way, such as economically, or who lacked access to early learning and therefore are unfairly labeled *low* performers

The students who fit into these groups possess thinking and learning assets. However, some teachers possess limiting beliefs about them, which results in lowered expectations for these students. This dynamic of unfairly setting inappropriate expectations can inadvertently sabotage students' success:

> Such judgments about capability often apply stereotypes about social groups such as about race and gender, reflect myths about development and behavior, confuse what is with what could be, and put too much weight on test scores rather than daily performance as evidence of ability. The actions taken in response to these judgments often determine very different learning opportunities and convey strong messages about capability. (Weinstein, 2002, p. 4)

Consider a common, unintentional mistake that leads to inherent inequities in access to education: Educators often think a student identified as an English learner lacks skills and cannot achieve the standards. Educators spend a significant amount of time focusing on those prerequisite language skills and fail to provide instruction in the actual grade-level standards prior to the end of the academic school year. This propels a vicious cycle in which the student cannot catch up, resulting in lost learning opportunities. When this occurs, the teachers miss the importance of having a learning progression to achieve a standard (chapter 3, page 61), nor do they use individual student data to drive instruction (chapter 5, page 121). Further, these teachers neglect to design optimal literacy instruction (chapter 7, page 163). Making inaccurate assumptions that lead to lower expectations may lead teachers to use less-rigorous strategies, groupings, and materials, producing less growth or no growth for students in this population.

Therefore, teachers must realize their influence on students and present possibilities for them. Teams can examine the following examples and formulate concrete ways to apply the strategies in classrooms (Budge & Parrett, 2018):

- Articulate the belief that students can achieve at high levels
- Create warm social-emotional relationships focused on strengths, funds of knowledge, cultural understandings, interests, and aspirations
- Provide informative feedback on performance to scaffold learning
- Teach content and use tasks with high cognitive demand
- Ask frequent, high-level questions
- Encourage a productive struggle (refraining from giving answers, allowing wait time, guiding to answer)
- Maintain close physical proximity
- Interact frequently
- Use positive nonverbal communication (p. 81)

Another detrimental situation that aligns to limiting expectations is when we assign labels to students. For example, students with disabilities are often named *SPED* (short for *special education*) or *IEP kids*. Students who work to acquire English are often referred to as *limited* in some way, which is shortsighted since they may understand conceptual ideas but not yet be able to communicate that understanding in English. Further, some students are called *low* due to a disadvantage they encountered at some point in their life that might be ill-defined.

In reality, these students are capable of learning grade-level standards; their learning needs just look different than other students' needs do (DuFour et al., 2016). Unfortunately, no positive asset orientation is associated with these students, as unwarranted expectations and labels cloud teachers' vision, misrepresent students, and communicate what students cannot do rather than what they can.

Education authors Kathleen M. Budge and William H. Parrett (2018) provide a powerful insight into the negative ramifications of using labels that has merit in this discussion. How can teachers reframe the way educators refer to students in these subgroups?

> How we think about and refer to our students is an important consideration. . . . Words are powerful, and they often can perpetuate or challenge our beliefs. Have you ever thought about the various ways we describe our students who live in poverty—*Title I kids, free and reduced-priced meals kids, low-SES kids, high-poverty kids,* or *poverty-kids*? What do we mean when we use these labels? What is a "high-poverty kid"? What do the kids and others think when they hear these terms? (p. 22)

Further, these labels also lead to assumptions about students' abilities. Instead of making assumptions, educators must gain accurate estimations of students' learning needs and knowledge. As John Hattie (2012) presents in *Visible Learning for Teachers*, educator estimates of student achievement have a profound impact on students' learning. In fact, students can yield four years' worth of academic growth in one school year when educators have positive estimates of student achievement, or clear data, as this gives teachers more accurate knowledge of the students in their classes. Accurate knowledge of students results in more-rigorous learning opportunities, learning materials, instructional strategies, and questioning techniques that closely match students' needs, which produces academic growth. Making inaccurate assumptions, in the absence of data, may lead teachers to use less-rigorous strategies, groupings, and materials, producing less growth or no growth for students. Therefore, whatever we think students are capable of will become their ceiling, as we are the drivers who create the ceiling.

Teachers need to address the question, "How can our team and school avoid excluding any student from rigorous learning opportunities and promote high expectations for all students?" If there are teaching practices that exclude some students from grade-level learning, teachers must work collaboratively to identify how to include all students, or educators run the risk of creating a low ceiling for students. For example, can they shift from an English learner pull-out model, in which students are removed from Tier 1 instruction, to a model that allows these students to participate in classroomwide Tier 1 instruction? Similarly, teams must address if the needs of students who qualify for an IEP can be met with accommodations or modifications within the classroom.

In our experience, some teachers catalog the obstacles that deter them from supporting these students as a means to justify limiting students' access to the curriculum; for example, they record the ideas that programmatic shifts are larger than any one person can consider or implement, that these shifts take time and resources, and that administrators and the board of education generally need to approve them. If discouragement sets in within your team, endeavor to adopt the mindset that change certainly can occur, and begin to educate and engage in supportive, critical conversations as an ally to your most vulnerable students. Remind teachers that they must maintain high expectations for all students within literacy instruction (and across content areas) since the key learning associated with literacy skills supports students in success beyond school. Excluding students risks further marginalizing populations that have been historically treated as peripheral.

Access to Resources

In addition to providing all students with a rigorous education that prepares them for their futures, teachers should provide students with diverse perspectives through access to a plethora of culturally rich resources. It's not enough to simply select texts that align to learning targets; teachers must ensure students read texts that are written from culturally diverse perspectives. As a result, all educators need to ask and address the crucial question, "How can I ensure the resources I select or am asked to use authentically reflect the demographics of my students, diverse perspectives, and the experiences of others?" To attend to this question, teachers should aim to provide a variety of culturally responsive classroom texts that create both mirrors and windows for students. As such, reflect on this quote from Aline O'Donnell (2019): "Curriculum can serve as a mirror when it reflects your own culture and identity, as well as a window when it offers a view into someone else's experience" (p. 19).

Critical to student identity development is a sense of belonging and acceptance (Brendtro, Brokenleg, & Van Bockern, 2019). Teachers can help provide students with this sense of inclusion by ensuring that students see pieces of their identity positively represented in the texts that they read, discuss, and analyze in the classroom. In this regard, teachers invite students to hold up mirrors. Additionally, resources can create windows for them by exposing them to a breadth and depth of perspectives and experiences that expand their own view of the world. These windows give students an opportunity to appreciate diverse perspectives from their immediate surroundings, the greater community, and beyond. When students of a dominant culture do not experience "windows into the realities of the multicultural world," they are at risk of "developing a false sense of their own importance in the world" in relation to others (Bishop, 1990, p. 9). So, let's be clear about the meaning of *diversity*.

People often use the term *diversity* in reference to race, class, or gender identity or expression; however, it encompasses so much more. It also includes ethnicity, age, sexual or affectual orientation, geographic background, spirituality or religious beliefs, learning style and abilities, marital or partner status, parental or caregiver status, national origin, language, economic status and background, work experiences, personality, and education. The totality of an individual derives from his or her fixed and fluid traits, characteristics, and experiences. As teachers make decisions about selecting diverse texts, they must commit to learning about each individual student, including his or her preferences and experiences. Additionally, teachers must exercise caution to avoid making assumptions about people who might outwardly appear to have similar characteristics when they may perhaps differ completely. It is a teacher's charge to use classroom resources to create learning experiences and environments that further the belief that all humans are created equally and that everyone can appreciate what makes each individual unique.

Part of this challenge is that teachers often do not have experience in the vast array of cultures represented by their students. Therefore, they may find it very difficult to know how to successfully incorporate these cultures when choosing resources to support instruction. As a result, teachers commonly make the mistake of believing they must understand *everything* about their students' backgrounds before they can adopt a *culturally responsive pedagogy*—that is, instruction that helps students connect their learning to their own cultural experience. In "Partnering With Families and Communities," Katherin Garland and Kisha Bryan (2017) explain why this isn't accurate:

The most successful implementation happens when teachers partner with families and community members to negotiate classrooms' cultures and curricula that actually reflect the communities where students develop and grow. Family and community members can play a major role in teachers' plans to (1) communicate high expectations to all students, (2) help students learn within the context of their cultures, and (3) value students' cultural backgrounds through content integration. (p. 52)

With this in mind, and at the onset of your team's audit of current resources for diverse representation or selecting new resources, consider the fact that the very nuances that we identify by are not monoliths. In other words, one story does not tell the story of all who identify with a cultural group. Not all individuals that identify as female, for example, have similar stories, preferences, or experiences. Therefore, it is impossible and not expected that teachers know everything about all dimensions of diversity that make individuals different from one another. But educators must have a willingness to learn and gain perspective through asking questions of others. Colleagues, parents, and students can be incredible allies in our own education, and most prove willing to tell their story. However, teachers often hold back when they have a curious impulse. They may not ask questions for fear of offending someone or saying the wrong thing. While it is true that some people may not appreciate educating others about their background, the vast majority of people are happy to share with educators about their identities, recognizing that helping others learn creates a more inclusive society. Teachers have to engage in and commit to the vulnerable act of learning from others.

Consider the following example: Our team member worked in a suburban school district outside Chicago where Katie Sheridan, director of language and early literacy, asked each administrator from across the district to interview a parent from a background different from their own. Many families in the school community were immigrants, and this exercise was intended to create connections between the school and home environments as a part of a district goal to build cultural proficiency and intercultural skills. The experience would allow administrators to gain insight into their students' cultures and share what they learned with colleagues in the school community so they could positively impact students' experiences at school (K. Sheridan, personal communication, May 2, 2019).

Many administrators wished they had a prepared script of questions to pose, as they felt anxious about approaching parents for a candid conversation on potentially sensitive topics. Intentionally, Katie did not provide a script since she hypothesized the administrators might have cycled through the protocol of questions rather than truly concentrate and engage in effortless dialogue. Instead, they were instructed to begin the conversation by asking, "What do you think I need to know about you—for example, your country of origin, background, family, religion, or culture—that will help me better educate your child or children?" Authentically listening to what parents had to share presented a lesson unto itself.

Based on the reason they selected a particular parent, the administrators each steered the conversation and posed questions. Unsurprisingly, responses were diverse and often centered on differences in education systems in other countries. Some parents pointed out the deficit of diverse resources and the lack of images of people who resembled their families on the school or classroom walls. Parents shared stories of their children feeling uncomfortable in school because teachers used resources that included stereotypes of the children's background. As the administrators probed further to learn more, an easy, fluid exchange of conversation emerged and lasted longer than anticipated.

After the discussions, the administrative team members met to share what they each gleaned from parents to educate one another. At times, they discovered conflicting views among the parents. For example, some parents thought their children's homework lacked rigor because their experience of homework had been different as students. Other parents felt strongly that homework intruded on quality family time in the evenings. In this case, the administrative team admitted it was unable to make changes that catered to every perspective on homework.

Another recurring concern the administrators learned from families was that many students did not see themselves represented in the school. They took this feedback to heart. As a result, they guaranteed change since the inadequate display of diversity on the walls was unintentional and certainly lacked presence of mind. For the team, this meaningful experience launched a journey to discover what else they had overlooked by neglecting key cultural implications; thus, the team committed to continuous learning and improvement to inculcate diversity into the fabric of the school and across the district.

The most significant lesson the administrators learned from this experience was to refrain from making assumptions, learn about diverse perspectives, and be forthright and comfortable to ask questions. Educators must engage in and commit to the vulnerable act of learning from others. As educators, we sometimes hold back when we have a curious impulse. We recoil from asking questions for fear of offending someone or saying something wrong. In truth, there are those who may not appreciate educating others about their background. But many willingly share about their identities and recognize that helping others learn about myriad cultures creates a more inclusive society for everyone, their children included.

As your team audits and enhances the current resources in your classrooms in concert with the demographics of your community, work with your best resources: your colleagues, your students, and your students' parents. To further this effort to select culturally responsive texts, Sharroky Hollie (2019) advises teachers to be cognizant of three text types. This knowledge will assist your team in wisely choosing core texts that reflect students culturally and linguistically.

1. **Culturally authentic texts:** This preferred text type refers to fiction or nonfiction that mirrors authentic cultural experiences of a certain group. It might focus on religion, gender, ethnicity, geographic location, or other aspects of culture. (Access www.responsivereads.com to find culturally authentic titles.)

2. **Culturally generic texts:** Although these texts center on characters with racial identities, they include few or superficial cultural details about these characters within the overall storyline.

3. **Culturally neutral texts:** This least-preferred culturally responsive type of text is considered neutral because, although the text focuses on a character of color, the other aspects of the story—its plot, theme, or methods of characterization—are largely traditional or mainstream. Teachers might select these texts for other purposes, such as to focus on the author's strong use of figurative language, vocabulary, or suspense. But in doing so, they should not mistake these texts for culturally responsive texts when their value is more predicated on the author's craft.

When selecting a text, if possible, select texts that are culturally authentic, and use what you've learned from your students and their parents to help in this endeavor. Keep in mind that one story does not tell the whole narrative of all who identify with a gender or cultural group. It is impossible to know everything about all dimensions of diversity that make us different from one another. Therefore, solicit input from your colleagues, your students, and your students' parents, many of whom are incredible allies and will likely prove willing to educate teacher teams and freely share about their cultures. Be receptive to learning by asking them questions that allow you to gain perspective, as this can ultimately prove useful when selecting texts.

Works from authors of all different cultures and backgrounds artfully bring stories and the world to life that touch on a variety of topics and themes that students might find relevant and interesting. In addition, provide a spotlight on authors who craft texts that reflect their own personal experiences and, therefore, provide an additional dimension into a culture. Of chief importance is your team's awareness of the impact the literature it selects will have on every student in its classrooms. No single text will resonate immediately to the experience of all students, but providing an array of rich texts that positively contribute to building students' knowledge, cultural awareness, and acceptance will ensure students grow not only as readers and writers but as human beings.

EXERCISE

Answer Important Questions About Access

Educators' job includes creating an inclusive environment in which students appreciate differences. Literacy can serve as a vehicle for expanding students' thinking and exposing them to the richness of the world. Through culturally responsive texts, they experience people, places, and situations perhaps previously unfamiliar to them. Engage in discussions with your team to determine how you and your team members can make classrooms more inclusive and literacy materials more diverse and culturally authentic.

Use the following questions to guide this exercise.

★ Do we send unintended messages about student identities through our day-to-day instructional practices? If so, how might we reconsider our actions or words?

★ How can we positively shift our collective mindset and language we use when referring to students that need something different? What language can we adopt that shows an asset-based orientation?

★ Do the resources that we select, or that we are asked to use, reflect the demographics of students in our classroom in an authentic way? Do they reflect diverse perspectives and experiences of others?

★ As we audit the demographics in our classrooms, do the resources we use show a balanced representation of who is in our classrooms and the rest of the world? Or do texts predominantly reflect one perspective? If so, how can we alter our plans to appeal to our students' characteristics?

★ How do we know our resources support diverse cultural experiences? Have we engaged with an ally of that demographic background? Have we considered the author of the text and to what degree the author's experience is authentic?

Summary

We have the opportunity to substantially improve the education experience and outcomes of our students. Literacy instruction is the place to begin this change. Each and every student of a different gender, race, ethnic background, language ability, disability, or other difference contributes to the collective composition and uniqueness of a classroom, school, and community. Educators of literacy, in particular, are privileged to provide students with access to learning experiences and resources that highlight and celebrate what each student brings to the classroom and world. With literacy instruction, students read about, write about, talk about, and listen to issues and discussions surrounding equity. Engaging in diverse texts and thoughtful discussions that spawn a change in perspective engenders appreciation for the lives others live and the way they think, which might be different from our own way of living and thinking.

Through teachers' thoughtful guidance, students can transfer what they learn within the class to their communities and make inclusive contributions. This chapter is but a starting point to a potentially rich conversation, and a launching point for action through which teams can use literacy education as a powerful tool toward inclusivity.

EPILOGUE

Undeniably, possessing strong literacy skills can benefit all members in our society. The International Literacy Association (2019) asserts in its position statement that "the ability to identify, understand, interpret, create, compute, and communicate using visual, audible, and digital materials across disciplines and in any context—and access to excellent and equitable literacy instruction are basic human rights" (p. 1).

Whether teaching students to function as generators or receivers of written, digital, or oral discourse, a teacher's obligation is to advance students' literacy capabilities so they can actively and fully engage in our world. Building capacity around literacy instruction is truly the strongest catalyst for supporting student growth in every area of school curriculum.

As schools commit to exemplary instruction to advance learning, the power of a PLC must not be overlooked. Regardless of the team structure in your PLC, this work always begins with teaming teachers who are focused on improving their own capacity to impact student learning. Teams dedicate themselves to working collaboratively to position students for success. Specifically, these teams of professionals engage in the PREP process to unwrap standards and identify learning targets, create a learning progression, design assessment tasks and rubrics, develop differentiated lessons, collect and analyze data to inform instruction, and intervene to provide necessary support all in an effort to move students' learning forward.

Teachers possess an awesome responsibility to increase students' literacy capacity that opens the doors wide to myriad and boundless opportunities. Teachers working in cohesive, effective, and goal-oriented teams can more capably educate students who will forge ahead with more confidence to meet the next challenge that lies ahead for them. Preparing them amply is our responsibility. Let us embrace this awesome duty.

APPENDIX A:

PREP TEMPLATE AND OTHER TOOLS

This appendix provides a series of reproducible tools your team can use as teachers build literacy-focused curriculum and supporting instruction. Here you will find the complete version of the PREP template (including slots for adding essential understandings and guiding principles) and other tools.

PREP Template

Unit: _____   Time Frame: _____

Grade: _____

Unit Standards

Essential Understandings (optional)	Guiding Questions (optional)

Strand (Reading Literature, Reading Informational Text, Writing, Language, and so on):

-
-
-
-
-

Reading and Writing Instruction for PreK Through First-Grade Classrooms in a PLC at Work © 2020 Solution Tree Press
SolutionTree.com • Visit **go.SolutionTree.com/literacy** to download this free reproducible.

Strand (Reading Literature, Reading Informational Text, Writing, Language, and so on):

-
-
-
-
-

Strand (Reading Literature, Reading Informational Text, Writing, Language, and so on):

-
-
-
-
-

Strand (Reading Literature, Reading Informational Text, Writing, Language, and so on):

-
-
-
-

Unwrapped Unit Priority Standards	Knowledge Items	Skills (Learning Targets and DOK Levels)

Learning Progression and Assessments Template

Priority Standard (or Standards):			

	Learning Progression Steps	Learning Progression Components	Assessments
	Step ____	**Priority Standard (or Standards):**	
	Step ____	**Learning Target (Skill) or Knowledge**	
	Step ____	**Learning Target (Skill) or Knowledge**	
	Step ____	**Learning Target (Skill) or Knowledge**	

page 1 of 2

Step ____	**Learning Target (Skill) or Knowledge**	
Step ____	**Learning Target (Skill) or Knowledge**	
Step ____	**Learning Target (Skill) or Knowledge**	
Step ____	**Learning Target (Skill) or Knowledge**	
Step ____	**Learning Target (Skill) or Knowledge**	
Step ____	**Learning Target (Skill) or Knowledge**	

Protocol to Unwrap Priority Standards

Directions: To unwrap priority standards, answer the following questions.

1. **What priority standard (or standards) are we targeting?** Record the priority standard in the space provided.

2. **What will students need to do to be proficient?** Find and capitalize (or circle) pertinent verbs in the standard. The verbs—together with the content and concepts (step 3)—pinpoint the exact skills students need in order to achieve proficiency of this standard. List the verbs in the space provided

3. **With what content and concepts will students need to apply these skills?** Find and underline the nouns and phrases which represent the content and concepts to be taught, and list them in the space provided.

Tool to Unwrap Priority Standards

Unit Priority Standards	Knowledge	Skills (Learning Targets and DOK Levels)

Read-Aloud Text Complexity: Qualitative Measures Rubric—Informational Texts

In prekindergarten through first grade, use this rubric to determine the complexity of read-aloud texts. The majority of students in these grades will not read complex texts independently.

Text Title: _____   Text Author: _____

	Exceedingly Complex	Very Complex	Moderately Complex	Slightly Complex
Text Structure	○ **Organization:** Is intricate with regard to such elements as point of view, time shifts, multiple characters, storylines and detail ○ **Use of Graphics:** If used, illustrations or graphics are essential for understanding the meaning of the text	○ **Organization:** May include subplots, time shifts and more complex characters ○ **Use of Graphics:** If used, illustrations or graphics support or extend the meaning of the text	○ **Organization:** May have two or more storylines and occasionally be difficult to predict ○ **Use of Graphics:** If used, a range of illustrations or graphics support selected parts of the text	○ **Organization:** Is clear, chronological or easy to predict ○ **Use of Graphics:** If used, either illustrations directly support and assist in interpreting the text or are not necessary to understanding the meaning of the text
Language	○ **Conventionality:** Dense and complex; contains abstract, ironic, and/or figurative language ○ **Vocabulary:** Complex, generally unfamiliar, archaic, subject-specific, or overly academic language; may be ambiguous or purposefully misleading ○ **Sentence Structure**: Mainly complex sentences with several subordinate clauses or phrases; sentences often contain multiple concepts	○ **Conventionality:** Fairly complex; contains some abstract, ironic, and/or figurative language ○ **Vocabulary:** Fairly complex language that is sometimes unfamiliar, archaic, subject-specific, or overly academic ○ **Sentence Structure:** Many complex sentences with several subordinate phrases or clauses and transition words	○ **Conventionality:** Largely explicit and easy to understand with some occasions for more complex meaning ○ **Vocabulary:** Mostly contemporary, familiar, conversational; rarely unfamiliar or overly academic ○ **Sentence Structure:** Primarily simple and compound sentences, with some complex constructions	○ **Conventionality:** Explicit, literal, straightforward, easy to understand ○ **Vocabulary:** Contemporary, familiar, conversational language ○ **Sentence Structure:** Mainly simple sentences

Reading and Writing Instruction for PreK Through First-Grade Classrooms in a PLC at Work © 2020 Solution Tree Press
SolutionTree.com • Visit **go.SolutionTree.com/literacy** to download this free reproducible.

	Exceedingly Complex	Very Complex	Moderately Complex	Slightly Complex
Meaning	o **Meaning:** Multiple competing levels of meaning that are difficult to identify, separate, and interpret; theme is implicit or subtle, often ambiguous and revealed over the entirety of the text	o **Meaning:** Multiple levels of meaning that may be difficult to identify or separate; theme is implicit or subtle and may be revealed over the entirety of the text	o **Meaning:** Multiple levels of meaning clearly distinguished from each other; theme is clear but may be conveyed with some subtlety	o **Meaning:** One level of meaning; theme is obvious and revealed early in the text.
Knowledge Demands	o **Life Experiences:** Explores complex, sophisticated or abstract themes; experiences portrayed are distinctly different from the common reader o **Intertextuality and Cultural Knowledge:** Many references or allusions to other texts or cultural elements	o **Life Experiences:** Explores themes of varying levels of complexity or abstraction; experiences portrayed are uncommon to most readers o **Intertextuality and Cultural Knowledge:** Some references or allusions to other texts or cultural elements	o **Life Experiences:** Explores several themes; experiences portrayed are common to many readers o **Intertextuality and Cultural Knowledge:** Few references or allusions to other texts or cultural elements	o **Life Experiences:** Explores a single theme; experiences portrayed are everyday and common to most readers o **Intertextuality and Cultural Knowledge:** No references or allusions to other texts or cultural elements

Source: Achieve the Core. (n.d.). Reviewing using the IMET: ELA: Module 101—high-quality texts, evidence-based discussion and writing, and building knowledge. *Accessed at https://achievethecore.org/content /upload/Understanding%20the%20IMET_ELA.LIT_Handout_101.pdf on April 29, 2020.*

Read-Aloud Text Complexity:
Qualitative Measures Rubric—Literature

In prekindergarten through first grade, use this rubric to determine the complexity of read-aloud texts. The majority of students in these grades will not read complex texts independently.

Text Title: _____   Text Author: _____

	Exceedingly Complex	Very Complex	Moderately Complex	Slightly Complex
Text Structures	**Organization:** Text is complex in such elements as point of view, time shifts, multiple characters, storylines, and detail.	**Organization:** Text may include subplots, time shifts, and more complex characters.	**Organization:** Text may have two or more storylines and occasionally be difficult to predict.	**Organization:** Text is clear, chronological, or easy to predict.
	Use of graphics: If used, illustrations or graphics are essential for understanding the meaning of the text.	**Use of graphics:** If used, illustrations or graphics support or extend the meaning of the text.	**Use of graphics:** If used, a range of illustrations or graphics support selected parts of the text.	**Use of graphics:** If used, graphics or illustrations directly support and assist in interpreting the text or are not necessary to understand the meaning of the text.
Language Features	**Conventionality:** Dense and complex; contains abstract, ironic, and (or) figurative language	**Conventionality:** Fairly complex; contains some abstract, ironic, and (or) figurative language	**Conventionality:** Largely explicit and easy to understand with some occasions for more complex meaning	**Conventionality:** Explicit, literal, straightforward, easy to understand
	Vocabulary: Complex, generally unfamiliar, archaic, subject-specific, or overly academic language; may be ambiguous or purposefully misleading	**Vocabulary:** Fairly complex language that is sometimes unfamiliar, archaic, subject-specific, or overly academic	**Vocabulary:** Mostly contemporary, familiar, or conversational language; rarely unfamiliar or overly academic	**Vocabulary:** Contemporary, familiar, or conversational language
	Sentence structure: Mainly complex sentences with several subordinate clauses or phrases; sentences often contain multiple concepts	**Sentence structure:** Many complex sentences with several subordinate phrases or clauses and transition words	**Sentence structure:** Primarily simple and compound sentences, with some complex constructions	**Sentence structure:** Mainly simple sentences

page 1 of 2

Meaning	**Meaning:** Multiple competing levels of meaning that are difficult to identify, separate or interpret; theme is implicit or subtle, often ambiguous, and revealed over the entirety of the text	**Meaning:** Multiple levels of meaning that may be difficult to identify or separate; theme is implicit or subtle and may be revealed over the entirety of the text	**Meaning:** Multiple levels of meaning clearly distinguished from each other; theme is clear but may be conveyed with some subtlety	**Meaning:** One level of meaning; theme is obvious and revealed early in the text.
Knowledge Demands	**Life experiences:** Explores complex themes; sophisticated or abstract themes; experiences portrayed are distinctly different from the common reader's **Intertextuality and cultural knowledge:** Many references or allusions to other texts or cultural elements	**Life experiences:** Explores themes of varying levels of complexity or abstraction; experiences portrayed are uncommon to most readers **Intertextuality and cultural knowledge:** Some references or allusions to other texts or cultural elements	**Life experiences:** Explores several themes; experiences portrayed are common to many readers **Intertextuality and cultural knowledge:** Few references or allusions to other texts or cultural elements	**Life experiences:** Explores a single theme; experiences portrayed are every day and common to most readers **Intertextuality and cultural knowledge:** No references or allusions to other texts or cultural elements

Source: Achieve the Core. (n.d.). Reviewing using the IMET: ELA: Module 101—high-quality texts, evidence-based discussion and writing, and building knowledge. *Accessed at https://achievethecore.org/content /upload/Understanding%20the%20IMET_ELA.LIT_Handout_101.pdf on April 29, 2020.*

APPENDIX B:

ESSENTIAL UNDERSTANDINGS AND GUIDING QUESTIONS

If teams wish to extend the six-step process laid out in chapter 1 (page 11), they can craft essential understandings, which crystalize and articulate the conceptual thinking, and guiding questions, which set the purpose for learning. If teams are using a published or existing curriculum that includes these components, the information provided here might validate or lead to revising what is in their resources.

Craft Essential Understandings

Teams carefully review what they have input on the master PREP template to see how the components weave together for planning lessons and assessments. In doing so, teams focus on formulating deeper conceptual understandings, called essential (or enduring) understandings. These statements of understanding enable teams to capture the essence of a unit. They are predicated on key concepts that teachers want students to realize, such as literacy-related concepts like figurative language, perspective, patterns, phonemic awareness, and narrative.

Many leaders in education espouse the value of this aspect of curriculum design. Hattie (2012) states that "conceptual understandings form the 'coat hangers' on which we interpret and assimilate new ideas, and relate and extend them" (p. 115). H. Lynn Erickson (2007) states that the "synergistic interplay between the factual and conceptual levels of thinking" is critical to intellectual development (p. 2). Furthermore, she writes, "When curriculum and instruction require students to process factual information through the conceptual level of thinking, the students demonstrate greater retention of factual information, deeper levels of understanding, and increased motivation for learning" (Erickson, 2007, p. 2).

Teachers formulate essential understandings by using the unwrapped standards and the foundational information from the Knowledge Items section of the PREP template (figure 1.1, pages 14–16). The following examples, taken from the featured friendship and acceptance unit, help ensure that teachers fulfill the promise of high-level instruction and assessment.

- ▸ Readers ask and answer questions about the characters, settings, and events in a story as they read to monitor their comprehension.

- ▸ Authors write narratives to tell their reactions to important events in the order they occurred.

- ▸ Readers use many strategies to identify and read words.

Review the following points as your team solidifies essential understandings.

- ▸ Teachers write essential understandings in adult language to crystallize and articulate the conceptual thinking used to design curriculum.

- ▸ Each essential understanding can take into account two or more standards. Writing one essential understanding for each standard is cumbersome and overwhelming. For example, the essential understanding *Readers ask and answer questions about the characters, settings, and events in a story as they read to monitor their comprehension* takes into account the following priority standards from the friendship and acceptance unit.

  - **RL.K.1:** "With prompting and support, ask and answer questions about key details in a text" (NGA & CCSSO, 2010).

  - **RL.K.3:** "With prompting and support, identify characters, settings, and major events in a story" (NGA & CCSSO, 2010).

These two priority standards easily merge together since characters, settings, and major events represents the text's key details that students can address through their questions.

Essential understandings need to be transferable. To accomplish this, proper nouns or past-tense verbs should not be included since doing so would anchor them in a specific situation, context, or time frame. In fact, teachers in grade clusters can use the same essential understandings if they pertain to the content material since they are written in applicable, general terms. For example, teachers would avoid writing a statement that could only be applied to a specific resource used in a unit, such as this, based on Henkes's (1991) book *Chrysanthemum: Readers can ask and answer questions about Chrysanthemum, her friends, and their behavior toward her.* This statement does not represent what is important for students to retain beyond a course of study and is, therefore, not essential.

To craft stronger essential understandings, capitalize on action verbs (such as *determine, promote, challenge, support*) instead of forms of the verb *to be*. In the examples from the narrative unit for friendship and acceptance, these precise verbs connect concepts embedded in the essential understandings: *move, use, develop, show, reveal, employ, support,* and *decipher.* Figure B.1 is a verb list that shows relationships. Teams can call on a list like this as they craft essential understandings during unit design discussions.

While teaching, the intent is to have students come to realize an enduring truth embedded in the essential understandings. If your team keeps this end goal in mind while constructing these statements, you will have successfully addressed what education consultant Kathy Tuchman Glass (2012) calls the *importance factor.* To merely state that readers ask and answer questions about a text would lead us to wonder, "Who cares? Why do students need to know this?" Instead of sharing an

act	enhance	introduce	recommend
change	establish	invent	resolve
construct	estimate	manage	respond
contrast	examine	manipulate	separate
cooperate	expand	map	sequence
create	explain	model	share
define	express	modify	show
demonstrate	generate	offer	simplify
describe	identify	organize	solve
design	illustrate	perform	suggest
determine	improve	persuade	support
develop	infer	point to	transfer
differentiate	inform	produce	transition
discriminate	integrate	prompt	uncover
display	interact	propose	use
distinguish	interpret	provide	utilize

Figure B.1: Verb list showing relationships.

*Visit **go.SolutionTree.com/literacy** for a free reproducible version of this figure.*

essential understanding, we have simply stated a fact. However, if teachers write, *Readers ask and answer questions about the characters, settings, and events in a story as they read to monitor their comprehension*, then the team has crafted a complete and pertinent essential understanding that gets to the *why*. By using essential understandings that go beyond facts, teachers can plan deeper, more meaningful instruction and assessment.

Once teams craft essential understandings, they use them to build guiding questions to frame instruction and assessment. However, since teams develop guiding questions directly from their essential understandings, teachers might find it beneficial to work on building essential understandings and their corresponding guiding questions concurrently.

Develop Guiding Questions

Guiding questions establish a purpose for learning, provide an overarching focus that promotes higher-level thinking, and emanate from essential understandings. These questions encourage students to engage in the work ahead and make them aware of the connection between what they are doing and their learning outcomes. Teachers should post these questions so students are aware of the value in what they are learning, allowing them to derive meaning from their learning.

The guiding questions are purposefully brief. Their brevity means that teachers can plan and conduct a series of lessons around these questions, guiding students to discover for themselves the deeper meaning embedded in the essential understandings. If a question is leading, teachers offer the answer too easily rather than give students the opportunity to discover answers on their own. As teachers, we must be vigilant in our search to identify what we want students to understand; the succinctly stated guiding question helps frame and set the purpose for learning. To read examples, refer to figure B.2, which shows the pairing of essential understandings and guiding questions. As you review it, keep the following in mind.

▸ Guiding questions can be used across units or grades, so they are purposefully written for this transferability. For example, *How do characters change throughout time?* can apply to various complex texts in a school year and across grades.

▸ Answers to each guiding question, written in language students can understand, are found in an associated essential understanding.

Essential Understandings	Guiding Questions
Readers understand that characters in literary texts have different experiences and reactions.	How do readers identify character experiences and reactions?
Readers understand that there is a relationship between illustrations and words.	How do readers use both words and illustrations to understand text?
Readers can look closely at a story to identify its characters, settings, and major events.	Why do readers look closely at a story and its elements?
To gain deeper meaning, readers use questioning to uncover significant details about elements of a narrative.	How can I understand a narrative story better by asking questions?
Readers learn about letter names and sounds to help lay the foundation for blending and segmenting.	How can I blend letter sounds to read words?

Figure B.2: Paired essential understandings with guiding questions.

Visit **go.SolutionTree.com/literacy** *for a free reproducible version of this figure.*

▶ Ensure questions require open-ended, higher-order responses. Beginning with *why*, *how*, or *is* can foster such a response. If other question words achieve this goal, use them.

▶ Write the question in first person to personalize it for students, or in third person as appropriate.

▶ When referring to *writers* or *authors*, the guiding questions can pertain to students as well as authors of published material. This way, students can use the essential understanding and guiding question both when studying complex text and when students write their own stories.

▶ Post the guiding questions, and refer to them to set the purpose for learning.

APPENDIX C:

LIST OF FIGURES AND TABLES

*Reproducible figures are in italics. Visit **go.SolutionTree.com/literacy** to download free reproducible versions of these figures.*

REFERENCES AND RESOURCES

Achieve the Core. (n.d.). *Reviewing using the IMET: ELA: Module 101—high-quality texts, evidence-based discussion and writing, and building knowledge.* Accessed at https://achievethecore.org/content /upload/Understanding%20the%20 IMET_ELA.LIT_Handout_101.pdf on April 29, 2020.

Adams, M. J. (1990). *Beginning to read: Thinking and learning about print.* Cambridge, MA: MIT Press.

Ainsworth, L. (2013). *Prioritizing the Common Core: Identifying specific standards to emphasize the most.* Englewood, CO: Lead + Learn Press.

Ainsworth, L., & Vieagut, D. (2015). *Common formative assessments 2.0: How teacher teams intentionally align standards, instruction, and assessment.* Thousand Oaks, CA: Corwin Press.

Allington, R. L. (2001). *What really matters for struggling readers: Designing research-based programs.* New York: Longman.

Allington, R. L. (2002). What I've learned about effective reading instruction: From a decade of studying exemplary elementary classroom teachers. *Phi Delta Kappan, 83*(10), 740–747.

Allington, R. L. (2009). *What really matters in response to intervention: Research-based designs.* Boston: Pearson.

Allington, R. L. (2012). *What really matters for struggling readers: Designing research-based programs.* Boston: Pearson.

Allington, R. L. (2014). How reading volume affects both reading fluency and reading achievement. *International Electronic Journal of Elementary Education, 7*(1), 13–26.

Allington, R. L., & Gabriel, R. E. (2012). Every child, every day. *Educational Leadership, 69*(6), 10–15.

AllThingsPLC. (n.d.). *About PLCs.* Accessed at www.allthingsplc.info/about on May 25, 2019.

Anderson, L. W., & Krathwohl, D. R. (Eds.). (2001). *A taxonomy for learning, teaching, and assessing: A revision of Bloom's taxonomy of educational objectives.* Boston: Allyn & Bacon.

Annie E. Casey Foundation. (2010). *Early warning! Why reading by the end of third grade matters.* Accessed at www.aecf.org/resources/early-warning-why-reading-by-the-end-of-third-grade-matters on April 1, 2020.

Armbruster, B. B., Lehr, F., & Osborn, J. (2006). *Put reading first: The research building blocks for teaching children to read. Kindergarten through grade 3.* Washington, DC: National Institute for Literacy.

Atwell, N. (2007). *The reading zone: How to help kids become skilled, passionate, habitual, critical readers.* New York: Scholastic.

Audet, L. (2018, January 15). *Supporting oral language development in writing workshop, 1–4* [Blog post]. Accessed at https://blog.heinemann.com/tcrwp-supporting-oral-language-development-writing-workshop on November 19, 2019.

BabyCenter. (2018, October 21). *Your 4 1/2-year-old: A growing attention span.* Accessed at www.babycenter.com/6_your-4-1-2-year-old-a-growing-attention-span_10329691.bc on April 3, 2020.

Bailey, K., & Jakicic, C. (2017). *Simplifying common assessment: A guide for Professional Learning Communities at Work.* Bloomington, IN: Solution Tree Press.

Bailey, K., Jakicic, C., & Spiller, J. (2014). *Collaborating for success with the Common Core: A toolkit for Professional Learning Communities at Work.* Bloomington, IN: Solution Tree Press.

Bates, C. C. (2013, May). Flexible grouping during literacy centers: A model for differentiating instruction. *Young Children, 68*(2), 30–33.

Bear, D. R., Invernizzi, M., Templeton, S., & Johnston, F. (2012). *Words their way: Word study for phonics, vocabulary, and spelling instruction.* Boston: Pearson/Allyn and Bacon.

Beck, I. L., & Beck, M. E. (2013). *Making sense of phonics: The hows and whys* (2nd ed.). New York: Guilford Press.

Beck, I. L., McKeown, M. G., & Kucan, L. (2013). *Bringing words to life: Robust vocabulary instruction* (2nd ed.). New York: Guilford Press.

Begin to Read. (n.d.). *What is phonemic awareness?* Accessed at www.begintoread.com/articles/phonemic-awareness.html on November 20, 2019.

Bennett-Armistead, V. S. (n.d.). *What is dramatic play and how does it support literacy development in preschool?* Accessed at www.scholastic.com/teachers/articles/teaching-content/what-dramatic-play-and-how-does-it-support-literacy-development-preschool/ on July 14, 2019.

Billen, M. T., & Allington, R. L. (2013). An evidence-based approach to response to intervention. In D. M. Barone & M. H. Mallette (Eds.), *Best practices in early literacy instruction* (pp. 305–321). New York: Guilford Press.

Bishop, R. S. (1990). Windows, mirrors, and sliding glass doors. *Perspectives: Choosing and Using Books for the Classroom, 6*(3).

Blachman, B. A. (1991). Getting ready to read: Learning how print maps to speech. In J. F. Kavanagh (Ed.), *The language continuum: From infancy to literacy* (pp. 1–22). Parkton, MD: York Press.

Blanch, N., Forsythe, L. C., Van Allen, J. H., & Roberts, S. K. (2017). Reigniting writers: Using the literacy block with elementary students to support authentic writing experiences. *Childhood Education, 93*(1), 48–57.

Blevins, W. (2013). *Phonics: Ten important research findings.* Accessed at www.wileyblevins .com/classroom_spotlight/phonics-ten-important-research-findings on November 3, 2019.

Blevins, W. (2017). *A fresh look at phonics, grades K–2: Common causes of failure and 7 ingredients for success.* Thousand Oaks, CA: Corwin.

Block, M. K., & Duke, N. K. (2015, March). *Letter names can cause confusion and other things to know about letter–sound relationships.* Accessed at www.naeyc.org /resources/pubs/yc/mar2015/letter-sound-relationships on April 1, 2020.

Bockting, W. O. (2008, October—December). Psychotherapy and real-life experience: From gender dichotomy to gender diversity. *Sexologies, 17*(4), 211–224.

Bourque, P. (2017). Building stamina for struggling readers and writers. *Educational Leadership, 74*(5). Accessed at www.ascd.org/publications/educational-leadership /feb17/vol74/num05/Building-Stamina-for-Struggling-Readers-and-Writers. aspx on July 8, 2019.

Boushey, G., & Moser, J. (2014). *The daily 5: Fostering literacy independence in the elementary grades* (2nd ed.). Portland, ME: Stenhouse.

Brendtro, L. K., Brokenleg, M., & Van Bockern, S. (2019). *Reclaiming youth at risk: Futures of promise* (3rd ed.). Bloomington, IN: Solution Tree Press.

Brookhart, S. M. (2013). *How to create and use rubrics for formative assessment and grading.* Alexandria, VA: Association for Supervision and Curriculum Development.

Bruner, J. S., Goodnow, J. J., & Austin, G. A. (1956). *A study of thinking.* New York: Wiley.

Brynie, F. H. (2009). *Brain sense: The science of the senses and how we process the world around us.* New York: American Management Association.

Budge, K. M., & Parrett, W. H. (2018). *Disrupting poverty: Five powerful classroom practices.* Alexandria, VA: Association for Supervision and Curriculum Development.

Buffum, A., & Mattos, M. (2020). *RTI at Work plan book.* Bloomington, IN: Solution Tree Press.

Buffum, A., Mattos, M., & Malone, J. (2018). *Taking action: A handbook for RTI at Work.* Bloomington, IN: Solution Tree Press.

Buffum, A., Mattos, M., & Weber, C. (2010). The why behind RTI. *Educational Leadership, 68*(2), 10–16.

Buffum, A., Mattos, M., & Weber, C. (2012). *Simplifying response to intervention: Four essential guiding principles.* Bloomington, IN: Solution Tree Press.

Calkins, L. (2013). *A guide to the Common Core writing workshop*. Portsmouth, NH: Heinemann.

Cannon, J. (1993). *Stellaluna*. San Diego: Harcourt Brace.

Casbergue, R. M., & Strickland, D. S. (2016). *Reading and writing in preschool: Teaching the essentials*. New York: Guilford Press.

Clay, M. M. (1993). *Reading recovery: A guidebook for teachers in training*. Portsmouth, NH: Heinemann.

Clay, M. M. (2004). *Talking, reading, and writing*. Accessed at www.literacylearning.net /uploads/3/7/8/8/37880553/jrr_3.2-clay.pdf on November 19, 2019.

Clay, M. M. (2013). *An observation survey of early literacy achievement* (Rev. ed.). Portsmouth, NH: Heinemann.

Clements, A., & Yoshi. (1991). *Big Al*. New York: Scholastic.

Coleman, D., & Pimentel, S. (2012a). *Revised publishers' criteria for the Common Core State Standards in English language arts and literacy, grades 3–12*. Accessed at www .corestandards.org/assets/Publishers_Criteria_for_3-12.pdf on May 25, 2019.

Coleman, D., & Pimentel, S. (2012b). *Revised publishers' criteria for the Common Core State Standards in English language arts and literacy, grades K–2*. Accessed at www .corestandards.org/assets/Publishers_Criteria_for_K-2.pdf on July 15, 2019.

Connell, R. (2009, February). Accountable conduct: "Doing gender" in transsexual and political retrospect. *Gender & Society, 23*(1), 104–111.

Connor, C. M., Alberto, P. A., Compton, D. L., & O'Connor, R. E. (2014). *Improving reading outcomes for students with or at risk for reading disabilities: A synthesis of the contributions from the Institute of Education Sciences Research Centers*. Washington, DC: National Center for Special Education Research.

Darling-Hammond, L. (1999). *Teacher quality and student achievement: A review of state policy evidence*. Seattle, WA: Center for the Study of Teaching and Policy.

Deussen, T., Autio, E., Miller, B., Lockwood, A. T., & Stewart, V. (2008). *What teachers should know about instruction for English language learners*. Accessed at https://educationnorthwest.org/sites/default/files/resources/what-teachers -should-know-about-instruction-for-ells.pdf on March 26, 2020.

Dimich, N. (2015). *Design in five: Essential phases to create engaging assessment practice*. Bloomington, IN: Solution Tree Press.

Donohoo, J., & Katz, S. (2017). When teachers believe, students achieve. *Learning Professional, 38*(6), 20–27.

DuFour, R. (2004). *What is a professional learning community?* Accessed at www.ascd .org/publications/educational-leadership/may04/vol61/num08/What-Is-a -Professional-Learning-Community%C2%A2.aspx on May 24, 2020.

DuFour, R., DuFour, R., & Eaker, R. (2008). *Revisiting Professional Learning Communities at Work: New insights for improving schools*. Bloomington, IN: Solution Tree Press.

DuFour, R., DuFour, R., Eaker, R., & Many, T. (2010). *Learning by doing: A handbook for Professional Learning Communities at Work* (2nd ed.). Bloomington, IN: Solution Tree Press.

DuFour, R., DuFour, R., Eaker, R., Many, T. W., & Mattos, M. (2016). *Learning by doing: A handbook for Professional Learning Communities at Work* (3rd ed.). Bloomington, IN: Solution Tree Press.

DuFour, R., & Marzano, R. J. (2011). *Leaders of learning: How district, school, and classroom leaders improve student achievement.* Bloomington, IN: Solution Tree Press.

Dweck, C. (2016). *What having a "growth mindset" actually means.* Accessed at https://hbr. org/2016/01/what-having-a-growth-mindset-actually-means on April 1, 2020.

Dweck, C. S. (2007). *The perils and promises of praise.* Accessed at www.ascd.org/publications/educational-leadership/oct07/vol65/num02/The-Perils-and-Promises-of-Praise.aspx on May 23, 2020.

Ehlert, L. (1996). *Eating the alphabet: Fruits & vegetables from A to Z.* San Diego: Harcourt.

Ehri, L. C. (2013). Orthographic mapping in the acquisition of sight word reading, spelling memory, and vocabulary learning. *Scientific Studies of Reading, 18*(1), 5–21.

Ehri, L. C., & Roberts, T. (2006). The roots of learning to read and write: Acquisition of letters and phonemic awareness. In D. K. Dickinson & S. B. Neuman (Eds.), *Handbook of early literacy research* (Vol. 2, pp. 113–131). New York: Guilford Press.

Elkonin, D. B. (1963). The psychology of mastering the elements of reading. In B. Simon & J. Simon (Eds.), *Educational psychology in the U.S.S.R.* (pp. 165–179). London: Routledge & Kegan Paul.

Erickson, H. L. (2002). *Concept-based curriculum and instruction: Teaching beyond the facts.* Thousand Oaks, CA: Corwin Press.

Erickson, H. L. (2007). *Concept-based curriculum and instruction for the thinking classroom.* Thousand Oaks, CA: Corwin Press.

Evans, S. (2018). *Helpers in your neighborhood.* Washington, DC: National Geographic Kids.

Fawcett Society. (2019). Fawcett research shows exposure to gender stereotypes as a child causes harm in later life. Accessed at www.fawcettsociety.org.uk/news/fawcett-research-exposure-gender-stereotypes-child-causes-harm-later-life on February 2, 2019.

Ferlazzo, L. (2014, December 6). *Response: The best ways to engage students in learning* [Blog post]. Accessed at http://blogs.edweek.org/teachers/classroom_qa_with_larry_ferlazzo/2014/12/response_the_best_ways_to_engage_students_in_learning.html on April 3, 2020.

Fisher, D. (2008). *Effective use of the gradual release of responsibility model.* Accessed at www.mheonline.com/_treasures/pdf/douglas_fisher.pdf on November 20, 2019.

Fisher, D., & Frey, N. (2008). *Better learning through structured teaching: A framework for the gradual release of responsibility.* Alexandria, VA: Association for Supervision and Curriculum Development.

Fisher, D., & Frey, N. (2012). Close reading in elementary schools. *The Reading Teacher, 66*(3), 179–188.

Fisher, D., & Frey, N. (2014a). Closely reading informational texts in the primary grades. *The Reading Teacher, 68*(3), 222–227.

Fisher, D., & Frey, N. (2014b). Scaffolded reading instruction of content-area texts. *The Reading Teacher, 67*(5), 347–351.

Fisher, D., & Frey, N. (2014c). *Better learning through structured teaching: A framework for the gradual release of responsibility* (2nd ed). Alexandria, VA: Association for Supervision and Curriculum Development.

Fisher, D., & Frey, N. (2018). Six factors define assessment-capable learners who are cognitively engaged. *Principal, 98*(1), 14–17.

Folgueira, R., & Bernatene, P. (2013). *Ribbit!* New York: Knopf.

Foorman, B., Beyler, N., Borradaile, K., Coyne, M., Denton, C. A., Dimino, J., et al. (2016). *Foundational skills to support reading for understanding in kindergarten through 3rd grade.* Accessed at https://ies.ed.gov/ncee/wwc /Docs/PracticeGuide /wwc_foundationalreading_070516.pdf on November 19, 2019.

Fountas, I. C., & Pinnell, G. S. (2006). *Teaching for comprehending and fluency: Thinking, talking, and writing about reading, K–8.* Portsmouth, NH: Heinemann.

Fountas, I. C., & Pinnell, G. S. (2019). *Level books, not children: The role of text levels in literacy instruction.* Accessed at www.fountasandpinnell.com/shared/resources /FPL_LevelBooksNotKids_Whitepaper.pdf on November 19, 2019.

Fountas & Pinnell Literacy Team. (2019, February 1). *What is shared reading?* [Blog post]. Accessed at https://fpblog.fountasandpinnell.com/what-is-shared-reading on November 20, 2019.

Freeman, D. (1968). *Corduroy.* New York: Viking Press.

Frey, N., Fisher, D., & Everlove, S. (2009). *Productive group work: How to engage students, build teamwork, and promote understanding.* Alexandria, VA: Association for Supervision and Curriculum Development.

Fried, M. D. (2013). Activating teaching: Using running records to inform teaching decisions. *The Journal of Reading Recovery,* 5–16.

Fritz, J. (1987). *Shh! We're writing the Constitution.* New York: Putnam.

Friziellie, H., Schmidt, J. A., & Spiller, J. (2016). *Yes we can!: General and special educators collaborating in a professional learning community.* Bloomington, IN: Solution Tree Press.

Gallagher, K. (2009). *Readicide: How schools are killing reading and what you can do about it.* Portsmouth, NH: Stenhouse.

Gallimore, R., Ermeling, B. A., Saunders, W. M., & Goldenberg, C. (2009). Moving the learning of teaching closer to practice: Teacher education implications of school-based inquiry teams. *Elementary School Journal, 109*(5), 537–553.

Gareis, C. R., & Grant, L. W. (2008). *Teacher-made assessments: How to connect curriculum, instruction, and student learning.* Larchmont, NY: Eye on Education.

Gareis, C. R., & Grant, L. W. (2015). *Teacher-made assessments: How to connect curriculum, instruction, and student learning* (2nd ed.). New York: Routledge.

Garland, K., & Bryan, K. (2017). Partnering with families and communities: Culturally responsive pedagogy at its best. *Voices From the Middle, 24*(3), 52–55.

Gender Spectrum. (n.d.a). *Gender across the grades.* Accessed at www.genderspectrum .org/articles/gender-across-the-grades on April 3, 2020.

Gender Spectrum. (n.d.b). *Understanding gender and the experience of gender diverse youth and their families.* Accessed at https://gender-spectrum.cdn.prismic.io/gender -spectrum/272f57e7-70a9-476d-b919-fff47b0aab3b_FinalPacketcombinepdf .pdf on April 3, 2020.

Genishi, C. (1998). *Young children's oral language development.* Urbana, IL: ERIC Clearinghouse on Elementary and Early Childhood Education.

Gibson, S. A. (n.d.). *Write alouds.* Accessed at www.readwritethink.org/professional -development/strategy-guides/write-alouds-30687.html on April 1, 2020.

Glass, K. T. (2012). *Mapping comprehensive units to the ELA Common Core standards, K–5.* Thousand Oaks, CA: Corwin Press.

Glass, K. T. (2015). *Complex text decoded: How to design lessons and use strategies that target authentic texts.* Alexandria, VA: Association for Supervision and Curriculum Development.

Glass, K. T. (2017). *The fundamentals of (re)designing writing units.* Bloomington, IN: Solution Tree Press.

Glass, K. T. (2018). *(Re)designing narrative writing units for grades 5–12.* Bloomington, IN: Solution Tree Press.

Glass, K. T., & Marzano, R. J. (2018). *The new art and science of teaching writing.* Bloomington, IN: Solution Tree Press.

Gonzalez, J. (2018). *To learn, students need to DO something* [Blog post]. Accessed at www.cultofpedagogy.com/do-something on November 20, 2019.

Graham, S., Bollinger, A., Booth Olson, C., D'Aoust, C., MacArthur, C., McCutchen, D., & Olinghouse, N. (2012). *Teaching elementary school students to be effective writers: A practice guide* (NCEE 2012-4058). Washington, DC: National Center for Education Evaluation and Regional Assistance, Institute of Education Sciences, U.S. Department of Education. Accessed at https://ies.ed.gov/ncee /wwc/Docs/PracticeGuide/writing_pg_062612.pdf on November 22, 2019.

Graham, S., & Hebert, M. (2010). *Writing to read: Evidence for how writing can improve reading.* Washington, DC: Alliance for Excellent Education.

Graham, S., & Hebert, M. (2011). Writing to read: A meta-analysis of the impact of writing and writing instruction on reading. *Harvard Educational Review,* *81*(4), 710–744.

Graham, S., & Perin, D. (2007). *Writing next: Effective strategies to improve writing of adolescents in middle and high schools—A report to Carnegie Corporation of New York.* Washington, DC: Alliance for Excellent Education.

Gronlund, G. (2013). *Planning for play, observation, and learning in preschool and kindergarten.* St. Paul, MN: Redleaf Press.

Guido, M. (2017, March 2). *The guide to cooperative learning: Principles and strategies for each type* [Blog post]. Accessed at www.prodigygame.com/blog/cooperative-learning-principles-strategies on April 3, 2020.

Guskey, T. R. (2010). Lessons of mastery learning. *Educational Leadership, 68*(2), 52–57.

Harris, K. R., Graham, S., Friedlander, B., & Laud, L. (2013). Bring powerful writing strategies into your classroom! Why and how. *The Reading Teacher, 66*(7), 538–542.

Harris, T. L., & Hodges, R. E. (Eds.). (1995). *The literacy dictionary: The vocabulary of reading and writing.* Newark, DE: International Reading Association.

Harrison, J., Grant, J., Herman, J. L. (2012). A gender not listed here: Genderqueers, gender rebels, and otherwise in the National Transgender Discrimination Survey. *LGBTQ Public Policy Journal at the Harvard Kennedy School, 2*(1), 13–24.

Harstad, E. (n.d.). *Is my preschooler overly distractible? How can I tell?* Accessed at www.understood.org/en/learning-thinking-differences/child-learning-disabilities/distractibility-inattention/is-my-preschooler-overly-distractible-how-can-i-tell on April 2, 2020.

Hattie, J. (2012). *Visible learning for teachers: Maximizing impact on learning.* New York: Routledge.

Hemingway, E. (2012). *Bad apple: A tale of friendship.* New York: Putnam.

Henkes, K. (1988). *Chester's way.* New York: Greenwillow Books.

Henkes, K. (1991). *Chrysanthemum.* New York: Greenwillow Books.

Heritage, M. (2008). *Learning progressions: Supporting instruction and formative assessment.* Washington, DC: Council of Chief State School Officers.

Hiebert, E. H., & Reutzel, D. R. (2014). *Revisiting silent reading: New directions for teachers and researchers.* Accessed at http://textproject.org/assets/library/resources/Hiebert-Reutzel-2014-Revisiting-Silent-Reading.pdf on April 20, 2020.

Himmele, W., & Himmele, P. (2012). *Why read-alouds matter more in the age of the Common Core Standards.* Accessed at www.ascd.org/ascd-express/vol8/805-himmele.aspx on January 23, 2020

Hollie, S. (2019, May 22). *Steps to authenticity* [Blog post]. Accessed at https:// literacyworldwide.org/blog/literacy-daily/2019/05/22/steps-to-authenticity on July 14, 2019.

International Literacy Association. (2019). *Children's rights to excellent literacy instruction.* Accessed at https://literacyworldwide.org/docs/default-source/where-we-stand /ila-childrens-rights-to-excellent-literacy-instruction.pdf on April 2, 2020.

Irons, A. (2008). *Enhancing learning through formative assessment and feedback.* London: Routledge.

Johnson, D. W., & Johnson, R. T. (n.d.). *What is cooperative learning?* Accessed at www .co-operation.org/what-is-cooperative-learning on November 20, 2019.

Kagan, S. (n.d.). *Cooperative learning: Seventeen pros and seventeen cons plus ten tips for success.* Accessed at www.kaganonline.com/free_articles/dr_spencer_kagan/259 /Cooperative-Learning-Seventeen-Pros-and-Seventeen-Cons-Plus-Ten-Tips-for -Success on November 19, 2019.

Kagan, S. (2013). *Kagan cooperative learning structures.* San Clemente, CA: Kagan.

Kagan, S., & Kagan, M. (2009). *Kagan cooperative learning.* San Clemente, CA: Kagan.

Kagan, S., Kagan, M., & Kagan, L. (2016). *59 Kagan structures: Proven engagement strategies.* San Clemente, CA: Kagan.

Keats, E. J. (1967). *Peter's chair.* New York: Harper & Row.

Kelly, L. B., Ogden, M. K., & Moses, L. (2019). *Collaborative conversations: Speaking and listening in the primary grades.* Accessed at www.naeyc.org/resources/pubs /yc/mar2019/speaking-listening-primary-grades on April 3, 2020.

Kid Sense. (n.d.). *Writing readiness (pre-writing) skills.* Accessed at https://childdevelopment .com.au/areas-of-concern/writing/writing-readiness-pre-writing-skills on April 3, 2020.

Killion, J. (2008). *Coaches help mine the data.* Accessed at https://issuu.com/dmsmathcoach /docs/nsdc_feb._atricle on February 22, 2020.

Kilpatrick, D. A. (2016). *Equipped for reading success: A comprehensive, step-by-step program for developing phonemic awareness and fluent word recognition.* Syracuse, NY: Casey & Kirsch.

Kirkland, L. D., & Patterson, J. (2005). Developing oral language in primary class-rooms. *Early Childhood Education Journal, 32*(6), 391–395.

Kishel, A. (2007). *U.S. symbols.* Minneapolis: Lerner Publications Company.

Kraus, R., & Aruego, J. (1971). *Leo the late bloomer.* New York: Windmill Books.

Lapp, D., Moss, B., Grant, M., & Johnson, K. (2015). *A close look at close reading: Teaching students to analyze complex texts, grades K–5.* Alexandria, VA: Association for Supervision and Curriculum Development.

Lee, J., Grigg, W. S., & Donahue, P. L. (2007). *The nation's report card: Reading 2007.* Washington, DC: National Center for Education Statistics, Institute of Education Sciences, U.S. Department of Education. Accessed at http:// nationsreportcard.gov/reading_2007 on July 5, 2019.

Lester, H., & Munsinger, L. (1999). *Hooway for Wodney Wat.* Boston: Walter Lorraine Books.

Liben, D., & Liben, M. (2017). *"Both and" literacy instruction K–5: A proposed paradigm shift for the Common Core Standards ELA classroom.* Accessed at https://achievethecore .org/page/687/both-and-literacy-instruction-k-5-a-proposed-paradigm-shift-for -the-common-core-state-standards-ela-classroom on November 3, 2019.

Liben, M., & Pimentel, S. (2018). *Placing text at the center of the standards-aligned ELA classroom.* Accessed at https://achievethecore.org/page/3185/placing-text-at-the -center-of-the-standards-aligned-ela-classroom on July 14, 2019.

Liebman, D. (2018). *I want to be a firefighter.* Buffalo, NY: Firefly Books.

Lyons, S. (2013). *Safety in my neighborhood.* North Mankato, MN: Capstone Press.

Many, T. W. (2009). Three rules help manage assessment data. *TEPSA News.* Accessed at https://absenterprisedotcom.files.wordpress.com/2016/06/many_tepsa_ datarules90.pdf on June 30, 2019.

Marzano, R. J. (2003). *What works in schools: Translating research into action.* Alexandria, VA: Association for Supervision and Curriculum Development.

Marzano, R. J. (2004). *Building background knowledge for academic achievement: Research on what works in schools.* Alexandria, VA: Association for Supervision and Curriculum Development.

Marzano, R. J. (2010). *Formative assessment and standards-based grading.* Bloomington, IN: Marzano Resources.

Marzano, R. J. (2017). *The new art and science of teaching.* Bloomington, IN: Solution Tree Press.

Marzano, R. J. (2019). *The handbook for the new art and science of teaching.* Bloomington, IN: Solution Tree Press.

Marzano, R. J., & Kendall, J. S. (2008). *Designing and assessing educational objectives: Applying the new taxonomy.* Thousand Oaks, CA: Corwin Press.

Meister, C. (2014a). *Mail carriers.* Minneapolis: Bullfrog Books.

Meister, C. (2014b). *Police officers.* Minneapolis: Bullfrog Books.

Mesmer, H. A. (2019). *Letter lessons and first words: Phonics foundations that work.* Portsmouth, NH: Heinemann.

Messner, K., & Rex, A. (2020). *The next president: The unexpected beginnings and unwritten future of America's presidents.* San Francisco: Chronicle Kids.

Mindset Works. (n.d.). *Programs that motivate students and teachers.* Accessed at www .mindsetworks.com/science on November 19, 2019.

Moats, L., & Tolman, C. (n.d.). *Why phonological awareness is important for reading and spelling.* Accessed at www.readingrockets.org/article/why-phonological -awareness-important-reading-and-spelling on November 20, 2019.

Moats, L. C., & Tolman, C. A. (2019). *LETRS* (Vol. 1). Longmont, CO: Sopris West Educational Services.

Mora, B. (n.d.). *Talk before you write* [Blog post]. Accessed at http://heretohelplearning .com/hometohome/talk-before-you-write on November 20, 2019.

Morrow, L. M., & Gambrell, L. B. (Eds.). (2011). *Best practices in literacy instruction* (4th ed.). New York: Guilford Press.

National Association for the Education of Young Children. (n.d.). *Learning to read and write: What research reveals.* Accessed at www.readingrockets.org/article /learning-read-and-write-what-research-reveals on November 19, 2019.

National Association for the Education of Young Children. (2009a). *Developmentally appropriate practice in early childhood programs serving children from birth through age 8.* Accessed at www.naeyc.org/sites/default/files/globally-shared /downloads/PDFs/resources/position-statements/PSDAP.pdf on May 12, 2020.

National Association for the Education of Young Children. (2009b). *Key messages of the position statement.* Accessed at www.naeyc.org/files/naeyc/file/positions /KeyMessages.pdf on March 27, 2020.

National Early Literacy Panel. (2008). *Developing early literacy: Report of the National Early Literacy Panel.* Accessed at https://lincs.ed.gov/publications/pdf /NELPReport09.pdf on May 24, 2020.

National Governors Association Center for Best Practices & Council of Chief State School Officers. (n.d.). *Common Core State Standards for English language arts and literacy in history/social studies, science, and technical subjects: Appendix A— Research supporting key elements of the standards.* Washington, DC: Authors. Accessed at www.corestandards.org/assets/Appendix_A.pdf on May 18, 2020.

National Governors Association Center for Best Practices & Council of Chief State School Officers. (2010). *Common Core State Standards for English language arts and literacy in history/social studies, science, and technical subjects.* Accessed at www .corestandards.org/assets/CCSSI_ELA%20Standards.pdf on May 28, 2019.

National Reading Panel. (2000). *Teaching children to read: An evidence-based assessment of the scientific research literature on reading and its implications for reading instruction.* Bethesda, MD: National Institute of Child Health and Human Development.

Neuman, S. B., Kaefer, T., & Pinkham, A. (2014). Building background knowledge. *The Reading Teacher, 68*(2), 145–148.

Northern Illinois University. (2015). *Instructional scaffolding to improve learning.* Accessed at www.niu.edu/spectrum/archives/scaffolding.shtml on July 8, 2019.

O'Donnell, A. (2019). Windows, mirrors, and sliding glass doors: The enduring impact of Rudine Sims Bishop's work. *Literacy Today, 36*(6), 16–19.

O'Neill, A., & Huliska-Beith, L. (2002). *The recess queen.* New York: Scholastic.

Office of the High Commissioner for Human Rights. (n.d.). *Gender stereotyping.* Accessed at www.ohchr.org/en/issues/women/wrgs/pages/genderstereotypes. aspx on February 2, 2019.

Opitz, B., Ferdinand, N. K., & Mecklinger, A. (2011). *Timing matters: The impact of immediate and delayed feedback on artificial language learning.* Accessed at www .frontiersin.org/articles/10.3389/fnhum.2011.00008/full on April 2, 2020.

Owocki, G., & Goodman, Y. (2002). *Kidwatching: Documenting children's literacy development.* Portsmouth, NH: Heinemann.

Pearson, P. D., & Gallagher, M. C. (1983). The instruction of reading comprehension. *Contemporary Educational Psychology, 8*(3), 317–344.

Pegis, J. (2017). *Why do we need rules and laws?* New York: Crabtree Publishing Company.

Pett, M. (2014). *The girl and the bicycle.* New York: Simon & Schuster.

Piasta, S. B., & Wagner, R. K. (2010, April). Learning letter names and sounds: Effects of instruction, letter type, and phonological processing skill. *Journal of Experimental Child Psychology, 105*(4), 324–344.

Pikulski, J. J., & Chard, D. J. (2005, March). Fluency: Bridge between decoding and reading comprehension. *The Reading Teacher, 58*(6), 510–519. Accessed at https://pdfs.semanticscholar.org/8425/9b58db9d2d2d5989437d48019586 8b51c036.pdf on January 27, 2020.

Pinnell, G. S., Pikulski, J. J., Wixson, K. K., Campbell, J. R., Gough, P. B., & Beatty, A. S. (1995, January). *Listening to children read aloud: Data from NAEP's Integrated Reading Performance Record (IRPR) at grade 4.* Washington, DC: National Center for Education Statistics.

Popham, W. J. (2007, April). All about accountability: The lowdown on learning progressions. *Educational Leadership, 64*(7), 83–84.

Popham, W. J. (2008). *Transformative assessment.* Alexandria, VA: Association for Supervision and Curriculum Development.

Popham, W. J. (2011). *Transformative assessment in action: An inside look at applying the process.* Alexandria, VA: Association for Supervision and Curriculum Development.

Pressley, M., Allington, R. L., Wharton-McDonald, R., Block, C. C., & Morrow, L. M. (2001). *Learning to read: Lessons from exemplary first-grade classrooms.* New York: Guilford Press.

Price-Mitchell, M. (2015, March 20). *3 strategies to foster sociability* [Blog post]. Accessed at www.edutopia.org/blog/8-pathways-strategies-foster-sociability-marilyn-price -mitchell on April 3, 2020.

Rasinski, T. (2005). *Daily word ladders.* New York: Scholastic.

Rasinski, T. (2014). Fluency matters. *International Electronic Journal of Elementary Education, 7*(1), 3–12.

Rasinski, T. V. (2012). Why reading fluency should be hot! *The Reading Teacher, 65*(8), 516–522.

Reeves, D. B. (2002). *The leader's guide to standards: A blueprint for educational equity and excellence.* San Francisco: Jossey-Bass.

Reis, R. A. (2014). *The US Congress for kids: Over 200 years of lawmaking, deal-breaking, and compromising, with 21 activities.* Chicago: Chicago Review Press.

Richardson, J., & Dufresne, M. (2019). *The next step forward in word study and phonics.* New York: Scholastic Professional.

Richardson, J., & Lewis, E. (2018). *The next step forward in reading intervention: The RISE Framework.* New York: Scholastic Professional.

Riley-Ayers, S. (2013). Supporting language and literacy development in quality preschools. In D. M. Barone & M. H. Mallette (Eds.), *Best practices in early literacy instruction* (pp. 58–78). New York: Guilford Press.

Rochman, M. (2017). The importance of teaching reading: Emphasize for reading fluency or accuracy in improving students' reading comprehension in EFL context. *Ethical Lingua, 4*(1), 11–29.

Roskos, K., & Christie, J. (2011, Fall). The play-literacy nexus and the importance of evidence-based techniques in the classroom. *American Journal of Play, 4*(2), 204–224. Accessed at https://files.eric.ed.gov/fulltext/EJ985588.pdf on November 20, 2019.

Roth, K., & Dabrowski, J. (2014). *Extending interactive writing into grades 2–5.* Accessed at www.readingrockets.org/article/extending-interactive-writing-grades-2-5 on May 23, 2020.

Rowe, D. W., & Flushman, T. R. (2013). Best practices in early writing instruction. In D. M. Barone & M. H. Mallette (Eds.), *Best practices in early literacy instruction* (pp. 224–250). New York: Guilford Press.

RTI Action Network. (n.d.). *What is RTI?* Accessed at www.rtinetwork.org/learn/what/whatisrti on July 1, 2019.

Ryan, R. M., & Deci, E. L. (2009). Promoting self-determined school engagement: Motivation, learning, and well-being. In K. R. Wentzel & A. Wigfield (Eds.), *Handbook of motivation at school* (pp. 171–196). New York: Routledge.

Schimmer, T. (2019, February 19). *Should formative assessments be graded?* [Blog post]. Accessed at www.solutiontree.com/blog/grading-formative-assessments/ on July 14, 2019.

Schmitt, B. D. (2014). *Attention deficit/hyperactivity disorder (ADHD): How to help your child.* Accessed at www.summitmedicalgroup.com/library/pediatric_health/pa-hhgbeh_attention on November 20, 2019.

Searcy, J. (2006). *Signs in our world.* New York: DK Pub.

Searle, M. (2010). *What every school leader needs to know about RTI.* Alexandria, VA: Association for Supervision and Curriculum Development.

Sendak, M. (1962). *Alligators all around: An alphabet.* New York: HarperCollins.

Serravallo, J. (2010). *Teaching reading in small groups: Differentiated instruction for building strategic, independent readers.* Portsmouth, NH: Heinemann.

Serravallo, J. (2014). *The literacy teacher's playbook, grades 3–6: Four steps for turning assessment data into goal-directed instruction.* Portsmouth, NH: Heinemann.

Serravallo, J. (2015). *The reading strategies book: Your everything guide to developing skilled readers.* Portsmouth, NH: Heinemann.

Serravallo, J. (2017). *The writing strategies book: Your everything guide to developing skilled writers.* Portsmouth, NH: Heinemann.

Serravallo, J. (2018). *Understanding texts and readers: Responsive comprehension instruction with leveled texts.* Portsmouth, NH: Heinemann.

Shanahan, T. (2008). *Teaching students to read complex text* [PowerPoint slides]. Accessed at www.shanahanonliteracy.com/publications/teaching-with-complex -text-1 on November 19, 2019.

Shanahan, T. (2014, February 6). *To special ed or not to special ed: RtI and the early identification of reading disability* [Blog post]. Accessed at https://shanahanonliteracy .com/blog/to-special-ed-or-not-to-special-ed-rti-and-the-early-identification -of-reading-disability on November 20, 2019.

Shanahan, T. (2015). Common Core State Standards: A new role for writing. *The Elementary School Journal, 115*(4), 464–479.

Shanahan, T. (2016, September 6). *Eight ways to help kids to read complex text* [Blog post]. Accessed at https://shanahanonliteracy.com/blog/eight-ways-to-help-kids -to-read-complex-text on November 20, 2019.

Shanahan, T. (2017, February 23). *How should we combine reading and writing?* [Blog post]. Accessed at https://shanahanonliteracy.com/blog/how-should-we- combine-reading-and-writing on November 20, 2019.

Shanahan, T. (2018a, February 17). *How to teach writing in kindergarten* [Blog post]. Accessed at https://shanahanonliteracy.com/blog/how-to-teach-writing-in- kindergarten on November 20, 2019.

Shanahan, T. (2018b, February 25). *How to teach writing in kindergarten part II* [Blog post]. Accessed at https://shanahanonliteracy.com/blog/how-to-teach-writing -in-kindergarten-part-ii on November 20, 2019.

Shanahan, T. (2018c, October 27). *Gradual release of responsibility and complex text* [Blog post]. Accessed at https://shanahanonliteracy.com/blog/gradual-release-of -responsibility-and-complex-text on November 19, 2019.

Shanahan, T. (2019). *Teaching students to read complex text.* Accessed at www .shanahanonliteracy.com/publications/teaching-with-complex-text-1 on June 14, 2019.

Shanahan, T., Callison, K., Carriere, C., Duke, N. K., Pearson, P. D., Schatschneider, C., et al. (2010). *Improving reading comprehension in kindergarten through 3rd grade.* Accessed at https://ies.ed.gov/ncee/wwc/Docs/PracticeGuide/reading- comp_pg_092810.pdf on November 20, 2019.

Shanahan, T., Fisher, D., & Frey, N. (2012). The Challenge of challenging text. *Educational Leadership, 69*(6), 58–62.

Silverstein, S. (1974). *Where the sidewalk ends.* New York: HarperCollins.

Slavin, R. E. (2014). Making cooperative learning powerful. *Educational Leadership, 72*(2), 22–26.

Snow, C. E., Burns, M. S., & Griffin, P. (Eds.). (1998). *Preventing reading difficulties in young children.* Washington, DC: National Academy Press.

Spear-Swerling, L. (2006). *The importance of teaching handwriting.* Accessed at www .readingrockets.org/article/importance-teaching-handwriting on April 20, 2020.

Stachowiak, D. (2018a, July 2). *Part 1: Terms and definitions for gender-inclusive classrooms* [Blog post]. Accessed at www.literacyworldwide.org/blog/literacy-daily/2018/07 /02/part-1-terms-and-definitions-for-gender-inclusive-classrooms on December 12, 2019.

Stachowiak, D. (2018b, July 12). *Part 2: Interrogating bias* [Blog post]. Accessed at www .literacyworldwide.org/blog/literacy-daily/2018/07/12/part-2-interrogating -bias on December 12, 2019.

Stachowiak, D. (2018c, July 26). *Part 3: Classroom inventory* [Blog post]. Accessed at www.literacyworldwide.org/blog/literacy-daily/2018/07/26/part-3-classroom -inventory on December 12, 2019.

Stachowiak, D. (2018d, August 2). *Part 4: Supporting gender noncomforming students* [Blog post]. Accessed at www.literacyworldwide.org/blog/literacy-daily/2018/08/02 /part-4-supporting-gender-nonconforming-students on December 12, 2019.

Stachowiak, D. (2018e, August 9). *Part 5: Creating a gender-inclusive curriculum* [Blog post]. Accessed at www.literacyworldwide.org/blog/literacy-daily/2018/08/09 /part-5-creating-a-gender-inclusive-curriculum on December 12, 2019.

Stachowiak, D. (2018f). The power to include: A starting place for creating gender-inclusive literacy classrooms. *Literacy Today, 36*(1), 28–30.

Stahl, K. A. D. (2005). Improving the asphalt of reading instruction: A tribute to the work of Steven A. Stahl. *The Reading Teacher, 59*(2), 184–192.

Stahl, K. A. D. (2012). Complex text or frustration-level text: Using shared reading to bridge the difference. *The Reading Teacher, 66*(1), 47–51.

Stanford Center for Assessment, Learning and Equity. (n.d.). *Performance outcomes.* Accessed at https://scale.stanford.edu/student/assessment-system/performance -outcomes on May 24, 2020.

Stecker, P. M., & Lembke, E. S. (2011). *Advanced applications of CBM in reading (K-6): Instructional decision-making strategies manual.* Washington, DC: National Center on Student Progress Monitoring.

Stein, S. (2001). *Equipped for the future content standards: What adults need to know and be able to do in the 21st century.* Washington, DC: National Institute for Literacy. Accessed at https://eff.clee.utk.edu/PDF/standards_guide.pdf on November 19, 2019.

Steinbeck, J. (1939). *The grapes of wrath*. New York: Viking Press.

Stiggins, R. (2005). From formative assessment to assessment FOR learning: A path to success in standards-based schools. *Phi Delta Kappan, 87*(4), 324–328.

Sullivan, A., & Brown, M. (2013). *Social inequalities in cognitive scores at age 16: The role of reading*. Accessed at https://cls.ucl.ac.uk/wp-content/uploads/2017/04 /CLS-WP-2013-10-.pdf on February 1, 2020.

Tankersley, K. (2003). *The threads of reading: Strategies for literacy development*. Alexandria, VA: Association for Supervision and Curriculum Development.

TeacherVision. (2007). *Cooperative learning*. Accessed at www.teachervision.com /professional-development/cooperative-learning on November 19, 2019.

Tomlinson, C. A. (2000). *Differentiation of instruction in the elementary grades*. Champaign, IL: ERIC Clearinghouse on Elementary and Early Childhood Education.

Tomlinson, C. A., & Imbeau, M. B. (2010). *Leading and managing a differentiated classroom*. Alexandria, VA: Association for Supervision and Curriculum Development.

Tomlinson, C. A., & Moon, T. R. (2013). *Assessment and student success in a differentiated classroom*. Alexandria, VA: Association for Supervision and Curriculum Development.

Trehearne, M., Healy, L. H., Cantalini, M., & Moore, J. L. (2003). *Comprehensive literacy resource for kindergarten teachers*. Vernon Hills, IL: ETA/Cuisenaire.

Turner, J. (2018). *The purpose of rules and laws*. New York: PowerKids Press.

Understood Team. (n.d.). *Understanding your child's trouble with writing*. Accessed at www .understood.org/en/learning-thinking-differences/child-learning-disabilities /writing-issues/understanding-your-childs-trouble-with-writing on November 20, 2019.

Virginia Department of Education. (2017). *K–12 English standards of learning curriculum framework*. Accessed at www.doe.virginia.gov/testing/sol/standards_docs /english/index.shtml on February 3, 2019.

Webb, N. L. (1997). *Criteria for alignment of expectations and assessments in mathematics and science education* (Research monograph no. 6). Washington, DC: Council of Chief State School Officers.

Webb, N. L. (1999). *Alignment of science and mathematics standards and assessments in four states* (Research monograph no. 18). Madison, WI: Wisconsin Center for Education Research.

Weinstein, R. S. (2002). *Reaching higher: The power of expectations in schooling*. Cambridge, MA: Harvard University Press.

What Works Clearinghouse. (2017). *Teaching elementary school students to be effective writers: Practice guide summary*. Accessed at https://files.eric.ed.gov/fulltext /ED578427.pdf on November 20, 2019.

Wiggins, G. (2012). *Seven keys to effective feedback.* Accessed at www.ascd.org /publications/educational-leadership/sept12/vol70/num01/Seven-Keys-to -Effective-Feedback.aspx on January 17, 2020.

Wiggins, G., & McTighe, J. (2005). *Understanding by design* (Expanded 2nd ed.). Alexandria, VA: Association for Supervision and Curriculum Development.

Wiliam, D. (2011). *Embedded formative assessment.* Bloomington, IN: Solution Tree Press.

Wood, J., & McLemore, B. (2001). Critical components in early literacy: Knowledge of the letters of the alphabet and phonics instruction. *The Florida Reading Quarterly, 38*(2), 1–8.

Wooldridge, L. (n.d.). *The big five: Phonological and phonemic awareness—Part 1.* Accessed at https://ortongillinghamonlinetutor.com/the-big-five-phonological -and-phonemic-awareness-part-1 on April 3, 2020.

INDEX

Reading and Writing Instruction for Second- and Third-Grade Classrooms in a PLC at Work®
By Sarah Gord and Kathryn E. Sheridan
Edited by Mark Onuscheck and Jeanne Spiller
Fully prepare students to begin the pivotal transition from learning to read to reading to learn. Written for individual teachers and collaborative teams, this carefully crafted resource outlines a high-quality approach to literacy instruction for second and third grade.
BKF915

Reading and Writing Instruction for Fourth- and Fifth-Grade Classrooms in a PLC at Work®
By Kathy Tuchman Glass
Edited by Mark Onuscheck and Jeanne Spiller
Prepare students to succeed with increasingly sophisticated reading and writing challenges. Designed for teachers of grades 4–5, this book fully prepares individuals and collaborative teams to establish a rich and robust plan for quality literacy instruction, assessment, and intervention.
BKF902

The New Art and Science of Teaching Reading
Julia A. Simms and Robert J. Marzano
The New Art and Science of Teaching Reading presents a compelling model for reading development structured around five key topic areas. More than one hundred reading-focused instructional strategies are laid out in detail to help teachers ensure every student becomes a proficient reader.
BKF811

The New Art and Science of Teaching Writing
Kathy Tuchman Glass and Robert J. Marzano
Using a clear and well-organized structure, the authors apply the strategies originally laid out in *The New Art and Science of Teaching* to the teaching of writing. In total, the book explores more than one hundred strategies for teaching writing across grade levels and subject areas.
BKF796

"Tremendous, tremendous, tremendous!

The speaker made me do some very deep internal reflection about the **PLC process** and the personal responsibility I have in making the school improvement process work **for ALL kids**."

—Marc Rodriguez, teacher effectiveness coach, Denver Public Schools, Colorado

PD Services

Our experts draw from decades of research and their own experiences to bring you practical strategies for building and sustaining a high-performing PLC. You can choose from a range of customizable services, from a one-day overview to a multiyear process.

Book your PLC PD today!
888.763.9045

Solution Tree